BIG FOOD BIG LOVE

BIG FOOD
BIG LOVE

DOWN-HOME SOUTHERN COOKING FULL OF HEART
from Seattle's **WANDERING GOOSE**

HEATHER L. EARNHARDT

Photography by Jim Henkens

SASQUATCH BOOKS
SEATTLE

Printed in China

Published by Sasquatch Books
20 19 18 17 16   9 8 7 6 5 4 3 2 1

Editor: Susan Roxborough
Production editor: Em Gale
Design: Anna Goldstein
Photography: Jim Henkens
Poppy illustration: Frida Clements

Library of Congress Cataloging-in-Publication Data is available.
ISBN: 978-1-63217-061-3

Sasquatch Books
1904 Third Avenue, Suite 710
Seattle, WA 98101
(206) 467-4300
www.sasquatchbooks.com
custserv@sasquatchbooks.com

*To my granddaddy, Marion Joseph Corbett, for making
a childhood as magical and full as it should be.*

*To my grandmother, Evelyn Pegram Perkinson Earnhardt,
you shaped me in ways you couldn't possibly have known.
Whole worlds could have been tamed with your love.*

*To my daughter Evelyn "Evey" Pearl, named after your great-
grandmother. I wish you could be here for so many reasons but also
to eat all this food and feel all this love. Big Food. Big Love.*

CONTENTS

Lines Connect *1*   Southern Vagabond *5*   My Red Dirt Roots *12*
3, 2, 1 . . . Open! *17*

GRAZING *Snacks & Starters*   22

GRAVY *Where It All Begins*   46

BIG LOVE BIG BISCUITS *Savory & Sweet Biscuits*   60

SUPPER *The Midday Meal & More*   88

"AND ALL ON IT" SUPPER SIDES *Eat Your Veggies Y'all*   118

FOR THE BIG POT *Big Love for All!*   144

ALL ABOUT THE PICKLES *Jar It Up*   158

SAUCES & DRESSINGS *Dress It Up*   170

BIG BREAKFAST *No Seriously, Eat Breakfast*   182

JELLIES, JAMS & BUTTERS *Butter It Up*   200

BIG CAKES & BUNDTS *Bigger Is Better*   210

PIES & TARTS *It's Jus' Pie*   234

COOKIES, BARS & BREAD PUDDING *Big Treats*   252

FOR SIPPIN' *You Could Use a Drink*   270

A Big Love Thank-You 279   Acknowledgments 281   Index 283

RECIPE LIST

GRAZING *snacks & starters*

Cornmeal Fried Green Tomatoes
merv's tomatoes with comeback sauce 25

"Not Ruth's" Pimento Cheese Spread
for spreading & dipping.................................27

Walla Walla Sweet Onion Dip
with granddaddy's fried onions 28

Home-Wrecker Sleeping Dogs
with caramelized onions & honey mustard 30

Granny's Crunchy Cheese Straws
for your pockets & parties.............................33

Country Caviar *perfect deviled eggs*................34

Fried Squid, Pickle & Lemon Plate
with comeback sauce....................................37

Princess "Hush Now" Hush Puppies.............39

Angels on Horseback *bacon, oysters,
toast & warmed lemon butter* 42

Spiced Pralines
"no, they don't come from a praline tree" 44

GRAVY *where it all begins*

Mushroom Gravy..49

MJ's Chipped Beef on Toast
kid's white gravy 50

Sawmill Gravy *sausage & sage* 52

Country Ham with Redeye Gravy
& perfect fried eggs 55

Simple Roast Chicken & Pan Gravy.............57

BIG LOVE BIG BISCUITS *savory & sweet biscuits*

Best Buttermilk Biscuits 65

Maple, Bacon & Date Biscuits
with maple glaze...67

Everything Biscuits
with a baked egg on top 68

Cheddar Chive Biscuits..................................70

Sweet Potato Biscuits 71

Bacon, Cheddar & Scallion Biscuits 72

Sausage & Sage Biscuits 73

Mama Lil's Peppers &
Tillamook Cheddar Biscuits.........................74

Biscuit Cinnamon Rolls *with cream cheese
& buttermilk frosting* 77

Angel Biscuits *always with country ham* 79

Biscuit Croutons *for soups & salads* 81

SUPPER *the midday meal & more*

Zevely House Shrimp & Grits.......................91

Grits & Grillades
pork & grits & new orleans............................94

Big Love Buttermilk Fried Chicken...............95

Crunchy Cornmeal-Fried Oysters 98

Fried Oyster Rich Boys *with french
rémoulade & extra-spicy dills* 100

B.O.L.T. (Bacon, Fried Oysters, Lettuce
& Tomato) *with pepper jelly &
french rémoulade* 102

Smoked Salmon Pie
with peas & a liquored crust 104

Red Tomato Cheddar Pie
with a liquored crust 106

"Granddaddy's Coming to Visit"
Peel & Eat Shrimp 108

Pulled Pork Butt *with vinegar sauce &
red slaw* 111

Friday Night Fish Fry *with french rémoulade* ...113

Aunt Annie's Cornflake Chicken Tenders
with whipped honey butter 115

"AND ALL ON IT" SUPPER SIDES
eat your veggies y'all

MJ's Potato Salad *tried & true*........................121

Double-Order Fried Okra
"you want WHAT?" 122

Lowcountry Sea Island Red Peas
with chowchow...125

Little Gem Salad *with smoked tomatoes
& creamy blue cheese dressing* 126

Granny's Mess of Soft Greens
turnip, mustard & collard 127

Bluebird Grain Farms Farro
& Collard Green Salad *with watermelon
radish & roasted garlic–lemon vinaigrette* 128

Smoky Meat Collards
with benton's bacon & pot likker 130

Broiled Garden Tomatoes
with burrata & spiced pralines......................133

Pimento "Not Your Mama's"
Mac & Cheese...134

Granny's Salisbury Red Slaw 137

Tomato & Cucumber Salad
with sorghum syrup & black pepper 138

The Wandering Goose White Slaw 139

Coconut Rice 139

Granddaddy's Fancy New Potatoes
with parsley & salty butter..........................140

Watermelon Salad *with salt & spearmint*........140

Hot Skillet Corn Bread
sour cream & fresh corn 141

Skillet Ramps & Yukon Gold Potatoes
with benton's bacon & toast.........................143

FOR THE BIG POT *big love for all!*

West Coast–Style She-Crab Soup 147

Go to Church Brunswick Stew.....................149

Any Time of Year Tomato Soup
with biscuit croutons...................................150

Granny's Garden Vegetable Soup.................151

Loaded Chicken Potpie *with biscuit topping* ... 153

"Not Just for Monday" Red Beans & Rice.... 154

Southern Spaghetti Sauce 155

ALL ABOUT THE PICKLES *jar it up*

Granny's Watermelon Rind Pickles 161

Bread & Butter Pickles *salty & sweet* 162

The Wandering Goose Extra-Spicy Dills 163

Pickled Red Onions 166

Granddaddy's Fast Cukes in Vin 166

Pickled Okra 167

Pickled Green Beans 168

Chowchow 169

SAUCES & DRESSINGS *dress it up*

Comeback Sauce 173

Sweet Heat BBQ Sauce 176

Creole Mustard 176

Granddaddy's Hard-Boiled Egg
Salad Dressing 177

Creamed Blue Cheese Dressing
for fancy folks 177

French Rémoulade *for even more
fancy folks* 178

Homemade Mayonnaise 178

Roasted Garlic–Lemon Vinaigrette 179

Central Carolina Vinegar Sauce 180

Quick & Spicy Cocktail Sauce 180

BIG BREAKFAST *no seriously, eat breakfast*

Country Breakfast Sausage *with spice mix* 185

The Wandering Goose Granola
*sour cherries, sesame seeds &
steen's cane syrup* 187

Spicy Skillet Potatoes 188

Bluebird Grain Farms Farro Breakfast
Porridge *cinnamon & lemon* 190

Boonville Breakfast Grits 192

Bubble & Squeak *corned beef brisket with
potatoes, onions, poached eggs & spicy
bubble sauce* 195

Veggie Hash *with poached eggs
& red pepper coulis* 197

Granny's Perfect Poached Eggs 199

Cinnamon-Sugared Toast 199

JELLIES, JAMS & BUTTERS *butter it up*

Strawberry Vanilla Preserves 203

Granny's Strawberry Fig Preserves 204

Pepper Jelly 205

Tomato-Apricot Jam 208

Maternal-Side Apple Butter 209

BIG CAKES & BUNDTS *bigger is better*

"Bob's Last Meal" Chocolate Cake 213

Happy Birthday Cake 214

Browned Butter Banana Bundt Cake 216

Huckleberry Cardamom Bundt Cake 217

Brownstone Front Cake 219

Granny's Kitchen Table Cake
    with bittersweet chocolate frosting 222

Lusty Lemon Layer Cake
    with lemon cream cheese frosting 225

Southern Coconut Cake
    with coconut cream cheese frosting 227

Uncle Ray's Fresh Apple Cake
    with buttermilk soda frosting 229

Shortcakes *strawberries with*
    elderflower syrup 230

7Up Bundt Cake 232

PIES & TARTS *it's jus' pie*

Concord Grape Tart 237

Sour Cherry Hand Pies 238

Apple Rosemary Galette 241

Rhubarb Galette *with orange blossom water* 242

Sweet Tea Chess Pie 243

Lemon Buttermilk Chess Pie 244

Chocolate Chili Chess Pie 247

Key Lime Pie *with saltine cracker crust* 248

Tarte á la Bouillie 249

COOKIES, BARS & BREAD PUDDING *big treats*

Best Chocolate Chip Cookie in Seattle 255

Smoked Chocolate Chip Cookies
    bacon & ruffles 256

Chocolate Cherry Oat Cookies
    with toffee bits 258

Chocolate Chip Walnut Toffee Cookies 259

Cracklin' Cookies *chicken skin & toffee bits* 261

Charlie Brown Cookies
    peanut butter & chocolate at its best 263

Aunt Chubby Bars *peanut butter & jelly* 264

Gooey Butter Cake Bars 266

Bittersweet Chocolate Bread Pudding
    with salty whiskey caramel sauce 267

FOR SIPPIN' *you could use a drink*

Prince's Southern Iced Tea *not too sweet* 273

Old Dominican Hangover Helper 275

Carrot-Apple-Beet-Ginger Squeeze 275

The Wandering Goose Easy
    Michelada Mix 276

Granny, Mimi Perk (my great-grandmother), and baby Aunt Becky, 1943

Things don't fall apart. Things hold. Lines connect in thin ways that last and last and lives become generations made out of pictures and words just kept. —LUCILLE CLIFTON

LINES CONNECT

I am the same person I was at six years old. Except now I curse too much. The morals and values I was taught by that age and the love and excitement about food I witnessed have never left me.

I come from a family of food lovers on both sides. For us, food and stories intermingle and are as common as corn bread and molasses, fried chicken and collard greens, biscuits and grits. Wherever there is food, there is a story alongside it. This is the soul of my restaurant, The Wandering Goose—Southern hospitality with big, bold-tasting comfort food and lots of love.

Each dish I make is a reflection of a time, a place, a smell, a memory, and a moment in my life. Whether it was growing up in central North Carolina, eastern Virginia, or South Carolina's Lowcountry; spending summers at the Outer Banks and in the hill country of the Appalachian Mountains; or the years I lived in New Orleans—Southern hospitality, tradition, and comfort food were constants. This thread runs through me always and runs through The Wandering Goose today.

My restaurant is an extension of my home, which is an extension of both my granny's and granddaddy's homes and hospitality. It's where I know the names of my delivery drivers, how they take their coffee, and which pastry they prefer. It's where people celebrate birthdays, holidays, and anniversaries, where they come to meet an old friend or a newfound acquaintance, where first dates happen and hands in marriage are sought. It's a place where crowds eat until they're bursting and everyone is squeezed in a little bit tight around the supper table.

The South is not only a geographical region but also a state of being. It is the land where iced-tea pitchers, well-seasoned cast-iron skillets, and deviled-egg platters are handed down from generation to generation. Where Texas Pete hot sauce sits at the center of everyone's kitchen table alongside a glass cruet of white vinegar with red chilies inside for heat, to douse both dark collard greens and fried fish. It is the land of storytelling and "bless your heart" and "I declare" and wickedly great sweet iced tea. It is a feeling that takes place around tables where food is shared and stories are told, and where you have a moral obligation to feed your guests. It is the land of the little white-haired lady in front of you in line at the Piggly Wiggly talking to you like she knows you.

It's not until later, when you're back in your car, that you realize you've been away far too long—you remember that's how people talk to one another in the South. They talk and tell stories from their front porches, the grocery-store line, the sidewalk, the bank, and the hardware store. Almost all Southerners can cook and tell a good story, and true Southerners make friends standing in lines.

My sister, Chelsea, and me, West Virginia, 1977

I was raised in North Carolina by a circle of strong Southern women—my mother, grandmother, aunts, and great-aunts—and influenced by all that was around me: the sound of crickets and bullfrogs, the color and smell of the dark-red earth, chiggers and clouds of mosquitoes. I fell asleep to thunderstorms and awoke to the sound of clinking pots and pans, the smell of country ham, and the chatter of fourteen cousins. The dining room tables and kitchen tables were heavy with dish after dish of food, all meant to be shared.

As children we played under cathedrals of kudzu and honeysuckle vines bathed in that faded yellow light of the 1970s. I emerged from this upbringing as someone who hugs hard, laughs loudly, cries easily, listens carefully, and records things intently, filing them away in my memory bank. The sights and sounds and taste of the South permeated my skin, enveloping me in a Southern blanket. I carry this thread of who I am and where I'm from in my pocket, connecting me to the generations that came before me and the land that made me. The clinking of magnolia leaves, the smell of ramps and wild mountain strawberries, kudzu vines and joe-pye weed, cool creeks and the warm Atlantic ocean are really never far away.

(From left to right clockwise): Daddy and me, 1973; My sister, Chelsea, and me, West Avenue, 1975;
Me on Monument Avenue, Richmond, Virginia; Building sand castles with Daddy, Virginia Beach, 1974

SOUTHERN VAGABOND

I arrived in Seattle quite by accident, and it only took me twenty-five years of moving around to get here.

HICKORY, NORTH CAROLINA, AND RICHMOND, VIRGINIA

I was born in Hickory, North Carolina. My parents, both twenty-two and freshly graduated from Lenoir-Rhyne University, moved me at six weeks old to Richmond, Virginia. At Virginia Commonwealth University, my mother earned her master's and my father, his PhD. By the time I was five, they were divorced—but not before my memory was imprinted with the "Wagon Man," as I called my father.

Wagon Man came every Friday on a horse-drawn wagon, pulling peaches and watermelons and sweet white corn. I'm not sure if it was the warm peaches, the way he nestled them ever so gently in the thick paper bag before handing them off to me, trusting I would keep them from bruising, or the horse and the overalled man himself, calling in his singsong voice, *"PEEEaches! WaaaaMelon! Sweeeeee Corn!"* that drew me in so completely, but I would have to say my love of farmers' markets started right then at age five.

My sister was born while we lived in Richmond, and for those five years she and I slid down steep hillsides on flattened cardboard boxes at Byrd Park and rode bicycles up and down West Avenue. Daddy played tirelessly with us in the grassy, tree-lined median of Monument Avenue, where Confederate generals towered over us; by age three and five we knew them by heart: Robert E. Lee, Stonewall Jackson, Jefferson Davis, J. E. B. Stuart.

MJ, my mother, was the director of therapeutic recreation at the Virginia Rehabilitation Center for the Blind, and we spent many an afternoon with her and the blind adults swimming, bowling, and yes, even practicing archery. (MJ was a bit zany like that.) My memories of this time are flooded with our turntable endlessly playing Jackson Browne, Joni Mitchell, Carole King, Carly Simon, and John Denver. I remember a lot of fun parties and a lot of not-so-fun fights between my mom and dad. I remember climbing up on the kitchen counter and pouring bowls of cereal, eating cold bologna slices out of the fridge, and making a lot of sandwiches: pimento cheese, beefsteak tomato with ground pepper and mayo, banana and peanut butter smeared thick with Duke's mayo. All of this was surrounded by trips to Virginia Beach to build castles in the hot sand, holding Daddy's hand in the ocean waves, and cool dips in the wide James River.

NEW ORLEANS, LOUISIANA

After the divorce, when I was six years old, MJ moved us deep down to the Cajun country of New Orleans, where my great-aunt Mooie lived. New Orleans was a magical, spiritual city full of music, voodoo, the muddy Mississippi, and enormous clouds of mosquitoes. Aunt Mooie combated the swarms that surrounded us while we played outside by smearing us head to toe with the *oiliest, greasiest, most foul-smelling* repellent. I want to say it was called 6-12, because I looked it up recently and the small glass jar looks the same. (I also found out that it was discontinued due to evidence it caused developmental defects in animals. *Great.*) My sister and I swam in Lake Pontchartrain (gross) and the Gulf Coast (not as bad?), where chunks of tar from the oil fields would stick to your feet and thighs. We avoided stepping into fire ant mounds the best we could, but one time my sister walked through one and had to be thrown into Lake Pontchartrain.

Granddaddy would visit and always take us out to fancy places: Brennan's for brunch, Galatoire's for dinner. Even back then Galatoire's had a line, but somehow, with Granddaddy, we never had to wait for a table. We ate oysters Rockefeller, oysters *en brochette*, shrimp Marguery, shrimp étouffée, turtle soup, and fried frog legs. We went to the Superdome—the same one where MJ saw Muhammad Ali defeat Leon Spinks to win the world heavyweight title for the third time—to watch the New Orleans Saints (or the 'Aints, as they were then known) play football. We wore brown paper bags over our heads and booed the team with everyone else because they were so bad. And we went to Mardi Gras, where MJ wore her five-inch-high clogs and caught us buckets of beads to wear around our necks. (And one year our babysitter took us along to bail her boyfriend out from jail, begging us not to tell MJ.)

The years we spent here were filled with trips to Café Du Monde, for hot beignets and chicory coffee, and to Jackson Square, where we fed the pigeons, inhaled fluffy Sno Balls, and ate caramelized sweet praline confections. We ate barbecued shrimp (New Orleans–style with Italian dressing, butter, and onions), vats of gumbo, jambalaya, and red beans and rice. (Even now I can eat a bowl of red beans and rice daily without ever getting tired of it.) MJ learned to make gumbo and showed me how to make my first dark roux when I was eight. The New Orleans lifestyle was always about joie de vivre, or joy of living, and I was utterly entranced and enthralled with it all. That thick, hazy, humid feeling burrowed under my skin and has never left.

Feeding the pigeons in Jackson Square Park, New Orleans, 1977

DALLAS, PENNSYLVANIA

After New Orleans, which had just begun to feel like home, it was a new marriage for MJ and another move—this time to Dallas, Pennsylvania. I started fourth grade not knowing a single soul at Dallas Elementary. As I was writing this, I thought I could completely skip over this period in my life, but then I remembered our first Christmas there.

To ease our transition and introduce ourselves during the holidays, MJ baked lemon tea bread for the neighbors. I was given the task of delivering the still-warm loaves in their shiny, rustling red wrappers. I loved the grateful surprise on the neighbors' faces, and it was shortly after that I started to bake relentlessly at the ripe old age of eight. I baked MJ's lemon tea bread, made loaves of pumpkin bread that I still bake to this day, and anything I possibly could out of *Joy of Cooking* and *McCall's* cookbooks. I watched and helped MJ grind chicken liver pâté in our heavy glass blender, sauté liver and onions, and bake a chocolate layer cake with whipped cream filling for our birthdays. There were trips to Manhattan for smoked lox, bagels with schmear, pickled herring, matzo ball soup, sandwiches of pastrami and corned beef, knishes, and sweet noodle puddings, all guzzled down with black cherry seltzers. This was my beginning, where I really caught the baking and cooking bug that never let me go.

Washing dishes, Dallas, Pennsylvania, 1980

MYRTLE BEACH, SOUTH CAROLINA

Four years and another divorce later, we landed in Myrtle Beach, where MJ had a friend. At thirteen, I quickly adapted to wearing jelly sandals, sporting a new Flock of Seagulls haircut, wearing a lot of lace and animal prints, and smoking Camel nonfilter cigarettes, emulating Madonna in *Desperately Seeking Susan*. Myrtle Beach was even more foreign to me than Pennsylvania had been, so the Lowcountry outside of town was what I fell in love with. Pawleys Island, Murrells Inlet, Florence, Marion, Charleston, Beaufort, Bowen Island, dense marshland and swamps, saltwater, crepe myrtles, and Spanish moss draped over live oaks.

All through high school on Friday nights were huge beach bonfires and passed quart jars of clear moonshine. Our teenage nails got muddy and our hands a bit bloody as we roasted bushels of oysters over seaweed draped in ocean-soaked burlap. At fifteen, I got a job working in a fish market, weighing out local seafood for customers, learning how to tell exactly what was fresh or not and which seafood came from close by and where.

After five years in South Carolina, I was done. I was ready to go "home," so to speak, to North Carolina. A week after graduating high school at seventeen, I hooked up a U-Haul to my 1970 green Chevy Nova and headed north, ending up in Winston-Salem.

Thirteen years old, Myrtle Beach, South Carolina, 1984

NORTH CAROLINA AND TUCSON, ARIZONA

I spent the next eight years living and working in North Carolina (with a brief stint in Tucson, Arizona) in restaurants as a server and busser, and going to school for commercial photography. I met my best friends (the kind of friends that are there for you at your best and your worst even after more than twenty years) at photography school in Asheboro, North Carolina. Asheboro is in Randolph County, a dry county, and much of our school time was spent driving to the next county over to buy beer. We played poker every Thursday night and learned how to be disciplined with even the worst hangover ever.

After graduating I moved to Winston-Salem and got my first job waiting tables at a busy high-end café. With no experience serving (I lied my way into that job), the first week there I opened a bottle of wine while holding it between my legs. But I learned quickly and could remain calm even though the maniac chef threw hot sauté pans at us through the kitchen window. I didn't know any better. I thought all chefs were like that.

One time, a very quaffed woman sent her lamb chops back *twice* for not being rare enough. You know what that chef did? He came out of the kitchen and slapped a raw rack of lamb on the table, blood splattering over the white tablecloth, and said, "You want rare? *That's* rare!" I kid you not. Immune by then to the chaos, I simply turned my head and poured more wine.

Traveling through Santa Fe, New Mexico, 1995

SEATTLE, WASHINGTON

I arrived in Seattle on May 1, 1997, and it promptly rained for what seemed like every day for months. Coming from Tucson and the Sonoran Desert, where I never once saw rain, I was immediately taken in with this weird climate with leaves larger than my head, Dr. Seuss—esque bowed spruce, and the thick gray curtain of clouds surrounded by water everywhere.

My plan was to stay for the summer, then head back down to Tucson to pursue a career in photography. But I never left. I got a job serving at Carmelita, a vegetarian restaurant in the Phinney Ridge neighborhood, and worked there on and off for the next twelve years. During this time, I also worked as a freelance food photographer, alongside catering jobs, barista jobs, bakery jobs, and just about any kind of restaurant job I could get. I made friends, met my first husband, had three children, got divorced after fourteen years of marriage, met my current husband, became a stepmom to two more children, and in 2012 opened The Wandering Goose.

As a Southerner, I find familiarity in the food here in the Pacific Northwest—fresh fish, shellfish, local produce. In the South you catch catfish, speckled trout, puppy drum, spots, shrimp, oysters, and blue crab and grow tomatoes, corn, beans, peas, okra, peaches, and collard greens. Here in the Pacific Northwest we have salmon, cod, rockfish, and shellfish alongside chard, collards, sweet lettuces, apples, pears, and stone fruit all grown and harvested in Washington. The ingredients here are all familiar and things I'm comfortable cooking and serving. Find what is familiar to you and seek out your local produce. The recipes in this book can all be adapted to your region. Discover your local farmers' markets, talk to the farmers, and learn what grows nearby and when. Celebrate where you are and where you are from, what foods your culture has to offer, what smells you remember as a child.

MY RED DIRT ROOTS

My cooking style and the success of The Wandering Goose would not be what it is today if it weren't for the influences of my paternal grandmother and my maternal grandfather. They each shaped me in different ways with cooking styles as unique as their personalities. Granny and Granddaddy both learned from a long line of Southern cooks before them who created with abandon, with humor, and with stories behind every dish. What we all have left when we are gone from this world are the stories that are told about us, and the stories we have told. My granddaddy and granny were both full of them.

Evelyn "Granny" Perkinson Earnhardt, 1920s

GRANNY

I grew up watching my grandmother cook Southern food that was straightforward, full of flavor, and served with integrity. From the time I could stand on my own two feet, I was at her side—careful to stay out of the way—watching, listening, and learning.

Granny was known as the "Cake Lady" of Salisbury, North Carolina. For more than fifty years, from her blue-and-white kitchen on Wiley Avenue, she churned out three- to seven-tiered wedding cakes, petits fours, cheese straws, chocolate pies, lemon pies, pecan pies (with nuts from her backyard trees), chess pies, hand-pulled butter mints, fresh apple cake, corn pudding, angel biscuits stamped out with an old snuff can, buttermilk cakes, lemon cakes, baking powder biscuits, macaroni and cheese (it was so infamous in our family, my dad had a square of it shellacked), black walnut cake, lemony pound cakes, and peach cobbler, along with "pimmenocheese" sandwiches, butter beans, pinto beans, crowder peas, field peas, zipper peas, corn bread and red slaw, spaghetti sauce thick with meat and tomatoes, fried chicken, redeye gravy, pan gravy, giblet gravy, corn grits, stewed yellow crookneck squash, fried squash, fried okra, turnip greens and mustard greens, creamed corn, fried catfish, and thick slices of warm tomatoes—all made while I watched, drinking the perfect glass of ice-cold sweet tea.

Granny canned butter beans and sweet corn, pickled red beets and watermelon rind, sweet pickles, corn relish, green beans, and okra pods. She made bread-and-butter pickles, chowchow, red pepper jelly, apple butter, and strawberry-fig jam. Babies grew up in her kitchen gnawing on chicken bones when they were teething, licking chocolate frosting from her huge aluminum frosting bowl, nibbling on cheese straws that were just the perfect amount of salt and spice and crunch, and savoring her handmade pastel-colored frosting flowers, which melted in their throats. We weren't Catholic but always fried catfish or flounder or speckled trout for Friday supper, with glasses of white vinegar set on the mantel in the living room to absorb the odor.

Granny believed that to feed someone was the best thing you could do for them, and she did it well, with grace and an effortless way about her. Granny's food wasn't complicated, but it showed off technique and consistency that is only learned from hours and weeks and months and years upon years in the kitchen. It was from my almost thirty years of sitting near her at the round kitchen table, or standing by her side looking up at the mixing bowls (then years later, looking down into the same bowls), watching her soft hands work and work, that I learned how to be patient and kind, cook with grace and confidence, and always make time for people.

Granny made all of her food without the luxury of a prep cook, dishwasher, convection oven, or KitchenAid mixer. She spent well over twelve hours a day cooking and baking, most often from 7 a.m. until far past midnight. Her work ethic is part of my foundation and carries me to this day. The love I saw her show her family, friends, and customers has never left me, and how she cared for them all is ingrained in my bones and blood.

Granddaddy with eight of his eleven grandchildren, Rutherford College, North Carolina, 1970s

GRANDADDY

My granddaddy grew up on a small family farm in eastern North Carolina, one of eleven children who helped Eva Belle and Great-Granddaddy Norwood by taking turns in the kitchen, tobacco barn, and fields. Granddaddy *loved* to cook, and his cooking was "tornadic," according to my aunts. He made hand-rolled biscuits, yeast rolls, standing rib roasts, legs of lamb, fried apples, warm livermush sandwiches, and fat beefsteak tomato sandwiches smeared thick with Duke's mayonnaise and lots of black pepper. His hand-cut french fries, okra, and battered onion rings were all fried in an old Revere Ware saucepot, from which grease spattered over everything.

From his garden we ate Silver Queen corn, butter beans, green beans, and cucumbers sliced and soaked in white vinegar and black pepper and served chilled. For breakfast ("brefas," as he called it), we awoke to the smells of country ham and Neese's sausage, redeye and sawmill gravy, biscuit toast, and homemade strawberry preserves.

Granddaddy was funny and kind, and could charm the pants off a black snake. Always the jokester, he played with us as a kid would. He never tired of tickling us until we cried, telling ghost stories so believable the little ones peed the bed, and snapping us with wet kitchen towels, making our legs red with welts. His favorite thing to do—and one that always caught you off guard—was throwing an innocent bystander in the pool with all their clothes on!

As children we snapped green beans, shelled butter beans, shucked corn, and set the table when asked. But mostly we ran around in the summer heat eating muscadine grapes off the vine, sprinkling salt on heavy watermelons, sucking honeysuckle nectar from the flowers, pouring salty peanuts into tiny Coke bottles to drink, and turning flat stones over to look for crayfish in the cool tobacco-brown water of his creek.

Granddaddy fed us until our bellies were about to burst and then say, "There's plenty more in the kitchen!" He made banana pudding from real custard and Nilla Wafers, and cobbler and hand-cranked ice cream from peaches off his very own trees. Those peaches were as small as our fists and warm, tasting of rich brown sugar. He made blackberry loblolly served hot with homemade vanilla ice cream, and banana 1-2-3-4 Cake with seven-minute frosting and layers of ripe bananas. He made us virgin frozen daiquiris (extra sour on purpose to get a laugh when our faces puckered) and bought us sugar cereal we couldn't ever have at home and soft white-powdered doughnuts from Childer's Market. He adored she-crab soup, broiled grouper, peel-and-eat shrimp, Yuban coffee, making people laugh, and feeding us grandchildren.

When asked to describe my granddaddy, most everyone remembers his exemplary storytelling. His stories were never rushed, but slow and measured, his excitement building and his smile growing bigger as the punch line got closer. He was always cooking up something in the kitchen while telling a funny story or joke behind it.

When my mother was growing up, he worked long hours, but he would come home and play with his three young daughters, who learned to cook and be just as witty and funny as their father was. He, along with my mother and aunts, taught all eleven of us grandkids how to cook, speak loud and proud, make a proper bed and clean a kitchen correctly, sit up straight, say *please* and *thank you*, and look people square in the eye when talking with them. Granddaddy was generous, jovial, and hard working and these qualities never wavered his entire life. He never forgot his upbringing of being a poor farmer's son and also the value of a good joke delivered at just the right time. He passed along to all of us not only the value of hard work done well but to also have fun while working and to laugh, laugh, laugh.

3, 2, 1 . . . OPEN!

Most days you can find me in the tiny kitchen of The Wandering Goose, punching out buttermilk biscuits, rolling tart dough, scooping cookies, cooking a soup of the day, or putting together a biscuit special for the weekend. Lines form early on Saturday and Sunday mornings at The Goose. The crew and I prep all week for the weekend onslaught, keeping the pastries freshly baked and stocked and the kitchen prepped to the gills so everything can run as smooth as only a restaurant kitchen can. During the week, there is a steady stream of folks that stop in and come back to the kitchen to say "Hey," or "I'm a transplant from North Carolina too!" or to compliment the cooks and say, "Everything was great!" All of our food is made to order right there in the two-hundred-square-foot kitchen. The cooks and dishwashers and I dance around each other all day, arms lifted to sneak by a corner, sheet trays carried high overhead, backs pressed against a wall to let someone pass. Sometimes even sucking in your stomach can give your fellow coworker a few inches of room. We work hard, sweat a lot, and laugh loud. It's tight and cozy and it's our home away from home.

We opened at 7 a.m. on Monday, October 1, 2012, after having an opening party on Saturday night and prepping the entire menu for twenty hours on Sunday. The line formed immediately; there were customers waiting outside our doors as we unlocked them. We kept a steady pace for about an hour, and then the going got tough. Ticket after ticket came into the kitchen at a breakneck speed. The rail was full, and there was a stack of tickets shoved under each other at the end of the rail. Mike Law, the chef at the time and my dear friend of more than twenty-two years, was cooking on the line with our sous chef, and he looked at me and I looked at him, and he waved his spatula high above his head and shouted, "This is where the rubber hits the *roooooooooad*!" Meaning, this is where we find out what we're made of, how tough and trained we actually are. What was in our stuffin' and what kind of grit we were wearin', if you know what I mean. And you know what? We got through it. Not just that first day, but day after day, and we're still having fun.

But that's the pretty version. It wasn't easy. It was a long, hard, messy, and rough road to get to where I am, where the restaurant is now. There is nothing glamorous about owning and running a restaurant. Nothing. What you see now is the backbreaking work of more than thirty years in this unforgiving, exhausting business. This restaurant is the end result of working day in and day out, week after week, month after month, year after year, for three decades.

You have to make a lot of mistakes to learn how *not* to make those same mistakes over again. You have to remember your customers' names, which coffee drink they prefer, the names of their children and family dog. You have to know your vendors and forge a real and permanent relationship with your delivery drivers—one day you will have to call on all of them for help. (Yes, more than once you will forget a produce order and your delivery driver, Jeff, will send you a text as a gentle reminder. Or you will space out on your chicken order and Bernardo, your rep, will hand deliver it within an hour.)

There's a lot to be said for having one restaurant and running it well. In my opinion, it's way harder than having ten restaurants that someone else is running for you. I *like* being at The Goose every day. I really *like* hanging out with my staff and customers. I feel weird if I miss a day, like I'm missing out on something important or something fun is happening without me. And I still really love to bake every single day. There is something about the morning bake-off where within a few hours you can fill the pastry case to overflowing with gorgeous fresh baked goods while hanging out with people you enjoy.

Someone once told me that running a restaurant was akin to being a doctor in the emergency room, just without all the blood. I disagree. I've seen a lot of blood in our kitchen. I've seen tips of fingers cut off and jagged cuts in hands made by opening a can the wrong way. I've had grown men, twice the size of me (and I'm a big girl), go white and ashen as I convinced them they *were* in fact going to live from their wound and could *for sure* make it in to work their shift the next day. (Once a cook cut his finger pretty bad, and the line cook next to him took one look at it and promptly passed out, knocking his head on the floor and producing a big, bloody gash. *Both* cooks had to take a trip to the emergency room.)

I've had a sink full of dirty dishwater dump on my head while I was folded underneath the dishwasher trying to fix the thing. (I knocked the drainpipe loose, and its contents drained all over my hair, shirt, and jeans. I still had to work a twelve-hour shift with that gunk all over me.) Not cool or glamorous by any means.

Back when I started in restaurants, there was no *Top Chef*, no *Iron Chef* or Food Network. No one I knew or worked for had been to culinary school. The chefs simply worked for years in the business, climbing their way up from dishwasher to line cook to finally become "chef." The only cooking show I ever saw was Julia Child on PBS, and I watched her constantly. Her voice calmed me, and I thought what she could cook, *just like that*, was so magical.

Cooking in the restaurant business was never a glamorous job. The misfits, the weirdos, the artists, the creative types gravitated toward a restaurant job because you could instantly become a part of something with other folks that were mostly from the same kind of crazy you were. We made our own family and our own posse and found our own sense of belonging while having the freedom and flexibility that a restaurant job offered. You could always drop what you were doing for a cross-country trip. As long as you got your shifts covered, there was a job waiting for you when you got back.

But the business trained me. I saw all kinds of stuff happening and watched how managers or owners or staff handled it, and learned the right way and the wrong way to deal with the crisis at hand. Emotions run hot in the chaotic environment of a restaurant and you need to learn to brush stuff off real quick and get back to work. *Always* stay calm.

The most important ingredient in any recipe is memory. Each of the following recipes evokes a memory for me, sometimes faint, sometimes as clear as an hour ago. Some recipes are formed simply from a smell I remember growing up, some from watching Granny or Granddaddy, while other recipes are my own rendition of a classic or version of theirs. The stories I tell alongside the recipes are the way I locate myself in this world, through the intimate particularities of my family.

THOUGHTS ON COOKING

- If you have kids, cook with them (or someone else's). Involve them in every step. Give them a task to do and explain what you're cooking and how. Let them learn to enjoy the gift of making something, then giving.

- Kiss the cook! In our family, whenever anyone gets a bay leaf in their food, it means they get to kiss the cook. Try this even with grumpy teenagers, and you'll get laughs.

- Learn the names of your garbage worker, postal worker, and milk delivery person. Tie a bag of freshly baked cookies to the garbage can for a welcome surprise. Introduce yourself to new neighbors and make friends with old ones. Leave something baked and wrapped on their porch for no reason.

- Southerners don't serve on plates—they serve on platters. Keep in mind a lot of the yields in this book are large but they halve or even quarter easily. With that said, they also double or triple beautifully!

- When frosting cakes, keep in mind that rustic is beautiful! Don't worry if your cake isn't perfect. (Perfect cakes are boring and usually don't taste very good.)

- Play music while you cook, bake, or entertain. Atmosphere is everything.

- Cook using your instincts and all of your senses. Listen to the meat searing, smell the garlic sautéing, watch the liquid evaporating. Touch and taste everything.

- Converse with other cooks and read anything on cooking. Knowledge is power.

- Taste everything and adjust by adding a bit more salt, a touch of hot sauce, a splash of vinegar, or a squeeze of lemon or lime juice.

- Know that you will screw something up and know that it's okay if you do. Don't be hard on yourself (like I am); just start over and try it again.

- Practice, practice, practice. Make something over and over again. It gets easier each time.

GRAZING

SNACKS & STARTERS

CORNMEAL FRIED GREEN TOMATOES
merv's tomatoes with comeback sauce 25

"NOT RUTH'S" PIMENTO CHEESE SPREAD
for spreading & dipping 27

WALLA WALLA SWEET ONION DIP *with granddaddy's fried onions* 28

HOME-WRECKER SLEEPING DOGS
with caramelized onions & honey mustard 30

GRANNY'S CRUNCHY CHEESE STRAWS
for your pockets & parties 33

COUNTRY CAVIAR *perfect deviled eggs* 34

FRIED SQUID, PICKLE & LEMON PLATE *with comeback sauce* 37

PRINCESS "HUSH NOW" HUSH PUPPIES 39

ANGELS ON HORSEBACK *bacon, oysters, toast & warmed lemon butter* 42

SPICED PRALINES *"no, they don't come from a praline tree"* 44

I REMEMBER GRANNY ALWAYS BEING THE last to sit down for supper and the first to stand up to refill someone's plate. I also remember her servings being so small compared to my overflowing portions. Now I understand why. Oftentimes the only items I eat during an entire supper party are a few bites of pimento cheese on a cracker, some deviled eggs I popped in my mouth while filling them, and a handful of cheese straws with a glass of wine before company comes. This isn't by choice, but usually because I'm tasting the entire time I'm cooking and find myself almost full by the time supper rolls around. That said, I love to graze and do it so much more than eating a huge meal all at once.

I like to make sure there are enough starters for everyone to nibble on before the meal *and* after, because what usually happens is that the party goes late into the night and the company comes full circle and eats the rest of the onion dip or the last few cheese straws and scrapes the pimento cheese bowl clean. A Southern cook always has too much food. After all, it's a sin to run out and leave someone hungry!

CORNMEAL FRIED GREEN TOMATOES

merv's tomatoes with comeback sauce

MOST SOUTHERN COOKS MAKE FRIED GREEN TOMATOES. I've eaten a lot of not-so-good versions and wanted an easy recipe that had a crunchy cornmeal outside and firm tomato inside. Merv Dykstra brings me heirloom red and green tomatoes all through the months of July, August, and September here in Seattle. This is a good recipe for using up tomatoes that don't ripen before frost sets in or when you have a craving for something a bit different after eating all of those juicy, ripe tomatoes. Here in Seattle I can find green tomatoes throughout the summer and into late fall in many Asian grocery stores, and Uwajimaya sells them in the summer months. You can also use any firm red tomato if green are unavailable.

MAKES 4 TO 6 SERVINGS

6 green tomatoes

1 quart (4 cups) buttermilk

1 recipe Cornmeal Dredge (page 98)

Canola oil, for frying

Comeback Sauce (page 173), for serving

* Using a serrated knife, cut the tomatoes into ¼-inch-thick slices and set them in a large bowl. Pour the buttermilk over the tomatoes and set them aside while you heat the oil.

* Spread the cornmeal dredge out on a pie pan or plate next to the bowl. Line another plate with paper towels and set it aside.

* In a large cast-iron skillet or saucepot over medium heat, heat 1 inch of oil until it registers 350 degrees F on a deep-fry thermometer. Using your hands, pull the tomato slices from the buttermilk and dredge them in the cornmeal, working in small batches so the cornmeal doesn't clump. Gently place the coated tomatoes in the hot oil and fry them for 2 to 3 minutes per side, flipping once, until golden brown. Remove them with tongs or a slotted spatula to drain on the lined plate. Repeat with the remaining tomatoes. Serve them as a side or main dish with Comeback Sauce for dipping. They're also great on a biscuit burger.

"NOT RUTH'S" PIMENTO CHEESE SPREAD
for spreading & dipping

GROWING UP, SANDWICHES OF "PIMMENOCHEESE"—AS FOLKS in the South pronounce it—were something I ate with even more regularity than PB&Js. And most everyone's refrigerator shelf held a tub of store-bought Ruth's Pimento Spread. Layered between two slices of supersoft white bread and served cold as a quick snack, or grilled if I wasn't in a hurry, it's something I crave to this day.

I make my own pimento cheese now with fresh extra-sharp cheddar instead of the processed cheese in Ruth's. There are numerous recipes, but I've found this one to be foolproof. Just be sure to grate the cheese yourself—pre-grated grocery-store cheese is dry and lacking in flavor. For a gussied-up version, include the cup of chopped toasted walnuts or pecans. Try it in a grilled sandwich with slices of garden tomatoes and crispy bacon, or serve it as a dip with crackers and crudités.

MAKES 4 CUPS

1 pound extra-sharp cheddar cheese (we use Tillamook)

1¾ cups mayonnaise, such as Duke's or Best Foods

1 (4-ounce) jar diced pimento peppers

1 cup chopped, toasted pecans or walnuts (optional)

1 teaspoon freshly ground black pepper

¼ teaspoon cayenne

Kosher salt (optional)

* Grate the cheese into a large bowl. Using a rubber spatula, mix in the mayonnaise and pimento peppers with their liquid until incorporated, adding a bit more mayo if necessary to make a soft, moist mixture. Mix in the pecans, pepper, and cayenne. Cover and refrigerate until ready to serve. Before serving, taste and adjust the seasoning; you may need salt, depending on the brand of cheese you used. Leftover spread will keep for 10 days stored in the refrigerator.

WALLA WALLA SWEET ONION DIP
with granddaddy's fried onions

REMEMBER THE PACKET OF LIPTON ONION soup mix you stirred together with a tub of sour cream and ate with Ruffles? This is that dip, but even better than you remember. It's easy to make and perfect for parties (but you must have the Ruffles to go with it!). Serve it with a garnish of Granddaddy's fried onions, or cut the onions thick for a side of onion rings or a burger topping. Double this recipe for a big party.

MAKES 3 CUPS

¼ cup canola oil

2 tablespoons unsalted butter

3 large sweet onions, sliced (about 6 cups)

2 tablespoons sugar

2 teaspoons kosher salt

1 teaspoon freshly ground black pepper

For the fried onions:

1 small sweet onion

2 cups buttermilk, at room temperature

¼ recipe Cornmeal Dredge (page 98)

Canola oil, for frying

Kosher salt and freshly ground black pepper

6 ounces cream cheese, at room temperature

¾ cup sour cream, at room temperature

¾ cup mayonnaise, such as Duke's or Best Foods

2 pinches cayenne

Smoked paprika, for garnish

* In a large sauté pan over medium-high heat, heat the oil and butter until the butter has melted. Add the onions and sprinkle with the sugar, salt, and pepper. Stir to coat the onions with oil and butter. Reduce the heat to medium low and cook, stirring every few minutes, until the onions are dark and caramelized, 35 to 40 minutes. Transfer the onions to a medium bowl to cool.

* Meanwhile, prepare the fried onions. Slice the onion ½ inch thick, separating the rings, and set them in a large bowl. Pour the buttermilk over the onions and let them soak for at least 15 minutes, or up to 24 hours, in the refrigerator.

* When you're ready to fry the onions, spread the cornmeal out on a pie pan or plate and place it near the bowl of soaking onions, next to the stove. Line another plate with paper towels and set it aside. In a large cast-iron skillet or saucepot, heat 2 inches of oil over medium heat until it registers 350 degrees F on a deep-fry thermometer. Using your hands, pull the onions from the buttermilk and dredge them in the cornmeal, working in small batches so the cornmeal doesn't clump. Gently place the coated onions in the hot oil and fry them for 4 minutes, flipping once, until golden brown. Remove them with tongs or a slotted spatula to drain on the lined plate and season with salt and pepper. Repeat with the remaining onions.

* To finish the dip, in a large serving bowl, combine the cream cheese, sour cream, mayonnaise, and cayenne. Add the cooled caramelized onions to the mixture. Mix until combined, adjusting the seasoning as necessary. Top with the fried onions and a sprinkling of paprika and serve immediately.

HOME-WRECKER SLEEPING DOGS
with caramelized onions & honey mustard

WE ORDER UNCURED BEEF HOT DOGS from Zoe's Meats here in Seattle. They're huge beasts of a thing—just what a real hot dog is supposed to be—and nitrate-free. We wrap them in puff pastry nestled around caramelized onions with extra-sharp cheddar cheese and honey mustard. They sell out on the weekends, and let me just say, the guys aren't the only ones who love them.

MAKES 8 HOT DOGS

For the caramelized onions:
¼ cup canola oil
2 tablespoons unsalted butter
3 large sweet onions, sliced (about 6 cups)
Kosher salt and freshly ground black pepper
2 tablespoons sugar
Pinch of cayenne
1 tablespoon Steen's Louisiana cane vinegar or Worcestershire sauce

For the honey mustard:
½ cup Dijon mustard
¼ cup honey

2 sheets frozen puff pastry, thawed
2 cups (8 ounces) grated extra-sharp cheddar cheese
8 good-quality hot dogs
1 recipe Egg Wash (recipe follows)

* To make the caramelized onions, in a large sauté pan over medium-high heat, heat the oil and butter until the butter has melted and the oil is shimmering. Add the onions and stir to coat them. Season with salt and pepper to taste. Reduce the heat to medium low, stirring every few minutes. After 20 minutes, sprinkle with the sugar and cayenne. Keep cooking until the onions are a deep dark-brown color, 40 to 45 minutes. When the onions have finished cooking, add the cane vinegar and stir for 2 more minutes, scraping up any brown bits stuck to the bottom of the pan. Let the onions cool a bit while you make the honey mustard.

* To make the honey mustard, in a small bowl, whisk the Dijon and honey until combined, adding more of either to taste. Set it aside.

* Preheat the oven to 400 degrees F.

* Cut two sheets of puff pastry into eight even rectangles. Using a pastry brush, brush them evenly all over with the honey mustard. Sprinkle on the caramelized onions in a thin layer, leaving a ½-inch uncovered border. Sprinkle the cheddar cheese over the onions, leaving a ½-inch uncovered border, and put a hot dog at the bottom of each rectangle. Roll up the hot dog like a cigar, brushing egg wash at the top border to seal the pastry, then brush egg wash all over the outside of the pastry. (At this point, you can freeze the hot dogs in a ziplock bag for later baking, if you want.) Put the hot dogs on a parchment-lined baking sheet and bake them until the pastry is a deep golden brown and the hot dogs are starting to blacken on the edges, 22 to 25 minutes, rotating the sheet halfway through baking.

EGG WASH

MAKES ¾ CUP

1 egg, beaten
½ cup heavy cream

* In a small bowl, using a fork, beat the egg and cream together until combined. Leftover egg wash will keep for 1 week in the refrigerator.

GRANNY'S CRUNCHY CHEESE STRAWS
for your pockets & parties

IN THE SOUTH, CHEESE STRAWS ARE found at every single wedding reception, baby shower, birthday party, anniversary party—pretty much anytime a party gets a bit fancied up. You can make them into the traditional long straws or curled crescents.

This is Granny's recipe, with the perfect texture: crunchy, but not too hard, and with a bright cheese flavor. She catered hundreds of weddings, and she must have made thousands of these cheese straws over the years. I don't ever recall visiting her when there weren't some cooling on her blue linoleum counters or being boxed up between layers of wax paper. She used an old aluminum cookie press to squeeze the cheese and flour mixture into the perfect crescent shape. Many a press was broken over the years due to either high usage or if the cheese mixture wasn't the right temperature.

Set these out as appetizers with cool cocktails for a backyard garden party or take them along for road trips or picnics.

MAKES 6 DOZEN 2-INCH CRESCENT-SHAPED CHEESE STRAWS

8 ounces extra-sharp cheddar cheese (2 cups), grated, at room temperature

½ cup (1 stick) plus 2 tablespoons unsalted butter, at room temperature

1½ cups all-purpose flour

½ teaspoon kosher salt

½ teaspoon smoked paprika

Pinch of cayenne

* In a stand mixer fitted with the paddle attachment, cream the cheese and butter together on medium-high speed. In a small bowl, sift together the flour, salt, paprika, and cayenne. Add the flour mixture to the cheese and butter, half at a time, mixing until combined and scraping down the bowl once or twice. Be patient: the dough takes a little while to incorporate and will look a bit dry. When the dough comes together, turn it out on a work surface and knead it a little, using your hands to incorporate all of the dry bits.

* Preheat the oven to 350 degrees F.

* Fill a pastry bag or cookie press fitted with a star tip. (If you're using a disposable pastry bag, double up the bags and stagger the seams to avoid tearing.) Note that you'll get an arm workout as this dough is stiff—it's easier to pipe if you fill the bag three or four separate times. Pipe the dough into long straws or 2- to 3-inch bite-size pieces. Gently bend each piece to form a crescent shape, or leave them straight. Put the cheese straws on a baking sheet—they will all fit snugly on one or you can divide them onto two—and bake them until the cheese appears just a bit darker in color, 17 to 18 minutes, rotating the sheets front to back and top to bottom halfway through baking. Cool the cheese straws on the baking sheets. Leftover cheese straws will keep for 1 week stored in a lidded glass jar or ziplock bag.

COUNTRY CAVIAR
perfect deviled eggs

DEVILED EGG PLATTERS ARE HANDED DOWN among Southern families, and a back-yard barbecue or church gathering is never complete without "country caviar." Once you master the perfect hard-boiled egg, perfect deviled eggs are close behind. If you know in advance you want to make these, buy your eggs the week before: they will be much easier to peel. Make more than you need or think you'll need, because you'll end up eating at least five or six before your guests arrive. You wouldn't want that deviled egg platter to have empty spots! Personally, I can eat my weight alone in deviled eggs.

MAKES 36 HALVES

18 Perfect Hard-Boiled Eggs (recipe follows), peeled and halved lengthwise

¾ cup mayonnaise, such as Duke's or Best Foods

1 tablespoon Dijon or creole mustard

2 teaspoons pickle juice or white vinegar

½ teaspoon freshly ground black pepper

¼ teaspoon cayenne

⅛ teaspoon kosher salt

Smoked paprika, for garnish

* Carefully, using a spoon or clean fingers, remove the yolks from the halved eggs and put them in a medium bowl. Rinse off any remaining yolk from the egg whites. Place the whites on a deviled egg plate or platter, setting any broken ones aside.

* Place the yolks into the bowl of a food processor and pulse until no clumps remain. (Or you can push the yolks through the back of a sieve into a bowl.) Add the mayonnaise, Dijon, pickle juice, pepper, and cayenne. Pulse until combined, adding a bit more mayonnaise if the filling is too dry. Taste the filling and add the salt—deviled egg filling salts easily, and you need to season gradually. Pulse and taste again, adding another small pinch of salt if needed.

* Scrape the filling into a pastry bag fitted with a star tip and pipe the filling into each egg white. (Alternatively, you can use a ziplock bag: squeeze the filling to one side, cut off one corner of the bag, and proceed to fill the eggs.) Garnish the eggs with a dusting of paprika. Eat all of the ones that broke. I also like to add a sprinkling of sugar over the assembled eggs and then brûlée them with a blowtorch.

PERFECT HARD-BOILED EGGS

MAKES 18 EGGS

18 large eggs,
   preferably 1 week old

* Gently place the eggs in a saucepot and cover them with an inch of hot tap water. Turn the heat to high and bring the water to a boil. Right when it boils, turn off the heat, cover the pot with a lid, and remove it from the burner. Leave the pot covered for exactly 9 minutes. When the timer goes off, immediately pour out the hot water and run cold water over the eggs until you are able to handle them comfortably. Peel the eggs, rinsing any remaining shell off gently with cool water.

FRIED SQUID, PICKLE & LEMON PLATE
with comeback sauce

WE TAKE THE KIDS SQUID JIGGING in Seattle's cold, rainy months, when the squid migrate from the Pacific Ocean to Puget Sound. Squid feed at night and are attracted to light; we bring lanterns and buckets, hot chocolate for the kids, and whiskey for the adults. Jigging for squid is an easy thing for kids to do. It gets them out during the winter, and they love watching the squid turn colors after they're caught.

Fried pickles are common in much of the South. Once when I was frying up a batch for my kids when they were little, I had some extra lemons that were on their way out, so on a whim I added them. The kids and I fell in love, and since then we have this plate whenever I feel like making something a bit fun.

Note: Whole squid is much cheaper to buy than cleaned squid. Try cleaning it yourself; I provide directions below. (If you're squeamish, you can use thawed frozen squid or ask your fishmonger to clean it for you.) I plan on one squid per person after it's cleaned—we usually catch smallish squid that weigh less than ten ounces. I use Meyer lemons when they're around as they have a sweeter, milder taste. Any other fresh fish or shrimp can be substituted for the squid.

MAKES 6 SERVINGS

2 to 3 small lemons, thinly sliced

2 cups buttermilk

6 (10-ounce) fresh squid

1 recipe Cornmeal Dredge (page 98)

Canola oil, for frying

1 jar Wandering Goose Spicy Dills (or your favorite 24-ounce jar pickles), drained and sliced into ¼-inch rounds

3 to 4 chives, chopped, for garnish

Comeback Sauce (page 173), for serving

* Put the lemons in a large bowl and pour the buttermilk over them. Soak the lemons while you clean the squid.

* Holding a squid's head with one hand and its body with the other, pull it apart with a firm tug and twist, and the guts will slip out. Discard the guts. The tentacles and tube are what you eat. Cut the tentacles off the head right behind the eyes, and discard the head. Save the ink gland for another use such as a homemade squid ink pasta, rice, or risotto. Squeeze the tentacles where they connect with the head of the squid and the beak will pop out. Discard the beak. Pull the thin, clear

continued

sliver of cartilage from the tube and discard. Rinse the tube under cold water, then slice it into rings. Repeat with the remaining squid.

* Spread the cornmeal dredge out on a pie pan or plate and set it next to the bowl with the lemons. Line another plate with paper towels and set it aside.

* In a large cast-iron skillet or saucepot over medium heat, heat 2 inches of the oil until it registers 350 degrees F on a deep-fry thermometer. Working in small batches so the cornmeal doesn't clump, toss the pickles in the dredge, then gently add them to the oil. Fry them until golden brown, 2 minutes per side. Remove them with tongs or a slotted spatula to drain on the lined plate. Check the temperature of your oil often before continuing to fry so it maintains a steady 350 degrees F. Repeat the dredging and frying with the lemon slices. Finally, toss the squid pieces in the dredge and fry them quickly, about 1 minute, then drain. Arrange everything on a large platter, garnish with the chives, and serve with a bowl of Comeback Sauce in the middle.

PRINCESS "HUSH NOW" HUSH PUPPIES

GRANNY ALWAYS HAD A SMALL DOG OR TWO, and I remember at least four of them. The last one she had before she died was named Princess. Princess was a little black toy poodle that would scratch your legs when you came over and bark and bark and bark. Actually, more like yap. When Granny's doorbell rang, which was often, Princess would begin her incessant yapping, and all the while Granny would say, "Hush, Princess! Hush! Hush now!" For years, my dad simply called the dog "Hush" and it stuck.

The story goes that hush puppies were invented in North Carolina fish camps. The fishermen would be frying their fish over an open fire and started frying off bits of cornmeal to feed to the dogs to make them hush. I imagine them saying "Hush now!" much the way my Granny did. To give Princess a little bit of credit, when Granny died of a heart attack, she'd been hanging her house plants out on her back porch on an unseasonably warm February morning. When her neighbor Valeria came over to drop off Granny's broom, she found Granny lying on her back with Princess right on top of her. Princess wouldn't let anyone near Granny, and the EMT driver had to throw a coat over that little dog before they could get to her. Hush now, Princess. Hush.

MAKES 16 LARGE OR 36 SMALL PUPPIES

1¼ cups regular ground cornmeal (not coarsely ground)

½ cup all-purpose flour

1 teaspoon baking powder

½ teaspoon baking soda

1½ teaspoons kosher salt

¼ teaspoon cayenne

¾ cup grated sweet onion

3 scallions, green and white parts, thinly sliced

1 egg

¾ cup buttermilk

Canola oil, for frying

Whipped Honey Butter (page 116), for serving

continued

Granny and Princess on Wiley Avenue, Salisbury, North Carolina

* In a large bowl, whisk together the cornmeal, flour, baking powder, baking soda, salt, cayenne, onion, and scallions. Using a wooden spoon, make a well in the center and add the egg and buttermilk. Using a whisk, mix the egg and buttermilk in the well, then slowly incorporate the dry ingredients, being careful not to overmix. Use a rubber spatula to scrape down the bowl, making sure there are no clumps of cornmeal.

* Line a plate with paper towels and set it aside. In a deep cast-iron skillet or Dutch oven over medium-high heat, heat 3 inches of oil until it registers 375 degrees F on a deep-fry thermometer. Using a 1-ounce scoop or 1 heaping tablespoon (or 1 heaping teaspoon if making small puppies), scoop the batter and release it gently into the oil. Working in small batches so the oil maintains 375 degrees F, fry until golden brown on all sides, 2 to 3 minutes. Remove the puppies with tongs or a slotted spatula to drain on the lined plate. Serve immediately with the honey butter, or keep them warm in a 200-degree-F oven until ready to serve.

MAKE IT A PARTY

Our house is a revolving door of friends and family. When cooking, I always plan on having extra in case a friend or two (or four) happens to stop by or the teenagers have some of their hungry friends over. I love to cook a huge pot of something like Southern Spaghetti Sauce (page 155) with a big salad and French bread, or platters of Big Love Buttermilk Fried Chicken (page 95) and bowls of Smoky Meat Collards (page 130). Put on some music, dim the lights, and light some candles. Give everyone something to drink and one simple task to do.

You can also do a big fish fry (see page 113) or serve "Granddaddy's Coming to Visit" Peel and Eat Shrimp (page 108) along with the Princess "Hush Now" Hush Puppies. Make sure to set out bowls of Quick and Spicy Cocktail Sauce (page 180), French Rémoulade (page 178), and Whipped Honey Butter (page 116) for dipping; lemon wedges for squeezing; and *plenty* of ice-cold Dixie lager.

ANGELS ON HORSEBACK
bacon, oysters, toast & warmed lemon butter

THERE ARE TWO TRADITIONAL VERSIONS OF this recipe. One is a country appetizer where the oysters are wrapped in bacon, baked, and served on toast points. The other is the New Orleans–style oysters *en brochette*, where the oysters and bacon are skewered, dusted in flour, and deep fried. I love them both, so I combined them here. I've added the drizzle of honey because I keep bees and always have a mason jar of honey on my counter. (I drizzle honey on everything, including eggs, fried chicken, and pork.)

MAKES 8 APPETIZER SERVINGS

For the lemon butter:
½ cup (1 stick) unsalted
　　butter
2 tablespoons freshly
　　squeezed lemon juice
1 teaspoon Worcester-
　　shire sauce
½ teaspoon Texas Pete
　　or Crystal hot sauce
¼ teaspoon kosher salt

1 baguette, cut on the
　　bias into 16 (1-inch-
　　thick) slices
8 slices thick-cut bacon,
　　cut in half

16 small oysters,
　　shucked
1 cup buttermilk
1 egg
2 cups all-purpose flour
2 teaspoons kosher salt
1 teaspoon freshly
　　ground black pepper
½ teaspoon Old Bay
　　Seasoning
¼ teaspoon cayenne
Canola oil, for frying
Honey, for drizzling
3 to 4 chives, chopped,
　　for garnish

* To make the lemon butter, in a small saucepan over low heat, melt the butter. Stir in the lemon juice, Worcestershire sauce, hot sauce, and salt until well blended. Keep warm until you're ready to serve the appetizers.

* Preheat the oven to 300 degrees F. Line a plate with paper towels and set it aside.

* Lay the baguette slices on a baking sheet and toast until they're crispy but not brown, 4 to 5 minutes. Transfer the slices to a plate and set them aside.

* Increase the oven temperature to 350 degrees F. Lay the bacon slices on the baking sheet and cook them partway, just until the fat is starting to render and the bacon is starting to brown, 8 to 10 minutes. Transfer them to the lined plate to drain. Wrap each oyster in bacon and skewer the seam closed with a toothpick. Set the wrapped oysters aside on a plate.

* Pour the buttermilk into a small bowl and beat in the egg. In a medium bowl, whisk together the flour, salt, pepper, Old Bay, and cayenne. Arrange the plate of oysters next to the bowls of buttermilk and flour, assembly-line style, and put them near the stove.

* Line another plate with paper towels and set it aside. In a small Dutch oven or deep cast-iron skillet over medium heat, heat 2 inches of oil until it registers 325 degrees F on a deep-fry thermometer. Holding the top of the toothpick, dip each oyster in the buttermilk mixture, then dredge it in the flour mixture. Working in small batches, gently drop the oysters into the oil. Fry them until golden brown, about 2 minutes per side. Remove them with tongs or a slotted spatula to drain on the prepared plate. Repeat with the remaining oysters.

* To serve, arrange the toasted baguette slices on a platter and brush the lemon butter on top. Add a fried oyster (remove the toothpick) on each. Drizzle with honey and sprinkle with chopped chives.

TEXAS PETE

I know, I know, the label says "Texas," for goodness sake. But since the 1930s, Texas Pete has been made in Winston-Salem, North Carolina. I have never seen a dining table or kitchen counter in the state without this ubiquitous hot sauce. Crystal is good, and it's what we use at The Goose, but Texas Pete has a viscosity and a tanginess that surpass most other bottled hot sauces. I can find it out here in grocery stores or you can order it though Amazon. God bless Amazon, and God bless Texas Pete.

SPICED PRALINES

"no, they don't come from a praline tree"

GRANNY HAD TWO HUGE PECAN TREES in her backyard. Every fall, the pecans would start to drop, and my cousins and I would collect large grocery sacks full of them. Granny used the fresh nuts in her pecan pies for Thanksgiving and Christmas. Around the holidays, if you sat on the couch (mostly the men watching football), she would place a large bowl of whole pecans on your lap to crack. In the South, small paper sacks of whole pecans are often given as a hostess gift during the holidays; bagged in cellophane, these nuts would make a great gift. If you like a bit more heat like I do, increase the cayenne by a pinch or two.

MAKES 4 CUPS

2 egg whites

1 pound pecan halves
   (4 cups)

½ cup packed dark
   brown sugar

½ teaspoon ground
   cinnamon

½ teaspoon ground
   cumin

½ teaspoon kosher salt

¼ teaspoon cayenne

¼ teaspoon ground
   cloves

¼ teaspoon freshly
   grated nutmeg

* Preheat the oven to 300 degrees F.

* In the bowl of a stand mixer with the whisk attachment, beat the egg whites until they're frothy and have doubled in volume. Add the pecans and toss to coat them with the egg. In a medium bowl, thoroughly mix the sugar, cinnamon, cumin, salt, cayenne, cloves, and nutmeg and pour them into a paper sack. Add the pecans and shake to coat them. Spread the pecans out on a baking sheet and bake them until they have darkened in color and you can smell the spices, 20 to 25 minutes, stirring them and rotating the sheet halfway through baking. Cool them on the baking sheet, then pack them into cellophane bags for gifts or in a ziplock bag or lidded jar for up to 10 days.

Shortly after my husband and I got together, pralines came up in the conversation, and he asked me—I kid you not—"What does a praline tree look like?" As soon as he said it, he quickly realized the error of his ways and tried to backtrack. I couldn't fault him; after all, he was from Alaska and had never even had a biscuit until he met me.

GRAVY

WHERE IT ALL BEGINS

MUSHROOM GRAVY 49

MJ'S CHIPPED BEEF ON TOAST *kid's white gravy* 50

SAWMILL GRAVY *sausage & sage* 52

COUNTRY HAM WITH REDEYE GRAVY *& perfect fried eggs* 55

SIMPLE ROAST CHICKEN & PAN GRAVY 57

IKE BISCUITS, EVERYONE HAS THEIR own opinion about gravy. Gravy is basically made from combining meat drippings, flour, stock or milk, and salt and pepper—that's where you start, but where you end up is simply a matter of personality and preference. For me, it's butter or meat drippings, flour, milk, chicken stock, hot sauce, Worcestershire sauce, an herb of some kind, and salt and pepper. It's my belief that any good-tasting gravy will have some color and not be milk white. It's also my belief that gravy should have a bit of a kick from hot sauce and black pepper and the proper amount of salt. Nothing, I tell you—*nothing*—is sadder to me than pale and seasoning-challenged gravy.

MUSHROOM GRAVY

THIS MUSHROOM GRAVY IS PERFECT FOR a "Meatless Monday" meal on a chilly autumn day. Serve it over split, toasted biscuits with a couple of poached eggs for protein. Made with homemade mushroom stock, it has a rich mushroom flavor. This recipe can easily be doubled to feed a crowd.

MAKES 8 CUPS, OR ENOUGH FOR 10 TO 12 BISCUITS

For the stock

2½ pounds portobello or cremini mushrooms

1 large sweet onion, diced

2 ribs celery, diced

1 carrot, diced

2 sprigs fresh rosemary

8 sprigs thyme

1 bay leaf

2 teaspoons kosher salt

2 quarts (8 cups) cold water

¼ cup extra-virgin olive oil

Kosher salt and freshly ground black pepper

1 cup (2 sticks) unsalted butter

1 cup all-purpose flour

2 cups whole milk

¼ cup Worcestershire sauce

¼ cup Texas Pete or Crystal hot sauce

¼ cup chopped fresh flat-leaf parsley

¼ cup chopped fresh thyme leaves

2 tablespoons chopped fresh rosemary leaves

Zest and juice from ½ lemon

* First cut the stems off the mushrooms and the gills from the caps, reserving the caps for the gravy.

* In a large stockpot over medium-high heat, combine the mushroom stems and gills, onion, celery, carrot, rosemary and thyme sprigs, bay leaf, salt, and water and bring to a boil. Once it's boiling, reduce the heat to a simmer and cook until reduced by one-quarter, about 45 minutes. Skim any residue that rises and discard. Strain the stock through a sieve and discard the solids. You should have about 6 cups.

* Preheat the oven to 400 degrees F.

* Slice the reserved mushroom caps into thick slices. Put the mushroom slices on a baking sheet; drizzle them with the oil and season with a pinch of salt and pepper, tossing with your hands to evenly coat. Roast the mushrooms until they are dark brown, 20 to 30 minutes. Set them aside.

* In a large sauté pan, melt the butter over medium heat until it bubbles. Whisk in the flour and cook until it's golden brown, 3 to 5 minutes. Slowly add the milk, then the mushroom stock, whisking constantly to avoid lumps. Add the roasted mushrooms and stir in the Worcestershire, hot sauce, parsley, thyme and rosemary leaves, and lemon zest and juice. Bring to a simmer and cook, stirring frequently until thick. Season with salt and pepper to taste. Keep warm until ready to serve. Store the gravy in a lidded container for up to 1 week in the refrigerator.

MJ'S CHIPPED BEEF ON TOAST
kid's white gravy

THIS DISH IS ONE OF THE very first things I remember being taught to cook by MJ. I must have been about seven years old because my memory is of standing on tippy-toes to look into the skillet. I recently made it for my teenage boys, and between bites they said, "Why haven't you made this for us before?" I promptly showed them right then and there how to make this gravy.

I use thinly sliced *bresaola*, but any cured beef will work. For the bread, I buy *shokupan* (Japanese white bread) from a local Asian grocery, Uwajimaya. Thick-sliced, with a small crumb and buttery flavor, *shokupan* is a perfect vehicle for this thick white gravy. You can find many versions of it at Asian grocery stores, or substitute good ol' Texas toast, the white sandwich bread available in most grocery stores.

MAKES 4 TO 6 SERVINGS

½ cup (1 stick) butter

½ cup all-purpose flour

3½ cups whole milk

2 tablespoons Worcestershire sauce

2 teaspoons Texas Pete or Crystal hot sauce

2½ teaspoons kosher salt

½ teaspoon freshly ground black pepper

10 ounces thinly sliced *bresaola* or other cured beef

4 to 6 slices thick white bread, toasted

* In a large skillet over medium-high heat, melt the butter. When the butter starts to bubble, whisk in the flour to make a roux. Cook for 2 to 3 minutes, until the roux starts to smell nutty. Slowly whisk in the milk and bring the gravy up to a simmer. Cook until thickened, 3 to 4 minutes. Add the Worcestershire, hot sauce, salt, and pepper and mix to combine. Taste for seasoning and adjust as necessary. Reduce the heat to low and add in the beef. Keep warm until ready to serve. Spoon about ¾ cup of gravy over each slice of toast. Serve immediately.

Mama MJ and her new Pontiac she got for her twenty-first birthday, 1970

SAWMILL GRAVY

sausage & sage

SOME FOLKS IN THE SOUTH CALL sawmill "milk gravy," but for me, it means white gravy with sausage. The name supposedly comes from Appalachian lumberjacks. Some say the camp cook had to use sparse ingredients to feed a lot of hungry men, and a gravy flavored with meat drippings gave them less to complain about. Others say the name comes from the cook adding cornmeal to thicken the gravy, which caused the loggers to think there was in fact sawdust in it. No matter where the name comes from, sawmill is the backbone of all Southern gravies.

Wandering Goose's version is made with seasoned pork sausage, chicken stock, and milk. I add hot sauce and Worcestershire for taste and color. The chopped fresh sage and freshly grated nutmeg add an additional flavor layer. This makes a lot of gravy, but you can refrigerate the leftovers, heating up a portion for breakfast each day; the gravy will keep for a week. To reheat it, just add a little bit of milk and taste again for seasoning. Or invite all your friends over for a biscuits-and-gravy brunch with sides of country ham and bacon. This is a spicy gravy so cut the amount of hot sauce in half if you don't like spice.

MAKES 6 CUPS GRAVY OR ENOUGH FOR 6 TO 8 BISCUITS

1½ pounds ground pork

3 tablespoons Sausage Spice Mix (recipe follows)

2 tablespoons extra-virgin olive oil

½ cup (1 stick) unsalted butter

¾ cup all-purpose flour

4 cups whole milk

1½ cups chicken stock

3 tablespoons Texas Pete or Crystal hot sauce

3 tablespoons Worcestershire sauce

3 tablespoons chopped fresh sage

½ teaspoon freshly grated nutmeg

Kosher salt and freshly ground black pepper

* In a large bowl, put the pork and spice mix. Using your hands, mix them together, breaking up the pork and evenly distributing the seasoning. Line a plate with paper towels.

* In a large skillet over medium heat, heat the oil until it's shimmering. Add the pork and cook, stirring, until it's no longer pink inside, 4 to 5 minutes. Using a slotted spoon, transfer it to the lined plate to drain. Remove all but 2 tablespoons of the oil from the pan, leaving any browned bits in the skillet. Melt the butter in the same skillet. When it bubbles, increase the heat to medium high and whisk in the flour. Cook it slowly until it starts to smell nutty and looks golden brown, about 1 minute. Whisk in the milk slowly, 1 cup at a time, to avoid clumps. Once the gravy starts to thicken, about 2 minutes, whisk in the chicken stock. Add the pork back to the skillet along with the hot sauce, Worcestershire, sage, and nutmeg. Add the salt and pepper to taste and bring to a simmer.

Continue to cook until thick and bubbly, 2 to 3 minutes. Reduce the heat to low. Taste and adjust the seasoning with additional salt or pepper as needed and serve immediately, or keep warm until company comes.

SAUSAGE SPICE MIX

MAKES 1¾ CUPS

¾ cup kosher salt

3 tablespoons chili powder

3 tablespoons smoked paprika

2 tablespoons freshly ground black pepper

2 tablespoons packed dark brown sugar

1½ tablespoons white pepper

1 tablespoon cayenne

1 tablespoon ground coriander

1 tablespoon ground cumin

½ tablespoon crushed red pepper flakes

1¼ teaspoons dry mustard powder

* Sift all the ingredients into a large bowl and mix thoroughly. The spice mix will keep for up to 3 months stored in a lidded glass jar or ziplock bag.

THE SIGALA BROTHERS

Oscar Sigala has been with me as a cook from day one. A month after The Wandering Goose opened, he brought in his brother Daniel to cook as well. Oscar is a charismatic, social, and hardworking man with an exceptional sense of humor. He is constantly popping out from behind a corner to scare me (and I scream every time, even after all these years) and hides little plastic rats and rubber snakes for me to find. He runs out and checks my car for a mark from the meter maid when I've forgotten to. Most importantly, though, he makes me laugh every single day—which is so important in a busy restaurant, where you're surrounded by chaos and an unforgiving list of things to do. Restaurants across America could not sustain without men and women like Oscar and Daniel.

COUNTRY HAM WITH REDEYE GRAVY
and perfect fried eggs

GRANNY AND GRANDDADDY BOTH DRANK COFFEE, and they both made this redeye gravy the next morning with the dregs of the coffeepot. It's best served right away, poured onto a split, toasted buttermilk biscuit with a fried egg and country ham on top, or over a bowl of grits. Some things are just that simple and perfect.

There are a few different stories about how redeye gravy got its name, and part or all of them are true, I'm sure. Some say Andrew Jackson requested gravy "as red as the cook's eyes." For others, it's the oily fat that rises to the top when you add the coffee, resembling the red veins in your eyeball. Regardless, it's a darn good gravy—easy to make and a great way to not waste day-old coffee! We use Caffe Vita's signature espresso blend, Caffe del Sol, in ours.

MAKES 1 CUP GRAVY, OR ENOUGH FOR 4 BISCUITS

2 tablespoons canola oil

4 large slices
country ham

1 cup strong
brewed coffee

2 tablespoons unsalted
butter

Freshly ground black
pepper

4 Perfect Fried Eggs
(recipe follows)

* In a large skillet over medium-high heat, heat the oil until it's shimmering. Add the ham and cook until it's golden brown in most places, 3 to 4 minutes per side. (Depending on how large your ham slices are, you might need to work in two batches.) Place the ham slices on a plate while you make the gravy. Add the coffee to the skillet, scraping up any browned bits on the bottom. Reduce the heat to low and stir in the butter and pepper. Keep warm until ready to serve, along with the fried eggs.

PERFECT FRIED EGGS

MAKES 4 EGGS

1 tablespoon unsalted
butter

4 large eggs

Kosher salt and freshly
ground black pepper

* In a medium skillet over medium-high heat, melt the butter. Add the eggs and reduce the heat to medium low. Cover the skillet with a lid (or use a plate) and cook for 3 minutes. Turn off the heat and check to see if the eggs are cooked enough for you. If not, re-cover the pan and let them rest for 1 to 2 more minutes. Season them to taste with salt and pepper before serving.

CAFFE VITA

Caffe Vita is a local independent coffee roaster here in Seattle. Not only is it hands down some of the best coffee anywhere, the owners of the company, Mike and Liz McConnell, are some of the most generous people I know.

Mike started the business in 1995 at the age of 27. He had been working in the industry for a few years selling espresso machines and setting up distributors throughout the county when he came to realize his passion lay in the coffee itself. Mike and Liz not only own 11 Caffe Vita coffee houses in Seattle and around the country, but also more than 20 other restaurants and bars. Along the way, they've helped me and many others realize our dream of owning a restaurant by offering capital, support, and guidance. Mike and Liz never asked me for a business plan; they believed in me and my food, and helped make it happen. Without them, The Wandering Goose would still be a dream.

SIMPLE ROAST CHICKEN & PAN GRAVY

RECENTLY I TAUGHT MY TWO TEENAGE boys to make a good roast chicken and pan gravy. It's important to me that they can cook for themselves and their friends when they go to college, or at least have the option of knowing how to cook. Roast chicken is an easy supper to have on the table with a minimal amount of work. (I roast two chickens at a time to feed our family of seven.) If there is any chicken left over, the next day we eat it between slices of soft bread with thick smears of Duke's mayo and salt and pepper.

MAKES 4 TO 6 SERVINGS

1 (5- to 6-pound) whole chicken

¼ cup extra-virgin olive oil

Kosher salt and freshly ground black pepper

1 small sweet onion, quartered

1 head of garlic, top third cut off

1 medium lemon, quartered

1 bunch (about ¼ ounce) fresh thyme

½ cup (1 stick) unsalted butter

½ cup all-purpose flour

3 to 3½ cups chicken stock, depending on how thick you want the gravy

½ cup Big Herb Blend (recipe follows)

2 tablespoons Worcestershire sauce

1 tablespoon Texas Pete or Crystal hot sauce

* Preheat the oven to 425 degrees F.

* To roast the chicken, rinse it and discard the giblets. Pat it dry with paper towels. Drizzle the oil evenly all over the chicken, rubbing it into the skin, and sprinkle it liberally with salt and pepper inside and out. Place the chicken, breast side down, in a cast-iron skillet or Dutch oven. Stuff the inside of the chicken with the onion, garlic, lemon, and thyme. Roast the chicken until its juices run clear when you cut into the thigh, 65 to 75 minutes. The thigh should separate easily from the body once the chicken has finished cooking. Transfer the chicken to a plate to rest for 10 minutes while you make the gravy.

* Pour off all but 3 tablespoons of the fat and liquid left in the roasting pan (keeping the browned bits). Set the pan on the stove over medium-high heat and melt the butter. Once the butter is bubbling, whisk in the flour and cook until it's golden brown, 3 to 4 minutes. Slowly add the chicken stock, whisking constantly to avoid lumps. Bring the gravy to a simmer and cook until it's thick and bubbly, 6 to 7 minutes. (If it gets too thick, thin it with an additional ½ cup chicken stock.) Mix in the herb blend, Worcestershire, hot sauce, and ½ teaspoon salt. Taste and adjust the seasoning with additional salt and pepper as needed.

* Slice the chicken and pour the gravy over it to serve.

continued

BIG HERB BLEND

WE USE THIS IN OUR BUBBLE and Squeak (page 195), Veggie Hash (page 197), and just about everything that needs a blast of fresh herbs.

MAKES 1½ CUPS

1 bunch flat-leaf parsley,
  leaves chopped

3 tablespoons chopped
  fresh rosemary leaves

3 tablespoons chopped
  fresh thyme leaves

2 tablespoons chopped
  fresh sage leaves

* Mix all the herbs together and store in the refrigerator; the blend will keep for 1 to 2 days.

BIG LOVE
BIG BISCUITS

SAVORY & SWEET BISCUITS

BEST BUTTERMILK BISCUITS 65

MAPLE, BACON & DATE BISCUITS *with maple glaze* 67

EVERYTHING BISCUITS *with a baked egg on top* 68

CHEDDAR CHIVE BISCUITS 70

SWEET POTATO BISCUITS 71

BACON, CHEDDAR & SCALLION BISCUITS 72

SAUSAGE & SAGE BISCUITS 73

MAMA LIL'S PEPPERS & TILLAMOOK CHEDDAR BISCUITS 74

BISCUIT CINNAMON ROLLS
with cream cheese & buttermilk frosting 77

ANGEL BISCUITS *always with country ham* 79

BISCUIT CROUTONS *for soups & salads* 81

**M**ANY PEOPLE UNDERESTIMATE THE SKILL required to make a biscuit and have certain ways they think a biscuit should be made or opinions on how it should taste. To Southerners, biscuits are a reflection of your personality. They can be squat and flat, tall and towering, bumpy and rambunctious, light and flaky, crisp or cakey. Biscuits are the tie that binds Southerners in the same way the slick humidity settles on our skin and behind our necks. Not a single Southerner I know has ever turned down or criticized a biscuit, a biscuit maker, or the style of someone's biscuit. We are all simply grateful to cradle a steaming-hot, buttered biscuit in our hands.

The biscuit maker is not so much a technician but a person who works by feel, sound, and touch. We start with the flour, add some baking powder and salt, a wee bit of sugar, and diced cold butter. This is mixed until the butter is the size of small peas, then we add the thick, cold buttermilk. Not too many turns on the mixer here, y'all! (My granny used to say, "If you mixed it eleven times, that is ten times too many.")

Then everything is dumped out onto our lightly floured wooden tabletop. We fold it over just enough to incorporate the last of the dry crumbly bits and ever so gently punch out each biscuit by hand with a metal biscuit cutter. (The cutting is important too: you never want to twist the cutter or it can seal the sides of the biscuit, resulting in a flat, dense mess that never got a chance to rise to its glory.) Each biscuit is then brushed with a soft touch of melted butter and placed into a 425-degree-F oven. We rotate the trays exactly once, and after twenty-two minutes or so, we take out perfectly cooked biscuits with light and fluffy interiors and a crunchy, golden-brown exterior.

So if someone takes the time to make you a biscuit from scratch, not from a can, hug them hard and thank them twice—then go try to make your own.

For making biscuits, I like to start with a superhot oven, 450 degrees F, to ensure a high rise and crunchy exterior. You'll notice in the biscuit recipes that I set the oven temperature to 450 degrees F and then turn it down to 425 degrees F right after putting the biscuits in the oven. Some oven temperatures reduce by 25 degrees or more when you open the door, and doing it this way makes it foolproof for the best buttermilk biscuits.

BEST BUTTERMILK BISCUITS

THIS IS THE RECIPE FROM WHICH you can alter and change the flavor of your biscuit. Once you have this version down, try any of the recipes that follow. All are sure to please and easy to prepare.

MAKES 1 DOZEN 3-INCH BISCUITS

6½ cups flour (see below)

3 tablespoons sugar

2 tablespoons plus
  2 teaspoons baking
  powder

1 tablespoon kosher salt

1½ teaspoons baking soda

1½ cups (3 sticks)
  unsalted butter, diced
  and chilled

3 cups buttermilk,
  chilled

2 tablespoons butter,
  melted

* In the bowl of a stand mixer fitted with the paddle attachment, mix the flour, sugar, baking powder, salt, and baking soda on low speed until combined. Increase the speed to medium low and mix in the butter until it is the size of small peas. With the mixer running, add the buttermilk, mixing just until blended. Do not overmix; the dough will be a bit shaggy with bits of unincorporated dry ingredients.

* Preheat the oven to 450 degrees F.

* Turn the dough out onto a lightly floured surface. Using a floured rolling pin, roll it gently into a 1½-inch-thick circle. Cut out 12 biscuits using a 3-inch cutter, dipping it in flour between biscuits. Do not twist the cutter; this will seal the sides of your biscuits and they will not rise as high.

* Arrange the biscuits onto two baking sheets, and brush them with the melted butter. Right before baking, reduce the oven temperature to 425 degrees F. Bake the biscuits until golden brown on top, 22 to 25 minutes, rotating the sheets halfway through baking.

WHICH FLOUR TO USE?

At The Goose we use soft winter-wheat flour from Boonville Flour and Feed Mill in Boonville, North Carolina, where they have been milling flour since 1896. Soft winter-wheat is a variety grown mostly east of the Mississippi that has a low protein and gluten content, and hence a more delicate crumb. Granny used classic White Lily flour. If you can't find either of those, you can substitute half cake flour and half all-purpose flour, or use Bob's Red Mill organic unbleached white all-purpose flour or any unbleached all-purpose flour.

Depending on which flour you use, you might need to add a touch more buttermilk to your dry ingredients

MAPLE, BACON & DATE BISCUITS
with maple glaze

AT THE GOOSE, WE USE SUPER-SMOKY Benton's bacon from Tennessee. I wanted to complement the bacon's smokiness with something sweet and dense, like dates. You can also use dried figs, which are just as good (I use them interchangeably). The maple syrup glaze adds just the perfect amount of maple flavor.

MAKES 1 DOZEN 3-INCH BISCUITS

6½ cups flour
  (see page 65)
3 tablespoons sugar
2 tablespoons plus
  2 teaspoons baking
  powder
1 tablespoon kosher salt
1½ teaspoons baking
  soda
1½ cups (3 sticks)
  unsalted butter, diced
  and chilled
1 cup (8 ounces) pitted
  chopped dates

8 ounces chopped
  cooked bacon
3 cups buttermilk,
  chilled
1 tablespoon maple
  extract
2 tablespoons butter,
  melted

For the maple glaze:
1 cup sifted
  confectioners' sugar
⅓ cup pure maple syrup
2 teaspoons maple
  extract

* In the bowl of a stand mixer fitted with the paddle attachment, mix the flour, sugar, baking powder, salt, and baking soda on low speed until combined. Increase the speed to medium low and mix in the butter until it is the size of small peas. Mix in the dates and bacon, and then, with the mixer running, add the buttermilk and maple extract, mixing just until blended. Do not over-mix; the dough will be a bit shaggy with bits of unincorporated dry ingredients.

* Preheat the oven to 450 degrees F.

* Turn the dough out onto a lightly floured surface. Using a floured rolling pin, roll it gently into a 1½-inch-thick circle. Cut out 12 biscuits using a 3-inch cutter, dipping it in flour between biscuits. Do not twist the cutter; this will seal the sides of your biscuits and they will not rise as high.

* Arrange the biscuits onto two baking sheets, and brush them with the melted butter. Right before baking, reduce the oven temperature to 425 degrees F. Bake the biscuits until golden brown on top, 22 to 25 minutes, rotating the sheets halfway through baking.

* To make the glaze, in a medium bowl, whisk together the confectioners' sugar, maple syrup, and maple extract until smooth.

* After the biscuits have cooled, drizzle them with the glaze. Serve immediately or keep at room temperature until company comes.

EVERYTHING BISCUITS
with a baked egg on top

TOPPED WITH DRIED ONION FLAKES, POPPY seeds, and sesame seeds, this biscuit has the complexity I crave for breakfast. I like to hollow out a little dent in the top and crack an egg in there before I bake the biscuit. With the egg or without, this biscuit is reminiscent of the everything bagels I grew up with and it's just as good.

MAKES 1 DOZEN 3-INCH BISCUITS

6½ cups flour
  (see page 65)
3 tablespoons sugar
2 tablespoons plus
  2 teaspoons baking
  powder
1 tablespoon kosher salt
1½ teaspoons baking
  soda
1½ cups (3 sticks)
  unsalted butter, diced
  and chilled

3 cups buttermilk,
  chilled
1 cup dehydrated onion
  flakes
½ cup poppy seeds
½ cup sesame seeds
2 tablespoons butter,
  melted
12 large eggs (optional)

* In the bowl of a stand mixer fitted with the paddle attachment, mix the flour, sugar, baking powder, salt, and baking soda on low speed until combined. Increase the speed to medium low and mix in the butter until it is the size of small peas. With the mixer running, add the buttermilk, mixing just until blended. Do not overmix; the dough will be a bit shaggy with bits of unincorporated dry ingredients.

* Preheat the oven to 450 degrees F.

* Turn the dough out onto a lightly floured surface. Using a floured rolling pin, roll it gently into a 1½-inch-thick circle. Cut out 12 biscuits using a 3-inch cutter, dipping it in flour between biscuits. Do not twist the cutter; this will seal the sides of your biscuits and they will not rise as high.

* In a medium bowl, combine the onion flakes, poppy seeds, and sesame seeds.

* Arrange the biscuits onto two baking sheets, and brush them with the melted butter. Dip the tops of the biscuits in the "everything" topping and return them to the baking sheets.

* Dip a whole egg in flour, and gently press the egg into the middle of the top of one of the biscuits, twisting it around a bit to make a well but not going all the way through to the bottom. Crack the egg in the well. Repeat with the remaining eggs and biscuits. (If not using the eggs, proceed to the next step.)

* Right before baking, reduce the oven temperature to 425 degrees F. Bake the biscuits until golden brown on top, 22 to 25 minutes, rotating the sheets halfway through baking.

CHEDDAR CHIVE BISCUITS

You can cut these into tiny one-inch biscuits and serve them as hors d'oeuvres before a party or make them regular size and serve them as a side to a weeknight supper. Feel free to experiment with other cheese and herb combinations, such as chèvre and parsley or rosemary and Gruyère.

MAKES 1 DOZEN 3-INCH BISCUITS

6½ cups flour
   (see page 65)
3 tablespoons sugar
2 tablespoons plus
   2 teaspoons baking
   powder
1 tablespoon kosher salt
1½ teaspoons baking
   soda

1½ cups (3 sticks)
   unsalted butter, diced
   and chilled
8 ounces extra-sharp
   cheddar cheese,
   grated
¾ cup diced chives
3 cups buttermilk,
   chilled
2 tablespoons butter,
   melted

* In the bowl of a stand mixer fitted with the paddle attachment, mix the flour, sugar, baking powder, salt, and baking soda on low speed until combined. Increase the speed to medium low and mix in the butter until it is the size of small peas. Mix in the cheese and chives, and then, with the mixer running, add the buttermilk, mixing just until blended. Do not overmix; the dough will be a bit shaggy with bits of unincorporated dry ingredients.

* Preheat the oven to 450 degrees F.

* Turn the dough out onto a lightly floured surface. Using a floured rolling pin, roll it gently into a 1½-inch-thick circle. Cut out 12 biscuits using a 3-inch cutter, dipping it in flour between biscuits. Do not twist the cutter; this will seal the sides of your biscuits and they will not rise as high.

* Arrange the biscuits on two baking sheets, and brush them with the melted butter. Right before baking, reduce the oven temperature to 425 degrees F. Bake the biscuits until golden brown on top, 22 to 25 minutes, rotating the sheets halfway through baking.

DAY-OLD BISCUITS

If you by chance have a biscuit or two left over the day after making a batch, trust me, these day-olds haven't lost their glory. Split them and toast them in a cast-iron skillet cut side down, or in a toaster oven cut side up. Add a hefty pat of butter and some freezer jam, or fry an egg and sprinkle some sharp cheddar or a spoonful of leftover collards on top for a quick breakfast or snack. Or use them to make Biscuit Croutons (page 81).

SWEET POTATO BISCUITS

I LOVE SWEET POTATOES AND EAT them roasted with nothing more than a sprinkling of salt. For this recipe, use the lighter, pale-yellow-colored potatoes. They are a bit drier than the orange-fleshed ones and release less liquid. These are great for The Sweet Blonde biscuit sandwich (see page 82) or used in place of the dough base in many of the biscuit recipes. Sometimes I add one-quarter cup chopped sage.

MAKES 1 DOZEN 3-INCH BISCUITS

1 pound sweet potatoes
6½ cups flour
    (see page 65)
3 tablespoons sugar
2 tablespoons plus
    2 teaspoons baking
    powder
1 tablespoon kosher salt

1½ teaspoons baking
    soda
1½ cups (3 sticks)
    unsalted butter, diced
    and chilled
1½ cups buttermilk,
    chilled
2 tablespoons butter,
    melted

* Preheat the oven to 400 degrees F.

* Wrap the potatoes in aluminum foil and bake for 1 hour, until soft on the inside. Let them cool until you can easily handle them. Peel the skins and break apart the flesh into 1-inch chunks. You should have about 2 cups. Set aside.

* In the bowl of a stand mixer fitted with the paddle attachment, mix the flour, sugar, baking powder, salt, and baking soda on low speed until combined. Increase the speed to medium low and mix in the butter until it is the size of small peas. Mix in the sweet potatoes, and then, with the mixer running, add the buttermilk, mixing just until blended. Do not overmix; the dough will be a bit shaggy with bits of unincorporated dry ingredients.

* Increase the oven temperature to 450 degrees F.

* Turn the dough out onto a lightly floured surface. Using a floured rolling pin, roll it gently into a 1½-inch-thick circle. Cut out 12 biscuits using a 3-inch cutter, dipping it in flour between biscuits. Do not twist the cutter; this will seal the sides of your biscuits and they will not rise as high.

* Arrange the biscuits on two baking sheets, and brush them with the melted butter. Right before baking, reduce the oven temperature to 425 degrees F. Bake the biscuits until golden brown on top, 22 to 25 minutes, rotating the sheets halfway through baking.

BACON, CHEDDAR & SCALLION BISCUITS

THIS IS THE TOP-SELLING SAVORY BISCUIT at The Goose. A lot of our customers will substitute this biscuit for the regular buttermilk one that comes with the biscuit sandwiches. Make sure your bacon is cooked until crispy. There is not much worse than flabby bacon! (Oh yeah, a pale gravy . . .)

MAKES 1 DOZEN 3-INCH BISCUITS

6½ cups flour
  (see page 65)
3 tablespoons sugar
2 tablespoons plus
  2 teaspoons baking
  powder
1 tablespoon kosher salt
1½ teaspoons baking
  soda
1½ cups (3 sticks)
  unsalted butter, diced
  and chilled

8 ounces chopped
  cooked bacon
8 ounces extra-sharp
  cheddar cheese,
  grated
1 bunch scallions, green
  and white parts,
  thinly sliced
3 cups buttermilk,
  chilled
2 tablespoons butter,
  melted

* In the bowl of a stand mixer fitted with the paddle attachment, mix the flour, sugar, baking powder, salt, and baking soda on low speed until combined. Increase the speed to medium low and mix in the butter until it is the size of small peas. Mix in the bacon, cheese, and scallions, and then, with the mixer running, add the buttermilk, mixing just until blended. Do not overmix; the dough will be a bit shaggy with bits of unincorporated dry ingredients.

* Preheat the oven to 450 degrees F.

* Turn the dough out onto a lightly floured surface. Using a floured rolling pin, roll it gently into a 1½-inch-thick circle. Cut out 12 biscuits using a 3-inch cutter, dipping it in flour between biscuits. Do not twist the cutter; this will seal the sides of your biscuits and they will not rise as high.

* Arrange the biscuits onto two baking sheets, and brush them with the melted butter. Right before baking, reduce the oven temperature to 425 degrees F. Bake the biscuits until golden brown on top, 22 to 25 minutes, rotating the sheets halfway through baking.

SAUSAGE & SAGE BISCUITS

MY AUNT DEE-DEE MADE SAUSAGE BALLS every Christmas. The smell of the ground pork sausage, sage, and cheddar inspired me to make these savory biscuits. You can cut them into large biscuits as directed, or make like Dee-Dee and use a one-ounce scoop for the batter, then roll it gently into balls with your fingers. But don't wait for Christmas or the holidays: serve them at a brunch or potluck, or make a batch and freeze to use at an impromptu cocktail party.

MAKES 1 DOZEN 3-INCH BISCUITS OR 4 DOZEN 1-INCH BISCUIT BALLS

6½ cups flour
(see page 65)

3 tablespoons sugar

2 tablespoons plus
2 teaspoons baking
powder

1 tablespoon kosher salt

1 tablespoon Sausage
Spice Mix (page 53)

1½ teaspoons baking
soda

1½ cups (3 sticks)
unsalted butter, diced
and chilled

1 pound cooked break-
fast sausage

8 ounces extra-sharp
cheddar cheese,
grated

½ cup chopped
fresh sage

3 cups buttermilk,
chilled

2 tablespoons butter,
melted

* In the bowl of a stand mixer fitted with the paddle attachment, mix the flour, sugar, baking powder, salt, spice mix, and baking soda on low speed until combined. Increase the speed to medium low and mix in the butter until it is the size of small peas. Mix in the sausage, cheese, and sage, and then, with the mixer running, add the buttermilk, mixing just until blended. Do not overmix; the dough will be a bit shaggy with bits of unincorporated dry ingredients.

* Preheat the oven to 450 degrees F.

* Turn the dough out onto a lightly floured sur-face. Using a floured rolling pin, roll it gently into a 1½-inch-thick circle. Cut out 12 biscuits using a 3-inch cutter, dipping it in flour between biscuits. Do not twist the cutter; this will seal the sides of your biscuits and they will not rise as high.

* Arrange the biscuits on two baking sheets, and brush them with the melted butter. Right before baking, reduce the oven temperature to 425 degrees F. Bake the biscuits until golden brown on top, 22 to 25 minutes, rotating the sheets halfway through baking.

MAMA LIL'S PEPPERS & TILLAMOOK CHEDDAR BISCUITS

MAMA LIL'S PEPPERS, GROWN AND PACKED in Eastern Washington's Yakima Valley, are available in many stores across the United States and online. We use the spicy version rather than the mild, but feel free to experiment with both. You can substitute any brand of oil-packed peppers.

MAKES 1 DOZEN 3-INCH BISCUITS

6½ cups flour (see page 65)

3 tablespoons sugar

2 tablespoons plus 2 teaspoons baking powder

1 tablespoon kosher salt

1½ teaspoons baking soda

1½ cups (3 sticks) unsalted butter, diced and chilled

1 cup chopped Mama Lil's peppers

8 ounces extra-sharp cheddar cheese, such as Tillamook, grated

3 cups buttermilk, chilled

2 tablespoons butter, melted

* In the bowl of a stand mixer fitted with the paddle attachment, mix the flour, sugar, baking powder, salt, and baking soda on low speed until combined. Increase the speed to medium low and mix in the butter until it is the size of small peas. Mix in the peppers and cheese, and then, with the mixer running, add the buttermilk, mixing just until blended. Do not overmix; the dough will be a bit shaggy with bits of unincorporated dry ingredients.

* Preheat the oven to 450 degrees F.

* Turn the dough out onto a lightly floured surface. Using a floured rolling pin, roll it gently into a 1½-inch-thick circle. Cut out 12 biscuits using a 3-inch cutter, dipping it in flour between biscuits. Do not twist the cutter; this will seal the sides of your biscuits and they will not rise as high.

* Arrange the biscuits on two baking sheets, and brush them with the melted butter. Right before baking, reduce the oven temperature to 425 degrees F. Bake the biscuits until golden brown on top, 22 to 25 minutes, rotating the sheets halfway through baking.

BISCUIT CINNAMON ROLLS
with cream cheese & buttermilk frosting

THERE ARE HUNDREDS OF WAYS TO make a cinnamon roll. Many recipes involve time-consuming steps and long waiting periods for the dough to rise. These fat rounds are ready fast, but taste like you spent days making them. Make the filling and frosting and keep them handy while you make the biscuits.

MAKES 1 DOZEN 3-INCH ROLLS

For the cinnamon-sugar filling:
¾ cup packed dark brown sugar
¼ cup granulated sugar
1 tablespoon ground cinnamon
½ teaspoon kosher salt
¼ teaspoon ground cloves
1 tablespoon butter, melted, plus more if needed

For the frosting:
4 ounces cream cheese, at room temperature
1 cup confectioners' sugar, sifted
2 tablespoons buttermilk

1 teaspoon vanilla extract
Pinch of kosher salt

6½ cups flour (see page 65)
3 tablespoons sugar
2 tablespoons plus 2 teaspoons baking powder
1 tablespoon kosher salt
1½ teaspoons baking soda
1½ cups (3 sticks) unsalted butter, diced and chilled
3 cups buttermilk, chilled
2 tablespoons butter, melted

* To make the filling, in a large bowl, stir together the sugars, cinnamon, salt, and cloves. Stir in the butter; the mixture should look like wet sand. If needed, add a bit more melted butter. Set it aside.

* To make the frosting, in the bowl of a stand mixer fitted with the paddle attachment, mix the cream cheese on medium speed until it is very smooth and no lumps remain. Mix in the confectioners' sugar, then the buttermilk, vanilla, and salt. Scrape down the bowl with a rubber spatula and mix again until the frosting is smooth. Transfer the frosting to a small bowl and set aside, at room temperature, while you make the biscuits.

* To make the rolls, in the bowl of a stand mixer fitted with the paddle attachment, mix the flour, sugar, baking powder, salt, and baking soda on low speed until combined. Increase the speed to medium low and mix in the butter until it is the size of small peas. With the mixer running, add the buttermilk, mixing just until blended. Do not overmix; the dough will be a bit shaggy with bits of unincorporated dry ingredients.

* Preheat the oven to 450 degrees F.

continued

* Turn the dough out onto a lightly floured surface. Using a floured rolling pin, roll it gently into a 12-by-6-inch rectangle that is ½-inch thick. Brush the dough all over with the melted butter, and sprinkle the filling over it, leaving a 1-inch border. Using a bench scraper or your hands, gently roll up the long side of the dough into a log. Trim ½ inch off the ends and cut the log into 1½-inch-thick slices, for a total of 10 to 12 pieces. Arrange the pieces cut side down on a baking sheet.

* Right before baking, reduce the oven temperature to 425 degrees F. Bake the rolls until puffed and golden brown on top, 22 to 25 minutes, rotating the sheet halfway through baking.

* Let the rolls cool completely on the baking sheet, then frost them using a butter knife or offset spatula. Serve immediately or gently rewarm them in a 200-degree-F oven if serving later.

ANGEL BISCUITS
always with country ham

GRANNY HAD HUNDREDS OF THESE ETHEREAL pillows of flour, yeast, and buttermilk in her kitchen most times I visited her, made as one-inch, bite-size biscuits for parties. I can see clearly in my mind her long fingers, bent with arthritis from years of cooking and baking, using an old snuff can to cut out the rounds. These biscuits are traditionally garnished with nothing more than a triangle of country ham and its own grease. (Oh. My. "Garnished with Grease" should be my epitaph.) Pop would sometimes help her fry the wee bits of country ham for an order that was soon to meet the white-gloved ladies of a wedding shower or brunch. He would nibble as he fried, and Granny would scold him, "Leave some for the order!" This is Granny's recipe.

MAKES 16 TO 18 BISCUITS

2¼ cups buttermilk

4 tablespoons sugar, divided

2¼ teaspoons (1 package) Red Star active dry yeast

5 cups flour (see page 65)

4 teaspoons baking powder

1 teaspoon baking soda

2½ teaspoons kosher salt

1 cup (1 stick) vegetable shortening, chilled and cut into cubes, or 1 cup (2 sticks) unsalted butter, chilled and cut into cubes

3 tablespoons canola oil, for frying

1 pound country ham, sliced

2 tablespoons butter, melted

* In a small saucepan over medium heat, warm the buttermilk until it reaches 110 degrees F on an instant-read thermometer. Remove the pan from the heat and measure ¼ cup of the warm buttermilk into a small bowl, along with 1 tablespoon of the sugar. Sprinkle the yeast over the buttermilk and let the mixture sit until foamy, 10 to 15 minutes.

* While the yeast activates, sift the remaining 3 tablespoons sugar, the flour, baking powder, baking soda, and salt into a large bowl. Using a fork, cut in the shortening until the mixture resembles small peas. Stir in the remaining 2 cups warm buttermilk, then add the foamy yeast mixture, mixing just until all the flour is dampened.

* Turn the dough out onto a lightly floured surface. Knead it a dozen or so times, until it's soft and the flour is incorporated. Using a floured rolling pin, roll the dough gently into a 1½-inch-thick circle. Cut out 16 to 18 biscuits using a 3-inch cutter, dipping it in flour between biscuits. You can reroll any scraps you have but keep in mind they won't be as soft as the first ones.

* Arrange the biscuits, spacing them about 1 inch apart, on two baking sheets. Cut enough plastic wrap to cover each baking sheet, spray it lightly with cooking spray, and cover the sheets loosely. Let the biscuits rise in a warm place for 1½ hours.

continued

* While the biscuits are rising, fry the country ham. In a large skillet over medium-high heat, heat the oil until shimmering. Fry the ham slices in batches, 3 to 4 minutes per side, or until the ham is golden brown. Set it aside while you bake the biscuits.

* About 15 minutes before the biscuits have finished rising, preheat the oven to 400 degrees F.

* When the oven is heated and the biscuits have risen, gently remove the plastic wrap (it may stick a bit) and brush the biscuits with the melted butter. Right before baking, reduce the oven temperature to 375 degrees F. Bake the biscuits until golden brown, 20 to 22 minutes, rotating the sheets halfway through baking. Let the biscuits cool for 5 minutes on the baking sheets, then remove them to a cooling rack. While they are still warm, you can brush them with additional melted butter, if desired. Slice the biscuits open and serve with the slices of country ham. Sometimes I add a bit of Creole Mustard (page 176).

Here's what's cookin' Angel Biscuits Serves
Recipe from the kitchen of Granny
1 cake yeast
2 Tablesp. warm water
5 cup plain flour (sifted)
1 Teasp. soda
4 Teasp. baking powder
4 Tablesp. Sugar
2½ Teasp. salt
1 cup crisco
2 cups buttermilk
over

BISCUIT CROUTONS
for soups & salads

DON'T THROW AWAY YOUR DAY-OLD BISCUITS! Use them to make these quick and versatile croutons for Little Gem Salad (page 126) or Any Time of Year Tomato Soup (page 150), or grind them up with crispy bacon and sprinkle them on top of Pimento "Not Your Mama's" Mac and Cheese (page 134).

MAKES 5 CUPS

5 day-old biscuits, cut
   into 1-inch cubes
½ cup extra-virgin
   olive oil
¼ cup Big Herb Blend
   (page 58)

1 teaspoon onion
   powder
1 teaspoon garlic
   powder
Kosher salt and freshly
   ground black pepper

* Preheat the oven to 350 degrees F.

* In a large bowl, toss the cubed biscuits with the oil, herbs, and onion and garlic powders. Season to taste with salt and pepper. Spread the croutons evenly on a baking sheet and bake for 7 minutes. Rotate the baking sheet and bake until the croutons are lightly golden brown, an additional 7 to 8 minutes. Cool the croutons and store them in an airtight container for up to 1 week.

Granddaddy Corbett and my grandmother Ellie, 1940s

BIG BISCUIT SANDWICH SUGGESTIONS

AUNT ANNIE'S

Slice a warm biscuit in half and spread **Creole Mustard** (page 176) on the bottom half. Place a **Big Love Buttermilk Fried Chicken** (page 95) breast or thigh on top, then top with **Bread and Butter Pickles** (page 162) and drizzle with an ample amount of **honey**. Top with the other half of the biscuit. (Sometimes I even spread extra mustard on top!)

THE SWEET BLONDE

Fry **country ham** until crisp. Slice a warm biscuit in half and spread the bottom half with **Steen's Butter** (page 142). Top with the ham and a **Perfect Fried Egg** (page 55). Sprinkle **Tillamook extra-sharp cheddar cheese** on top of the egg, and top with the other half of the biscuit.

THE SAWMILL

Slice a warm biscuit in half and place a **Big Love Buttermilk Fried Chicken** (page 95) breast or thigh on the bottom half. Sprinkle **Tillamook extra-sharp cheddar cheese** over the chicken, followed by **Sawmill Gravy** (page 52), with a bit more cheese on top. Top with the other half of the biscuit.

BIG TROUBLE

Slice a warm biscuit and spread **peanut butter** on both halves. Place sliced **bananas** on the bottom half and top with **bacon**. Drizzle the bacon with **honey** and top with the other biscuit half.

THE EASY

Cook **2 Perfect Fried Eggs** (page 55) and just before they're finished, top with **Tillamook extra-sharp cheddar cheese** to melt. Slice a warm biscuit in half and place **bacon** or **Country Breakfast Sausage** (page 185) on the bottom half. Top with the cheesy eggs and the other biscuit half.

THE ORIGINAL

Slice a warm biscuit in half and place a large pat of **butter** on the bottom half. Put **3 tablespoons local raspberry freezer jam** over the butter and top with the other biscuit half. Warm the sandwich in a 400-degree-F oven for 5 minutes, or until hot.

SUPPER
THE MIDDAY MEAL & MORE

ZEVELY HOUSE SHRIMP & GRITS 91

GRITS & GRILLADES
pork & grits & new orleans 94

BIG LOVE BUTTERMILK FRIED CHICKEN 95

CRUNCHY CORNMEAL-FRIED OYSTERS 98

FRIED OYSTER RICH BOYS *with french rémoulade*
& extra-spicy dills 100

B.O.L.T. (BACON, FRIED OYSTERS, LETTUCE & TOMATO)
with pepper jelly & french rémoulade 102

SMOKED SALMON PIE *with peas & a liquored crust* 104

RED TOMATO CHEDDAR PIE *with a liquored crust* 106

"GRANDDADDY'S COMING TO VISIT"
PEEL & EAT SHRIMP 108

PULLED PORK BUTT
with vinegar sauce & red slaw 111

FRIDAY NIGHT FISH FRY *with french rémoulade* 113

AUNT ANNIE'S CORNFLAKE CHICKEN TENDERS
with whipped honey butter 115

**S**UPPER AND *DINNER* IN THE South mean different things to different folks, depending on the region and generation. To my family, supper means *dinner*, the last meal of the day, informal and friendly. But Chris Kloss, my friend and fabulous employee, who's also from the South, says the opposite. This is how his mama, Linda Lea, explains it:

> Some folks were raised that dinner was the main meal of the day, usually at or around noon. Supper was at night. We were rural people, and the noon meal was large to feed the men and children, often working in the fields. The meal was often taken to the fields, especially during harvest, and there were usually three generations of women cooking the food.
>
> The landowner, his sons, sometimes his daughters, and the hired employees all got a large meal. One example of that would be smothered steak, creamed potatoes, fried okra, pinto beans, cold iced tea, and melons and fresh tomatoes cut up. Desserts included chess pie or pound cake, and a one-hour rest! Then in the middle of the afternoon, everyone had tea and dessert again (whatever the women would bring).
>
> Sometimes they would all eat dinner at the house, and the men and boys would eat first so they could rest. The women and small children would eat after the men and boys finished. Sometimes certain dishes were empty, but there was plenty of food. Some of this, like the field workers eating first, may be a German custom, but it made sense to the rest of us. I forgot the homemade bread! Everything was homemade then, and it was so good!

However you say it, or whatever it means to you, you can count on the midday meal being filling comfort food that tastes real good.

ZEVELY HOUSE SHRIMP & GRITS

AFTER HIGH SCHOOL I LIVED IN Winston-Salem and got a job as a busser at the historic eighteenth-century Zevely mansion. The staff kept cigarettes in the ashtrays at the server station and would take deep drags between writing down orders—this was Winston-Salem after all, home of R.J. Reynolds Tobacco Company. You could see the smokestack of the huge redbrick cigarette factory from the second-floor window.

The chef was named Alex, a huge, sweet guy, and his sous-chef was a tiny gal whose name I forget now. While I worked there she had a baby, and I'll be darned if she didn't strap that baby on her back and work a relentless brunch shift. Staff smoking inside a restaurant and a baby on the hot line of a kitchen? I've never seen such a thing since Zevely House. That was where I learned to make this dish, which would be my last requested meal—if anyone's asking.

Note: You can prepare the shrimp stock up to three days ahead of time. It makes two cups, so you'll have enough to make this dish twice. Store it for up to six months in the freezer. It's best to make the grits before the shrimp, so I make the grits first and keep them on the back of the stove covered with a lid on while I do the rest. If it cools off too much, gently warm for a few minutes just before serving.

MAKES 6 SERVINGS

For the stock:

2 pounds (26- to 30-count) head-on shrimp

6 cups water

1½ teaspoons Old Bay seasoning

1 bay leaf

8 tablespoons unsalted butter, divided

4 ounces thick-cut bacon, diced

½ cup diced shallots

10 ounces cremini mushrooms, stemmed and sliced

1 cup white wine

1 teaspoon kosher salt

½ teaspoon freshly ground black pepper

Juice from 1 large lemon

Juice from 1 large lime

1 recipe Basic Grits (recipe follows)

Chopped parsley, for garnish

Texas Pete or Crystal hot sauce, for garnish

* To make the stock, preheat the oven to 375 degrees F.

* Snap the heads off the shrimp, reserving the heads. Peel and devein the shrimp, reserving the shells. Remove and discard the black digestive tract. Refrigerate the shrimp and spread the shells and heads on a baking sheet. Roast them until they're bright pink and fragrant, about 15 minutes.

continued

* Put the roasted shrimp shells and heads in a medium stockpot with the water. Add the Old Bay and bay leaf, and bring the water to a boil over high heat. Reduce the heat to medium and simmer the stock for 20 minutes while you cook the grits. The stock will be light brown in color and will reduce to 2 cups.

* In a large skillet or Dutch oven over medium-high heat, melt 4 tablespoons of the butter. While the butter melts, line a plate with paper towels and set it next to the stove. Add the bacon to the skillet and cook until it renders its fat, 4 to 5 minutes. Use a slotted spoon to transfer the bacon to the lined plate to drain. Add the shallots and sauté until a few are starting to darken, about 1 minute. Add the mushrooms and sauté until they're golden brown and soft, about 3 minutes. Add the wine, 1 cup of the stock, salt, and pepper, and cook for 5 to 6 minutes, scraping up the brown bits at the bottom of the pot, until the sauce reduces just a bit and is dark brown in color. Add the lemon and lime juices, the remaining 4 tablespoons butter, and the bacon and shrimp. Cook until the shrimp turn bright pink, 2 to 3 minutes.

* Serve over the grits, spooning the sauce over the top, and garnish with parsley and hot sauce.

BASIC GRITS

MAKES 6 SERVINGS

9 cups water
1½ cups stone-ground
   grits
6 tablespoons unsalted
   butter

4 teaspoons kosher salt
1 teaspoon freshly
   ground black pepper

* In a large saucepan over high heat, bring the water to a boil. When the water boils, add the grits, whisking continuously. Reduce the heat to medium and continue to whisk every few minutes, so the grits don't stick, for 15 minutes. Reduce the heat to low and add the butter, salt, and pepper. Cook for 10 more minutes, whisking every few minutes, until the grits are thick and sputtering in the pot. The grits should have a little bit of a "bite" or texture to them still, but not crunchy. Taste and adjust the seasoning with additional salt or pepper as needed.

GRITS & GRILLADES
pork & grits & new orleans

GRITS AND *GRILLADES* (PRONOUNCED "GREE-YAHDS") IS a popular New Orleans creole dish that first appeared in the late 1800s. Boneless pork loin is seared, then slow-cooked until fork-tender and smothered in a spicy, rich tomato gravy. Spooned over slow-cooked grits and topped with grated Gruyère cheese and diced fresh tomato, the *grillades* at The Goose have a steady following. One customer comes in twice a week to eat them for breakfast.

MAKES 6 SERVINGS

½ cup canola oil

1½ cups all-purpose
flour

1 (3- to 4-pound) bone-
less pork loin, cut into
1-inch-thick slices

1 large sweet onion,
diced

1 rib celery, diced

1 cup diced green
bell pepper

¼ cup chopped garlic

¼ cup tomato paste

1 (28-ounce) can whole
peeled tomatoes
with juice

1 quart (4 cups) chicken
stock

¼ cup Texas Pete or
Crystal hot sauce

¼ cup Worcestershire
sauce

10 to 12 sprigs (about
½ ounce) fresh thyme

1 bay leaf

Kosher salt and freshly
ground pepper

1 recipe Basic Grits
(page 92)

1 cup grated Gruyère
cheese, for garnish

2 diced roma tomatoes,
for garnish

* In a large Dutch oven over medium-high heat, heat the oil until shimmering. Spread the flour out on a plate. Working in batches, dredge each slice of pork in the flour and sear it until it's golden brown on both sides, about 3 minutes per side. Set the pork aside. The flour and oil in the pan will be dark brown. This is okay.

* In the same pan, add the onion, celery, and bell pepper and sauté until the onions are translucent, about 5 minutes. Add the garlic and sauté for 1 minute. Add the tomato paste and sauté until dark brown, 4 to 5 minutes. Add the whole tomatoes with juice and cook until just beginning to simmer, 5 more minutes. Add the pork back in, along with the chicken stock, hot sauce, Worcestershire, thyme, bay leaf, and salt and pepper to taste, and bring the liquid to a boil. Turn the heat down to maintain a simmer and cook until the pork is tender, about 1 hour. Use a slotted spoon to remove and discard any grease that forms at the top.

* When the pork is ready, taste it and adjust the seasoning with additional salt and pepper as needed. Serve it over the grits with plenty of gravy, sprinkled with Gruyère and tomatoes.

BIG LOVE BUTTERMILK FRIED CHICKEN

FRIED CHICKEN IS AN EMBLEM OF the South and loved the world over: there are as many styles and flavors as there are ways of eating it. Whether it's served hot over a buttermilk biscuit or eaten cold as a midnight snack standing in front of the refrigerator, fried chicken is good any time of day or night. And it's good for you! If your oil is at the correct temperature, the chicken won't absorb any excess and will come out with a crackling skin and hot, juicy interior.

My hope is that you fry enough of this chicken so that there are one or two pieces left for a midnight snack. I love thigh meat, so that's what I use in this recipe, but you can use legs as well. At The Goose we debone our thighs before serving them on a biscuit sandwich, but deboning yours is optional. Keep in mind with the bones in they take longer to cook fully through. Serve these with Sweet Heat BBQ Sauce (page 176) and Texas Pete. Double or triple the recipe for a fried chicken Friday dinner party!

Note: Be sure to start this recipe the day before serving to allow the chicken to marinate.

MAKES 6 SERVINGS

2 quarts (8 cups) buttermilk

2 large lemons, zested and quartered

10 to 12 sprigs (about ½ ounce) fresh thyme

¼ cup Texas Pete or Crystal hot sauce

¼ cup Worcestershire sauce

1 tablespoon kosher salt

2 teaspoons freshly ground black pepper

12 bone-in chicken thighs

For the dredge:

4 cups all-purpose flour

½ cup kosher salt

¼ cup freshly ground black pepper

¼ cup onion powder

¼ cup garlic powder

2 tablespoons cayenne

2 tablespoons smoked paprika

Canola oil, for frying

* In a large bowl, mix the buttermilk, lemon quarters and zest, thyme, hot sauce, Worcestershire, salt, and pepper. Put the chicken thighs in another large bowl, pour the marinade over, and marinate the thighs in the refrigerator for 24 hours. About 30 minutes prior to frying the chicken, take it out of the refrigerator so the chicken comes to room temperature.

* When you're ready to fry the chicken, preheat the oven to 200 degrees F. Meanwhile, make the dredge. Sift all the ingredients into a large bowl. (This can be made up to 1 month ahead and stored in a glass jar with a lid or a ziplock bag.)

* Spread the dredge out on a pie pan or plate and place it next to the stove. (Alternatively, you can put it in a large paper sack.) Have a baking

continued

sheet handy. In a large Dutch oven or cast-iron pot, heat 3 inches of oil over medium-high heat until it registers 325 degrees F on a deep-fry thermometer. Using your hands and working in small batches, remove the chicken from the marinade and press it into the dredge or shake the chicken pieces with the dredge in the sack. (This is a fun task for kids to help with.) You can dredge them up to 30 minutes before frying. Fry the chicken until golden brown, turning once, about 12 minutes. Keep the thighs warm on the baking sheet in the oven while you cook the rest of the chicken, discarding the marinade. Be sure to check the temperature of the oil before you start frying each batch.

* Serve immediately or serve cold the next day.

FRIED CHICKEN FRIDAY

When I decided to open 364 days a year (we are only closed on Christmas Day) and not serve dinner, a lot of people came up to me saying, "You *have* to do dinner! You should be open breakfast, lunch, *and* dinner!" But I have kids. *Five* of them. Five kids relying on me to read them bedtime stories, cook dinner, help with homework, do their laundry, and drive them to soccer, basketball, and Ultimate Frisbee practices. I had to make a compromise, and that's how "Fried Chicken Friday" came to be. Every Friday we open from 5 to 9 p.m. for our Fried Chicken Friday dinners. The customers (many of whom come every single Friday) we attract, the music we play, and the food we serve make Friday night at The Goose seem like one big dinner party.

CRUNCHY CORNMEAL-FRIED OYSTERS

IN HIGH SCHOOL WE WOULD CHIP in our money to buy bushels of oysters on Friday nights and roast them on the beach. They usually came from the Gulf of Mexico or Pamlico and Albemarle Sounds (Pamlico is the second-largest estuary system in the United States). We could buy a bushel back then for twenty bucks! Even now, oysters are relatively cheap, especially on the East Coast.

At The Goose we use "small" oysters from Taylor Shellfish (see page 102), and let me tell you, there's nothing small about them. Pacific oysters, full of brine and salt and sea, are the best for frying. Serve them in the Fried Oyster Rich Boys (page 100) or the B.O.L.T. (page 102), or as a substitute for the chicken in the Little Gem Salad (page 126). Double or quadruple the recipe for a party.

MAKES 4 SERVINGS

½ recipe Cornmeal Dredge (recipe follows)

Canola oil, for frying
2 (10-ounce) jars extra-small oysters

* Put the cornmeal dredge in a large bowl and line a plate with paper towels. Set them both next to the stove.

* In a cast-iron skillet or Dutch oven over medium-high heat, heat 2 inches of oil until it registers 325 degrees F on a deep-fry thermometer. Drain the oysters, toss them with the dredge, and slip them in batches into the hot oil. Fry them for 3 to 4 minutes, turning once. Using a slotted spatula, remove them to drain on the lined plate. Serve them warm with French Rémoulade (page 178), Quick and Spicy Cocktail Sauce (page 180), Red Pepper Jelly (page 205), or a side of Comeback Sauce (page 173) for dipping.

CORNMEAL DREDGE

MAKES 4½ CUPS

3 cups regular ground cornmeal (not fine or coarse)
1 cup all-purpose flour
3 tablespoons kosher salt
2 tablespoons freshly ground black pepper

1½ tablespoons onion powder
1½ tablespoons garlic powder
1 tablespoon cayenne
1 tablespoon smoked paprika

* In a large bowl, mix together all the ingredients. Store it in a glass jar with a lid or a ziplock bag.

FRIED OYSTER RICH BOYS

with french rémoulade & extra-spicy dills

PO'BOYS CAME OUT OF NEW ORLEANS in the early 1900s. Nowadays there are many versions, ranging from fried oysters, fried shrimp, and classic roast beef with gravy, to catfish, meatball, ham and cheese, and even a french fry version. A "dressed" po'boy has lettuce, tomato, pickle, and mayonnaise. Our version is dressed with our own house-made French rémoulade, dills, and a dollop of pepper jelly, thus garnering the "Rich Boy" name. We buy our *banh mi* bread from Tony's Bakery in Columbia City, but you can substitute any soft French bread that has a crusty exterior. If you love rémoulade like my husband does, add more.

MAKES 4 SERVINGS

½ cup French
    Rémoulade (page 178)

4 *banh mi* or French
    bread buns, split and
    toasted

1 head romaine lettuce,
    cored and shredded

2 tomatoes, sliced

1 recipe Crunchy
    Cornmeal-Fried
    Oysters (page 98)

2 tablespoons Pepper
    Jelly (page 205)

2 Extra-Spicy Dills
    (page 163), halved
    lengthwise

* Spread 2 tablespoons of rémoulade on each bun. Divide the shredded lettuce, tomato slices, and fried oysters among the buns. Top each sandwich with a bit of pepper jelly and garnish with a pickle half. Serve immediately.

FRIED CHICKEN PO'BOYS

Follow the recipe for Fried Oyster Rich Boys, substituting 4 pieces of Big Love Buttermilk Fried Chicken (page 95) (de-boned thighs or breast) for the oysters and omitting the pepper jelly.

B.O.L.T. (BACON, FRIED OYSTERS, LETTUCE & TOMATO)
with pepper jelly & french rémoulade

WE HAVE THIS SANDWICH ON AND off the menu, and whenever it's on, the customers go crazy for it. I love squishing the whole thing together flat and shoving it in my mouth when no one is looking. It's probably not a good first-date sandwich if you're worried about the mess. The combination of bacon, oysters, pepper jelly, and rémoulade take it over the top.

MAKES 2 LARGE SANDWICHES

¼ cup French Rémoulade (page 178)

4 slices toasted brioche

4 leaves butter lettuce

1 large tomato, cut into 4 slices

½ recipe Crunchy Cornmeal-Fried Oysters (page 98)

4 strips bacon (we use Benton's), cooked until crispy and drained

¼ cup Pepper Jelly (page 205)

* Spread half of the rémoulade on each of 2 slices of toast and top with 2 lettuce leaves and 2 tomato slices. Divide the oysters evenly between the toast and top each with 2 bacon strips, half of the pepper jelly, and the top bread slices. Cut both sandwiches in half and serve immediately.

TAYLOR SHELLFISH

Pacific Northwest oysters are different than those in much of the South, and a lot of that is due in part to Taylor Shellfish. Taylor has been farming in the Pacific Northwest for five generations. The largest producer of farmed shellfish, they employ more than 500 employees and harvest on 11,000 acres of Washington and British Columbia coastline. Growing up in the South, we usually had one kind of oyster, the most common being the Gulf oyster—a large, oftentimes muddy-tasting thing that we roasted over open beach fires. Here, Taylor has raised the bar with varieties such as Kumamoto, Totten Virginica, Olympia, and Shigoku; each has its own distinct flavor profile. At their Samish Bay store, you can buy a bucket of oysters to shuck yourself and eat on picnic tables overlooking the bay.

SMOKED SALMON PIE
with peas and a liquored crust

THE PACIFIC NORTHWEST IS KNOWN FOR its smoked salmon. Native tribes here have been smoking salmon over outdoor fires for thousands of years. King, sockeye, and coho are all popular species for smoking and abundantly available to buy or catch yourself. Smoked salmon can be pricey, so feel free to use half smoked and half regular cooked salmon. You can also leave out the salmon all together and substitute any other kind of firm whitefish such as snapper or rockfish. This recipe fills a two-quart casserole dish, but it can be doubled for a party and cooked straight in a Dutch oven. You can also make a quarter batch of the Best Buttermilk Biscuits (page 65) and use that for the topping instead of the pie dough.

Note: Depending on the type of fish stock you use, the salt content will vary widely. I've had to add as much as two and a half teaspoons of salt to the filling as most fish stock is rather bland.

MAKES 6 SERVINGS

½ recipe Liquored Pie Dough (recipe follows)

½ cup (1 stick) unsalted butter

½ pound Yukon Gold potatoes, chopped

1 large sweet onion, diced

1 leek, cleaned thoroughly, white and pale-green parts sliced into half moons

1 cup chopped celery, from 2 ribs

1½ teaspoons kosher salt

1 teaspoon freshly ground black pepper

½ cup all-purpose flour

2½ cups fish or seafood stock

¾ cup white wine

¼ cup heavy cream

2 teaspoons lemon zest

1 tablespoon finely chopped fresh dill

8 ounces smoked salmon, flaked (or substitute regular cooked salmon or whitefish such as cod for 4 of the ounces)

8 ounces frozen petite peas

¼ cup flat-leaf parsley, chopped

1 recipe Egg Wash (page 31)

* Begin by making sure the pie dough has chilled in the refrigerator for at least 1 hour. On a lightly floured surface, roll it out about ¼ inch thick into the shape of your casserole dish. Keep refrigerated until you are ready to bake the pie.

* Preheat the oven to 400 degrees F.

* In a large Dutch oven over medium-high heat, melt the butter. Add the potatoes, onion, leek, celery, salt, and pepper and sauté until the celery and leeks begin to soften, 7 to 8 minutes. Add the flour, stirring to coat the vegetables, and cook until the flour is sticking to the vegetables and you can see the bottom of the pot, about 1 minute. Add the stock and wine and stir until the sauce starts to thicken and bubble, 2 to 3 minutes. Turn the heat down to low and add the cream, lemon zest and juice, and dill and season with salt and pepper to taste. Continue to cook

over low heat until bubbling, 1 to 2 minutes. Turn off the heat and stir in the salmon, peas, and parsley. Taste and adjust for seasoning, adding more salt or pepper.

* Pour the mixture into the casserole dish and top with pie dough, tucking in the edges and then crimping around the sides of the casserole dish. Cut five 1-inch vents in the top of the crust. Brush the dough with the egg wash. Set the dish on top of a baking sheet to catch any drips, and bake until the pie is golden brown and the filling is bubbling, 40 to 45 minutes.

LIQUORED PIE DOUGH

THIS PIE DOUGH WILL MOST LIKELY make more than you need, but keep it in the freezer so you can pop it out to defrost and within a few minutes have a homemade crust ready for a sweet or savory pie. You can use a food processor or a stand mixer. If using a stand mixer, just be sure not to overmix the dough once you add the water or vodka. Use ice water if you don't have vodka, or half vodka and half water if you don't have a lot of vodka.

MAKES ENOUGH FOR TWO 9-INCH CRUSTS

3¾ cups all-purpose flour

3 tablespoons sugar

1½ tablespoons kosher salt

1½ cups (3 sticks) unsalted butter, cold (preferably frozen) and cut into ¼-inch dice

1 cup plus a few extra tablespoons chilled vodka (or ice water)

* In a food processor, pulse the flour, sugar, and salt five times. Add in the butter pieces and pulse until the butter is the size of small peas. (If using a stand mixer, mix everything on low speed until the butter is the size of small peas.) Turn the dough out into a large bowl. Add the vodka slowly, using a rubber spatula to gently mix it in. Keep adding vodka until the dough is cohesive and can be patted together easily. Form the dough into a 1-inch-thick disk and wrap it in plastic wrap. Chill it in the refrigerator for at least 1 hour before using.

RED TOMATO CHEDDAR PIE
with a liquored crust

TOMATOES ARE SO PROLIFIC IN THE South that cooks are always finding new ways to eat them. Tomato pie, a simple combination of tomatoes, cheese, and mayonnaise, is found all over the Carolinas. This pie is easy to make, quick to serve, and delicious both hot and cold. You can create a lattice top or just use a traditional fully covered top; just be sure to cut some slits or circles for vents.

MAKES 1 NINE-INCH PIE

4 large red tomatoes (about 4 pounds), cut into ¼-inch-thick slices

Kosher salt

1 recipe Liquored Pie Dough (page 105)

½ cup mayonnaise, such as Duke's or Best Foods

3 tablespoons plus 2 teaspoons cornstarch

2½ cups grated extra-sharp cheddar cheese, divided

1 bunch scallions, green and white parts, thinly sliced

1 recipe Egg Wash (page 31)

Fleur de sel, for sprinkling

* Lay the tomato slices on a paper towel–lined baking sheet and sprinkle them with a few pinches of kosher salt. Cover the tomatoes with more paper towels and let the liquid drain for 30 minutes. (You are doing this so the crust doesn't get soggy.)

* Meanwhile, roll out half of the pie dough on a lightly floured surface into a ¼-inch-thick, 12-inch round and place it in a pie tin. Crimp the edges and put the crust in the freezer for 30 minutes or until firm.

* While the crust chills, in a medium bowl, stir together the mayonnaise, cornstarch, and 2 cups of the cheese.

* When the crust is firm, sprinkle ¼ cup of the cheese on the bottom. Layer half of the tomato slices, then the mayo mixture. Sprinkle with the scallions and then layer the remaining tomatoes. Sprinkle with the remaining ¼ cup cheese.

* Preheat the oven to 425 degrees F.

* Roll out the top crust on a lightly floured surface into a ¼-inch-thick, 12-inch round. Use the rolling pin to drape it over the pie, and brush the egg wash on the sides of the dough to glue the top to the bottom crust. Follow along over your original crimp, trimming it to fit. Cut five vents in the top. Brush egg wash over the top and sprinkle it with a bit of *fleur de sel*. Bake until the crust is deep golden brown, 40 to 50 minutes.

"GRANDDADDY'S COMING TO VISIT" PEEL & EAT SHRIMP

Whenever Granddaddy came to visit it was an extra-special time because food was a huge centerpiece of his visit. He would arrive in his big Cadillac with his fedora and suspenders, and the first thing he would ask us was, "Whatareweeatin'?" his eyes lighting up with excitement. MJ would have shopped for his arrival and planned the meals weeks beforehand, and we always, *always* had this peel-and-eat shrimp. As a side there was boiled sweet corn and crusty French bread, nothing more.

Look for a shrimp count of twenty-six to thirty shrimp per pound and make more than you think you'll need. Some portion guides will tell you to plan for a pound of shrimp feeding four adults, which yields about eight pieces per person. Well, I can eat half a pound on my own, so I plan for a bit more, such as one pound per three adults. These are great with a Dixie lager or Abita amber beer.

MAKES 6 SERVINGS

1 cup (2 sticks) unsalted butter

¼ cup Worcestershire sauce

¼ cup Texas Pete or Crystal hot sauce

1 teaspoon kosher salt

½ teaspoon freshly ground black pepper

2 pounds (26- to 30-count) head-on shrimp

1 sweet onion, cut in half, then into ¼-inch-thick slices

Chopped fresh parsley, for garnish

Melted butter, for serving

1 loaf crunchy French bread, for serving

* Preheat the oven to 375 degrees F.

* In a medium saucepan over medium heat, melt the butter and then turn the heat off. Stir in the Worcestershire, hot sauce, salt, and pepper.

* In a large bowl, toss the shrimp with the onion and butter sauce. Transfer the shrimp mixture to a large baking sheet.

* Roast until the shrimp are bright pink, about 10 minutes. Serve them poured out onto a newspaper-covered table, garnished with parsley, accompanied by bowls of melted butter for dipping and chunks of French bread. You can also pour the leftover marinade from the baking sheet into a bowl for dipping.

PULLED PORK BUTT
with vinegar sauce & red slaw

THIS RECIPE IS A TRIBUTE TO College Barbeque on Statesville Boulevard in Salisbury where I used to go with Granny. It's one of the few places still smoking their own meat. You can see the smoke billowing up from the stack and smell the hickory wood from down the street. College opened in 1964 and still looks exactly the same. The wood chopping block where they chop the pork is concave a good six inches in the middle from all of the years of wear.

   If you have a bit left over, freeze it to mix into Go to Church Brunswick Stew (page 149).

MAKES 6 SERVINGS

¼ cup packed dark brown sugar

2 tablespoons smoked paprika

2 tablespoons kosher salt

1½ tablespoons garlic powder

1½ tablespoons onion powder

½ tablespoon freshly ground black pepper

1 (3- to 4-pound) boneless pork butt (pork shoulder)

Central Carolina Vinegar Sauce (page 180), for finishing

6 King's Hawaiian or other sweet rolls, for serving

Granny's Salisbury Red Slaw (page 137), for serving

* In a medium bowl, combine the brown sugar, paprika, salt, garlic and onion powders, and pepper. Using your fingers, press the dry rub all over the pork, covering it completely. Let it sit for at least 1 hour or overnight.

* When you are ready to cook the pork, preheat the oven to 225 degrees F.

* Put the pork butt in a roasting pan and cover it with aluminum foil. Roast it until the meat is completely falling apart, 6 to 7 hours. (If you have a smoker, you can smoke the pork for the first 3 hours, then finish it in the oven.) Remove the foil and let the pork rest until it's cool enough to handle, then pull it apart with your fingers to shred it. Toss it with the vinegar sauce and the pan juices and keep it warm until you're ready to serve it on rolls alongside Granny's slaw.

FRIDAY NIGHT FISH FRY
with french rémoulade

Down where the reeds and the catfish play
There lies a dream as soft as the water

—"CATFISH SONG," TOWNES VAN ZANDT

WHY NOT HAVE A BIG OL' FISH FRY? In the 1950s and '60s on Friday evenings, Granny and Pop would take their kids to the neighbors' and have a fish fry in their backyard. They dredged the fish in cornmeal and cooked it in lard in a flat cast-iron pan over an open fire.

Go out fishing or buy something local. Make a batch of the cornmeal dredge, premix some hush puppy batter, and sit back with a beer while you and your friends tell stories over an open fire. Add a bunch of outdoor lights and candles, and it makes for a memorable party. Or scale it down and make it inside on the stovetop for a Friday night supper for your family.

MAKES 18 TO 20 SERVINGS

10 pounds assorted fish
   fillets, such as catfish,
   snapper, rockfish, or
   ling cod
½ gallon buttermilk
Canola oil, for frying
Batter from 2 recipes
   Princess "Hush Now"
   Hush Puppies
   (page 39)

2 recipes Cornmeal
   Dredge (page 98)

For serving:
French Rémoulade
   (page 178)
Quick and Spicy
   Cocktail Sauce
   (page 180)
Lemon wedges

Granny fishing, Cherry Grove, South Carolina, Intracoastal
Waterway, 1970s

continued

* Preheat the oven to 200 degrees F.

* In a large stainless-steel bowl or plastic bucket, soak the fish in the buttermilk.

* In a large cast-iron skillet over medium-high heat, heat about 2 inches of oil until it registers 375 degrees F on a deep-fry thermometer. Fry the hush puppies according to the recipe, to yield 32 puppies. (Do them first, so they don't take on the flavor of the fish.) After frying, check the level of the oil and add more as needed. Turn down the heat so the oil registers 350 degrees F. Keep the hush puppies warm in the oven while you fry the fish.

* In a large bowl, put the cornmeal dredge. Have a big platter handy, along with several paper bags. Using your fingers, take the fish out of the buttermilk and press each fillet into the cornmeal on both sides. Set them on the platter and repeat until all the fillets are dredged. Working in batches, slide the fish gently into the hot oil and cook until golden brown, 3 to 4 minutes per side, flipping once. Using a slotted spatula, transfer the fish onto the paper bags to drain. Repeat until you've fried all the fillets. Check the temperature of your oil between batches so that it maintains 350 degrees F.

* Serve with the rémoulade, cocktail sauce, and lemon wedges, along with Prince's Southern Iced Tea (page 273) and ice-cold Dixie beer.

OUTDOOR COOKING

I cook outside at home often using a huge paella pan I've had for years. It has a tall stand, is connected to a propane tank, and is one of the most versatile kitchen items I've ever owned. I've fried more than 100 pounds of chicken in that thing, had a fish fry for 60 people, and cooked paella for Christmas Eve dinner in the rain. I love cooking outside using the paella pan or cooking over an open fire in a cast-iron skillet. At family gatherings I've cooked a full breakfast for 20 using nothing more than a fire pit and 1 cast-iron skillet (and some prep help from the family). So get outside, rain or shine, invite your friends, throw some wood on the fire pit, and start cookin'!

AUNT ANNIE'S CORNFLAKE CHICKEN TENDERS
with whipped honey butter

MY FRIEND ANNIE, WHO IS ALSO from the South, made these cornflake-crusted tenders for her kids when they were growing up. Serve them with the honey butter and the kids won't be the only ones to devour them. Annie serves them with curry ketchup she buys from the grocery store.

MAKES 4 TO 6 SERVINGS

2 pounds chicken
  tenders
½ cup maple syrup
3 cups cornflakes,
  smashed or ground in
  a food processor
½ cup all-purpose flour
¼ cup grated Parmesan
  cheese
¼ cup shredded
  Parmesan cheese

1 teaspoon kosher salt
½ teaspoon freshly
  ground black pepper
¼ teaspoon crushed red
  pepper flakes
2 eggs
Canola oil, for frying
Whipped Honey Butter
  (recipe follows),
  for serving

* In a mixing bowl, place the chicken and toss with the maple syrup. (I like to poke a few holes in the chicken with a fork so it absorbs more maple syrup.) Set it aside.

* In a medium bowl, whisk the cornflakes, flour, Parmesan, salt, pepper, and red pepper flakes and set it aside.

* In a small bowl, beat the eggs with a fork, then add them to the chicken mixture, tossing to coat the tenders.

* Place the bowl with the cornflakes mixture next to the stove. Line a plate with paper towels and set it aside.

* In a large cast-iron skillet or saucepot over medium-high heat, heat ½ inch of oil until it registers 325 degrees F on a deep-fry thermometer. Working in batches, dip each tender in the cornflake mixture, using your fingers to press the coating into the chicken so it adheres. Gently place the tenders in the hot oil and fry them until golden brown on both sides, 3 to 4 minutes, turning once. Remove them with tongs or a slotted spatula to drain on the lined plate. Repeat with the remaining tenders. Serve hot with honey butter on the side.

continued

WHIPPED HONEY BUTTER

HONEY BUTTER ON TOAST OR BISCUITS with cinnamon sugar sprinkled on top is just the beginning. Dip hot hush puppies in honey butter, slather corn bread with it, layer it between pancakes and waffles, or spread it over baked fish. Any way you do it, you can't go wrong.

MAKES 1 CUP

1 cup (2 sticks) unsalted
   butter, at room
   temperature

¼ teaspoon kosher salt

½ cup local honey

* In the bowl of a stand mixer fitted with the whisk attachment, cream the butter on medium-high speed until light and fluffy. With the mixer running, add the salt. Drizzle in the honey and whip until thoroughly mixed. It will keep at room temperature for up to 5 days or refrigerated for up to 2 weeks.

BEGINNING AND ENDING WITH FOOD

Before the Internet, when you were traveling for vacation or on your way to a friend's house, you used maps, but mostly relied heavily on verbal directions. Verbal directions are important to Southern folks because you can point out to someone where exactly they need to eat while driving through such and such town or off such and such exit or at mile marker such and such.

Southerners like to bookend *any* event with food. A trip to the auto parts store is bookended with a barbecue sandwich and hush puppies. A trip to the beach is bookended by breakfast first to start the trip, a picnic lunch of cold fried chicken and potato salad eaten at a rest area picnic table, and a supper of platters of fried seafood once you're at the beach. Many a funeral were bookended with a trip to College BBQ.

Days are planned around when to eat and what to eat. Meals are planned carefully around college basketball games and football games, and vacations are remembered and rehashed by talking about what you had to eat and what kind of fish you caught.

You could even say a Southern childhood is bookended by food. Without the food, any event or activity is somewhat lacking soul and a bit of a letdown. My memories of trips to the ocean are bookended by MJ's little red cooler filled with bologna and cheese sandwiches on soft white bread slathered with cool Duke's mayo and spicy brown mustard, Pringles potato chips, and ice-cold mini Cokes. To this day when I'm at the beach on a hot summer day, I find myself craving that same meal.

Picnic with Granny, Pop, and my sister, Chelsea, somewhere on the side of a Southern highway, 1970s

"AND ALL ON IT"

SUPPER SIDES

EAT YOUR VEGGIES Y'ALL

MJ'S POTATO SALAD *tried & true* 121

DOUBLE-ORDER FRIED OKRA *"you want WHAT?"* 122

LOWCOUNTRY SEA ISLAND RED PEAS *with chowchow* 125

LITTLE GEM SALAD *with smoked tomatoes
& creamy blue cheese dressing* 126

GRANNY'S MESS OF SOFT GREENS *turnip, mustard & collard* 127

BLUEBIRD GRAIN FARMS FARRO & COLLARD GREEN SALAD
with watermelon radish & roasted garlic–lemon vinaigrette 128

SMOKY MEAT COLLARDS *with benton's bacon & pot likker* 130

BROILED GARDEN TOMATOES *with burrata & spiced pralines* 133

PIMENTO "NOT YOUR MAMA'S" MAC & CHEESE 134

GRANNY'S SALISBURY RED SLAW 137

TOMATO & CUCUMBER SALAD *with sorghum syrup
& black pepper* 138

THE WANDERING GOOSE WHITE SLAW 139

COCONUT RICE 139

GRANDDADDY'S FANCY NEW POTATOES
with parsley & salty butter 140

WATERMELON SALAD *with salt & spearmint* 140

HOT SKILLET CORN BREAD *sour cream & fresh corn* 141

SKILLET RAMPS & YUKON GOLD POTATOES
with benton's bacon & toast 143

WHEN WE'D ASK GRANDDADDY WHAT we were having for dinner, he'd always reply something to the effect of, "We are having rib-a-roast, rice an' gravy, butter beans, fried okra, and all on it." The "all on it" meant "etcetera," which we knew was the cukes in vinegar, rolls, biscuits, sweet tea, and banana pudding that accompanied every meal. He even proposed to one of his girlfriends by saying "Okay! Let's get married, and all on it!" (A good term for dinner, but not for a marriage proposal.) On the back page of his funeral flyer, the very last words were "And all on it."

As children, when supper was ready at Granddaddy's, we lined up youngest to oldest, and I was always convinced my eight younger cousins would leave none for the rest of the family. But somehow Granddaddy knew just how much food to make so that there was more than enough and not one of us went without. You could pile your plate high, and with all of the sides he cooked there was always more than enough for one more round at the kitchen island.

Use the sides in this chapter interchangeably as a main attraction at your supper table.

MJ'S POTATO SALAD
tried & true

THIS IS THE POTATO SALAD I grew up with. I serve it with hot fried chicken at supper or cold fried chicken for a picnic. I haven't changed it much from how MJ prepared it, except for the addition of hot sauce and white vinegar.

Don't overcook your potatoes or they will fall apart in the water and the entire thing will turn mushy: they should have a firm bite and be able to be sliced. But don't undercook them either—they should be starting to break down a bit.

MAKES 6 CUPS

2 pounds Yukon Gold potatoes

2 cups mayonnaise, such as Duke's or Best Foods

4 ribs celery, diced (2 cups)

4 Perfect Hard-Boiled Eggs (page 35), chopped

1 small sweet onion, diced (¾ cup)

2 tablespoons Creole Mustard (page 176)

2 teaspoons white vinegar

2 teaspoons Texas Pete or Crystal hot sauce

1 teaspoon kosher salt

1 teaspoon freshly ground black pepper

* Put the potatoes in a large saucepan, cover them with cold water, and bring the water to a boil. Turn the heat down just a bit, and boil the potatoes until you can pierce them gently with a fork, about 20 minutes. Drain the potatoes and set them aside to cool. Once they're cool, cut them into bite-size pieces, reserving 2 whole potatoes.

* Put the cut potatoes in a large bowl, add the mayonnaise, celery, eggs, onion, mustard, vinegar, hot sauce, salt, and pepper, and mix thoroughly. Mash the 2 whole potatoes in a small bowl and add them to the potato mixture. Mix and taste to adjust the seasoning and texture; the salad may need a few more tablespoons of mayonnaise to make it creamier. Chill it in the refrigerator until you're ready to serve it.

Brand-new baby me with Mama MJ, 1971

DOUBLE-ORDER FRIED OKRA

"you want WHAT?"

FRIED OKRA IS HANDS DOWN MY favorite vegetable: I can eat two pounds of it all by myself. K&W Cafeteria in Winston-Salem, North Carolina, has good fried okra, and ordering there is quite an adventure. You get in line (there is always a line) and grab a tray first thing. Then come the Jell-O and salads and aspic. Skip over these and head straight to the vegetables, but be ready, because those women don't give you a chance to get your thoughts together or change your mind before they start yelling at you. "WHAT'CHUWANT?" "YOUWANNAVEGETABLE?" "WHATVEGETABLE?!"

I would recite my order in my head over and over throughout the Jell-O and aspic because if I wavered, I would hold up the line, which doesn't make them happy (not to mention that the line continues to push you even if you aren't ready). So I would be ready, and I had to say it *fast*: "May-I-please-have-green-beans-mashed-potatoes-macaroni-and-cheese-and-a-double-order-of-fried-okra?" Then they would repeat your order—GREENBEANSMASHEDTATERSMACANCHEESE—up until they got to the okra. "YOUWANTWHAT?" "A double order of fried okra, please." "DOUBLEORDERFRIEDOKRA," they repeated back, and I would breathe a sigh of relief and move on down to grab my chocolate cream pie.

I can find okra in most Asian grocery stores here in Seattle. Try to buy it fresh when you can, and use it within a day or two.

MAKES 6 TO 8 SERVINGS

3 pounds fresh okra
2 quarts (8 cups) buttermilk

1 recipe Cornmeal Dredge (page 98)
Canola oil, for frying

* Slice the okra into ½-inch rounds and put them in a large bowl. Cover them with the buttermilk and let them sit while you get the cornmeal dredge and oil ready.

* Spread the cornmeal dredge out on a pie pan or plate and place it to the left of the bowl with the okra, next to the stove. Line a plate with paper towels and set it aside.

* In a large cast-iron skillet or Dutch oven over medium-high heat, heat 1½ inches of oil until it registers 325 degrees F on a deep-fry thermometer. Using your fingers, pull the okra slices from the buttermilk and dredge them in the cornmeal. Gently place the cornmeal-coated okra in the hot oil (you can fill up the skillet, but leave some room around the pieces) and fry them until golden brown, 4 to 5 minutes. Remove them with tongs or a slotted spatula to drain on the lined plate. Serve the okra as you fry it or keep it warm in a 200-degree-F oven while you fry the rest. Serve it plain or with Comeback Sauce (page 173) on the side for dipping.

LOWCOUNTRY SEA ISLAND RED PEAS
with chowchow

SEA ISLAND RED PEAS ARE HEIRLOOM field peas that were first grown in the southeastern United States in the early 1700s. Nowadays Sea Island peas are grown on fewer than five hundred acres. We buy ours from Anson Mills in South Carolina, and you can order them online. They are smaller than black-eyed peas, stay firm when cooked, and have a distinct nutty flavor. You can substitute black-eyed or crowder peas, but the cooking time will be a lot shorter. I love these served with fried chicken or as a main dish over rice.

MAKES 6 CUPS

3 tablespoons extra-virgin olive oil

1 small sweet onion, diced (½ cup)

1 rib celery, diced (½ cup)

1 small carrot, diced (¼ cup)

1 small jalapeño, seeded and diced

2 cloves garlic, chopped

2 cups Sea Island red peas

1 quart (4 cups) chicken or vegetable stock

2 tablespoons Texas Pete or Crystal hot sauce

2 tablespoons Worcestershire sauce

2 tablespoons chopped fresh thyme

1 bay leaf

Kosher salt and freshly ground black pepper

Chowchow (page 169), for serving

* In a large saucepan over medium-high heat, heat the oil. When it's shimmering, add the onion, celery, carrot, and jalapeño, and sauté until the vegetables begin to soften, 5 to 6 minutes. Add the garlic and sauté until fragrant but not brown, 1 to 2 minutes more. Add the peas, chicken stock, hot sauce, Worcestershire, thyme, and bay leaf and bring to a simmer. Simmer over medium-low heat until the peas are soft, 1½ to 2 hours. Season to taste with salt and pepper. Serve warm, with chowchow on top.

SWEET ONIONS

Granny used to tell me that when she was little she would eat a Vidalia onion just like an apple, with nothing on it but a sprinkling of salt. I never asked her why, but I now realize it was most likely during the Great Depression. She never talked about being hungry then, only that she learned not to waste a thing. Buy sweet onions near where you live, and use them anytime a recipe calls for yellow.

LITTLE GEM SALAD
with smoked tomatoes & creamy blue cheese dressing

LITTLE GEM IS A LETTUCE THAT tastes sweet like butter lettuce and is crunchy like romaine. It is full of little nooks and crannies that make secret spots for your salad dressing to hide. If you can't find Little Gem, substitute baby romaine or romaine hearts, or use a combination of romaine and butter lettuce. If you don't have a home smoker, substitute oil-packed sun-dried tomatoes, or simply oven-roast the tomatoes for two and a half to three hours instead. The undressed salad will keep in the refrigerator in a lidded glass container for up to one week. I love adding pieces of cold leftover Big Love Buttermilk Fried Chicken (page 95) to this salad.

MAKES 4 SERVINGS

6 Roma tomatoes, halved

1 tablespoon kosher salt, plus more for seasoning

1 teaspoon freshly ground black pepper, plus more for seasoning

1 teaspoon garlic powder

3 heads little gem lettuce, cored, leaves washed and dried, and chilled

¾ to 1 cup Creamed Blue Cheese Dressing (page 177)

1 cup Biscuit Croutons (page 81)

8 ounces cooked crispy bacon, chopped

6 fresh chives, chopped

* Preheat the oven to 225 degrees F.

* To make the smoked tomatoes, lay the tomato halves on a baking sheet and sprinkle them with the salt, pepper, and garlic powder. Smoke them according to the directions for your smoker, (approximately 30 minutes), then transfer them to the oven and roast them until most of their liquid is gone and they look a little shriveled, 1½ to 2 hours. Cool and slice the tomatoes.

* In a beautiful, large serving bowl, toss the lettuce with the dressing. Sprinkle with a pinch of salt and pepper and toss a bit more. Top with the croutons, bacon, and tomatoes. Garnish with the chives. Serve immediately.

GRANNY'S MESS OF SOFT GREENS
turnip, mustard & collard

GRANNY COOKED TURNIP, COLLARD, AND MUSTARD greens all together in one pot until they were so soft you could almost spread them on toast. She grew the greens in her garden and would add in the tiny, creamy turnip bulbs. After cooking them, we doused the greens with hefty splashes of white vinegar with chilies from her cruet.

MAKES 8 SERVINGS

¼ cup canola oil

8 ounces smoky bacon, such as Benton's, cut into ¼-inch dice, or 1 smoked ham hock

1 large sweet onion, cut into ½-inch dice

3 cloves garlic, finely minced

2 bunches turnip greens, tough ribs removed and leaves thinly sliced (chiffonade)

2 bunches collard greens, tough ribs removed and leaves thinly sliced (chiffonade)

2 bunches mustard greens, tough ribs removed and leaves thinly sliced (chiffonade)

4 to 5 baby turnips, trimmed and quartered

1 quart (4 cups) chicken stock

½ cup packed dark brown sugar

¼ cup Texas Pete or Crystal hot sauce

¼ cup Worcestershire sauce

¼ cup red wine vinegar

Kosher salt and freshly ground black pepper

2 tablespoons heavy cream

White vinegar with chilies, for serving

* In a large Dutch oven, heat the oil over medium-high heat. Add the bacon and onion and cook until the bacon has rendered its fat and is crispy (don't let it burn) and the onions are translucent, 6 to 7 minutes. Add the garlic and sauté for 1 minute. Add the greens, turnips, and chicken stock and cook until the greens begin to soften, about 10 minutes. Reduce the heat to low, cover the pot halfway, and simmer the greens gently for 1 hour.

* Stir in the brown sugar, hot sauce, Worcestershire, and vinegar. Season to taste with salt and pepper. Simmer for another 30 minutes, then taste and adjust the seasoning with additional salt and pepper as needed. Stir in the cream just before serving. Serve with a few splashes of white vinegar with chilies.

Granny in her garden, 1930s

BLUEBIRD GRAIN FARMS FARRO & COLLARD GREEN SALAD

with watermelon radish & roasted garlic–lemon vinaigrette

FARRO IS AN ANCIENT GRAIN THAT some say is the ancestor of all the wheat species. It has a nutty, chewy texture that holds up well in soups and salads without getting mushy. This salad is hearty and crunchy and has just the right amount of acidity. Make a batch, keeping the components refrigerated and tossing them with the dressing right before serving. Use any leftover roasted vegetables you have in place of the beets and turnips. The watermelon radish adds a pretty pink color, but you can substitute another variety.

A mandoline is helpful to achieve extra-thin slices of the vegetables. An alternative is you can slice them by hand (carefully) into one-eighth-inch-thick slices.

MAKES 4 SERVINGS

2 medium red beets (about 1 pound), peeled and cut into 1-inch chunks

2 medium turnips (about 1 pound), peeled and cut into 1-inch chunks

¼ cup extra-virgin olive oil

1 teaspoon kosher salt, plus more for seasoning

Freshly ground black pepper

1 cup uncooked farro

5 to 6 sprigs fresh thyme

2 to 3 collard greens, tough ribs removed and leaves thinly sliced (chiffonade)

1 carrot, sliced paper thin

1 small watermelon radish, sliced paper thin

1 small fennel bulb, sliced paper thin

¾ cup Roasted Garlic–Lemon Vinaigrette (page 179)

½ cup toasted sesame seeds, for garnish

* Preheat the oven to 400 degrees F.

* Line as many baking sheets as you need with parchment paper and spread the beets and turnips on them. Drizzle the oil over the vegetables and season them to taste with salt and pepper. Roast until tender when pierced with a fork, 35 to 45 minutes.

* Meanwhile, cook the farro. In a medium saucepot over medium-high heat, bring 6 cups water to a boil. Add the farro, salt, and thyme. Cook the farro until soft but still chewy, about 25 minutes. Drain in a strainer and set aside to cool.

* In a large bowl, combine the collards, carrot, radish, and fennel with the roasted beets and turnips. Add the farro with a few pinches of salt and pepper and toss everything together. Pour in the dressing and mix with your hands or a spoon until thoroughly coated. Taste for seasoning, adding a bit more dressing, salt, and pepper as needed.

* To serve, divide the salad equally among four plates or serve on a platter, garnished with the sesame seeds. I like to eat my salad with one or two Perfect Hard-Boiled Eggs (page 35).

SMOKY MEAT COLLARDS
with benton's bacon & pot likker

COLLARDS GROW YEAR-ROUND AND ARE AVAILABLE in almost every part of the country. I grow them here in the Pacific Northwest and love them best after the first frost has sweetened the leaves. In this recipe, they have the perfect balance of sweet, heat, and vinegar. (They're quite spicy, so if you aren't up for the heat, cut the hot sauce by half.) Serve them as a dinner side, or for breakfast in a bowl with corn bread to soak up the pot "likker" (see Pot Liquor on the opposite page). You can also make a collard biscuit sandwich with a fried egg and melted cheese served with likker on the side for dipping.

For vegetarian collards, omit the bacon and use vegetable stock instead of chicken stock. Add a few teaspoons of liquid smoke if you're missing the smoky flavor of the bacon. Serve them with Lowcountry Sea Island Peas (page 125) and Coconut Rice (page 139) for a Meatless Monday supper.

MAKES 12 SERVINGS

¼ cup canola oil

8 ounces smoky bacon, such as Benton's, cut into ¼-inch dice

1 large sweet onion, cut into ¼-inch dice

6 cloves garlic, minced

6 bunches collard greens, tough ribs removed and leaves cut into 1-inch-wide strips

2 quarts (8 cups) chicken stock

1 cup packed dark brown sugar

½ cup Crystal hot sauce

½ cup Worcestershire sauce

¼ cup red wine vinegar

Kosher salt and freshly ground black pepper

* In a large Dutch oven over medium-high heat, heat the oil. Add the bacon and onion and cook until the bacon has rendered its fat and is crispy (don't let it burn), and the onions are translucent, 6 to 7 minutes. Add the garlic and sauté for 1 minute. Add half of the collard greens and 4 cups of the stock. Cook until the greens begin to soften, about 10 minutes, then add the remaining collard greens and remaining stock. Reduce the heat to low, cover the pot halfway, and simmer the greens gently for 1½ hours.

* Stir in the brown sugar, hot sauce, Worcestershire, and vinegar. Season to taste with salt and pepper. Simmer another 30 minutes, then taste and adjust the seasoning with additional hot sauce, salt, and pepper as needed.

POT LIQUOR

Collards simmering on back stoves are commonplace in much of the South. (The scent of a big pot of collards cooking is strong enough that you can smell it down the block.) And in the South, where there's collards, there's "pot liquor" (also spelled "pot likker"). Pot liquor is the broth that's left in the pot after cooking any leafy greens. It's full of flavor and nutrient rich. You can drink it on its own, or save it to use as a base for soups or in place of water when making rice. Never discard the likker!

BROILED GARDEN TOMATOES
with burrata & spiced pralines

The first time I had *burrata* cheese was years ago at John Sundstrom's restaurant Lark here in Seattle. I had never even heard of it, and at the time it was only available from one distributor in Los Angeles. Now it's often sold in grocery stores next to the fresh mozzarella. *Burrata* is actually fresh mozzarella with *cream injected into the middle*. Cream injected into the middle of anything is good to me. It's great with collards and a sprinkling of red pepper flakes or, in this recipe, over garden tomatoes topped with spiced pecans. If you can't find *burrata*, substitute fresh mozzarella.

MAKES 8 SERVINGS

5 to 6 large heirloom tomatoes

Kosher salt and freshly ground black pepper

1 pound *burrata* cheese

1 cup Spiced Pralines (page 44)

Steen's cane syrup, for garnish

Pinch of Big Herb Blend (page 58), for garnish

* Preheat the oven to broil.

* Slice the tomatoes and sprinkle them with salt and pepper to taste. Lay the slices on two baking sheets and broil them until the tomatoes are soft and starting to turn black in places, 6 to 7 minutes. Remove the baking sheets from the oven and place dollops of cheese on the tomatoes (the cheese won't really slice, so cut it the best you can). Return the sheets to the oven and broil until the cheese has melted and is just a bit brown in places, another 2 to 3 minutes. Using a spatula, transfer the cheesy tomatoes to a platter. Top with the spiced pecans and a drizzle of syrup. Sprinkle with herbs and serve.

PIMENTO "NOT YOUR MAMA'S" MAC & CHEESE

IN THE SOUTH, MACARONI AND CHEESE is considered a vegetable. No joke. At cafés and diners that offer "meat and three" plates, mac and cheese is on the list of vegetables.

I grew up on Kraft Macaroni and Cheese, but only at MJ's. At Granny's, I never even saw a box of Kraft and I doubt she ever cooked one. Granny made hers from scratch using elbow noodles, sharp cheddar cheese, eggs, whole milk, and evaporated milk. She mixed it all on the stovetop, then finished it in the oven until it was thick and stiff and could be cut into squares. It was so famous in our family that one year my dad had a square of it shellacked and gave it to my uncle Ray for Christmas.

My version starts with a roux and adds four kinds of cheese; pimentos add a bit of sweetness and color, and cayenne packs a bit of a punch. Don't feel locked in with elbow macaroni: use whatever noodle you like best. I like mine with rigatoni.

MAKES 10 TO 12 SERVINGS (6 TO 8 AS A MAIN DISH)

1 pound elbow macaroni

½ cup (1 stick) unsalted butter

½ cup all-purpose flour

4 cups whole milk

½ cup half-and-half

1 pound extra-sharp cheddar cheese, grated (reserve 2 cups for topping)

4 ounces smoked Monterey Jack cheese, grated

4 ounces Gruyère cheese, grated

4 ounces cream cheese, diced

1 tablespoon Texas Pete or Crystal hot sauce

1 tablespoon Worcestershire sauce

1 tablespoon kosher salt

1 teaspoon freshly ground black pepper

½ teaspoon freshly grated nutmeg

¼ teaspoon cayenne

1 (4-ounce) jar diced pimentos, drained

* Preheat the oven to 375 degrees F.

* Cook the macaroni in a pot of boiling water with a tablespoon of salt, stirring occasionally, until al dente, about 6 minutes. Drain the macaroni and set it aside.

* In a large Dutch oven, melt the butter over medium heat. When it starts to bubble, add the flour and cook, whisking continuously, until the flour is fragrant and lightly golden brown, 3 to 4 minutes. Add the milk and half-and-half in a steady stream. Let the mixture come to a simmer, and cook, whisking frequently, until the sauce is thickened, about 10 minutes. Whisk in the cheddar (except the 2 reserved cups), Monterey Jack, Gruyére, and cream cheese until completely melted and smooth. Turn off the heat and whisk in the hot sauce, Worcestershire, salt, pepper, nutmeg, and cayenne. Taste and adjust the seasoning with additional salt and pepper as needed. Stir in the pimentos.

* Add the macaroni to the sauce and mix thoroughly. Top with the reserved cheddar. Bake the mac and cheese on the middle rack in the oven until the sauce starts to bubble, 25 to 35 minutes. Turn the oven to broil and brown the top for 4 to 5 minutes, being careful not to burn the cheese. Serve immediately.

GRANNY'S SALISBURY RED SLAW

THERE WAS NEVER A TIME WHEN I opened Granny's fridge and didn't see a mason jar of this red slaw. For most folks within a sixty-mile radius of Lexington, North Carolina, red slaw was *the only* slaw. Salisbury being a mere twenty minutes away from Lexington, we ate red slaw with almost every meal. It has the perfect balance of vinegar and heat. Granny's version is the only one I ever saw with small bits of tomato mixed in. Store it in the far reaches of your fridge, as it's best when it's completely chilled. Perfect served over pulled pork sandwiches.

MAKES 4 CUPS

1 head cabbage (a little over 1 pound)
1 (14.5-ounce) can whole peeled tomatoes with juice
½ cup white vinegar

3 tablespoons sugar
1 tablespoon Texas Pete or Crystal hot sauce
2 teaspoons kosher salt
1 teaspoon freshly ground black pepper

* Peel off and discard the cabbage's outer leaves, core it, and cut it into 1-inch chunks. Add half of the chunks to the bowl of a food processor and pulse a few times until the leaves are uniformly chopped. Put them in a large bowl. Pulse the rest of the cabbage and add it to the bowl. Add the tomatoes and juice and, using your hands, squish the tomatoes until no large pieces remain. Stir in the vinegar, sugar, hot sauce, salt, and pepper. Taste and adjust the seasoning with additional hot sauce, salt, and pepper as needed. It will keep stored in a lidded glass jar in the refrigerator for up to 1 week.

Granny, Spencer, North Carolina, 1930s

TOMATO & CUCUMBER SALAD
with sorghum syrup & black pepper

TOMATOES ARE EVERYWHERE IN THE SOUTH. Everyone grows them, and they're often served cut into fat slices with a sprinkling of salt and pepper as a simple supper side.

I remember one particularly hot Memorial Day with Granny and Pop. We drove out to the national cemetery, and Senator Jesse Helms walked by us. Granny shook his hand and said, "Well, I'll shake your hand, but I sure as heck won't vote for ya!" Democrats through and through, we chuckled as we folded ourselves back in the Buick and went to eat lunch: chilled cucumbers in vinegar, pimento cheese sandwiches, and this salad. I also like it with Hot Skillet Corn Bread (page 141) on the side.

MAKES 4 TO 6 SERVINGS

4 to 5 large tomatoes, quartered

2 cucumbers, peeled and cut into large chunks

¼ red onion, thinly sliced

4 to 5 tablespoons sorghum syrup

2 to 3 tablespoons Steen's cane vinegar or apple cider vinegar

Kosher salt and freshly ground black pepper

* In a large bowl, toss the tomatoes, cucumbers, and onion with the sorghum syrup and vinegar. Season to taste with salt and pepper. Serve immediately or chill until you're ready to serve, adding 1 more tablespoon of sorghum right before serving.

SORGHUM SYRUP

Thick and rich but labor intensive, sorghum syrup is made by boiling down the grassy sorghum plant. The drought-resistant plant was first grown in the southern United States in the mid-1800s for use as an affordable sweetener. Nowadays, it's grown by small farms specializing in producing limited batches of the syrup. This unique syrup tastes rich and caramel-y and is perfect for drizzling over biscuits, granola, pancakes, and ice cream. Sorghum syrup complements a cheese plate or a grilled cheese sandwich and is perfect poured over Hot Skillet Corn Bread (page 141). At The Wandering Goose, we use Muddy Pond Sorghum Syrup from Tennessee.

THE WANDERING GOOSE WHITE SLAW

THIS CREAMY COLESLAW HAS THE PERFECT balance of vinegar, sugar, and hot sauce. Serve it with Big Love Buttermilk Fried Chicken (page 95) or on top of a pulled pork sandwich with Cornmeal Fried Green Tomatoes (page 25) or hush puppies (see page 39) on the side.

MAKES 8 CUPS

2 pounds green cabbage, shredded

1 carrot, grated

1 cup mayonnaise, such as Duke's or Best Foods

½ cup sugar

⅓ cup apple cider vinegar

¼ cup Texas Pete or Crystal hot sauce

2 tablespoons honey

1½ teaspoons kosher salt

1 teaspoon freshly ground black pepper

* In a large bowl, mix all the ingredients until combined. Taste and add more salt, pepper, or hot sauce. It will keep stored in the refrigerator for 1 week.

COCONUT RICE

I USE COCONUT CREAM FOR THIS RICE, which is thicker and richer than coconut milk. Feel free to substitute coconut milk; just don't use light coconut milk, as it lacks the flavor that makes this rice so delicious. Try rinsing out the can with a little bit of water to get the entire amount of cream out. The recipe can easily be doubled.

MAKES 3 CUPS

1 (19-ounce) can coconut cream, such as Mae Ploy

1 cup jasmine rice

2 tablespoons unsalted butter

1½ teaspoons kosher salt

* In a large saucepan over medium-high heat, combine the coconut cream, rice, butter, and salt and bring it to a boil. Reduce the heat to low, cover the pan, and cook until the rice is soft and has absorbed all the cream, about 20 minutes.

GRANDDADDY'S FANCY NEW POTATOES
with parsley & salty butter

THIS WAS ONE OF GRANDDADDY'S "ALL ON IT" supper sides: little new potatoes cooked until soft but still able to hold their shape tossed in salted butter and mixed with chopped fresh parsley. He made them extra fancy by peeling the potato only in the middle. I don't know if he came up with that himself, but I still make these the same way.

MAKES 4 TO 6 SERVINGS

1½ pounds small red
  new potatoes
6 tablespoons unsalted
  butter

¼ cup fresh flat-leaf
  parsley, chopped
Kosher salt and freshly
  ground black pepper

* Peel the potatoes in one round strip just around the middle, leaving the peel on the top and bottom. Put the potatoes in a large saucepot and fill the pot with enough water to cover. Bring the water to a boil over medium-high heat and cook the potatoes until you can pierce them with a knife but they don't fall apart, about 15 minutes. Drain and return them to the pot. Add the butter and parsley and stir gently to coat. Season to taste with salt and pepper and serve warm.

WATERMELON SALAD
with salt & spearmint

I ADDED SPEARMINT TO THIS CLASSIC treat in memory of Granny, whose backyard mint patch would release its scent as I brushed past it to hook up the sprinkler on hot summer days. Reserve the rind for Granny's Watermelon Rind Pickles (page 161).

MAKES 4 TO 6 SERVINGS

1 (6-pound) watermelon,
  sliced, rind removed,
  seeded, and cut into
  2-inch chunks

½ ounce fresh
  spearmint, thinly
  sliced (chiffonade)
Fleur de sel

* In a large bowl, toss the watermelon with the spearmint. Sprinkle with *fleur de sel* and serve immediately or keep in the refrigerator until ready to serve.

HOT SKILLET CORN BREAD
sour cream & fresh corn

I'm certainly not ashamed to say I keep a supply of Jiffy Corn Muffin Mix in my pantry. I happen to like its sweet, cakey quality and often add grated pepper jack cheese and some freshly grated corn to gussy it up a bit. I've served it at parties and once had one of my best friends, who is a fancy chef in France half the year, tell me that it was the best corn bread he'd ever had! I didn't have the heart just then to tell him it was Jiffy. (Well, Jon, now you know!)

This is a quick corn bread recipe for when I want something heartier and happen to be out of Jiffy. Serve it with a generous helping of Steen's Butter (recipe follows). If you have any leftovers, warm them in the oven the next morning and serve them with strawberry jam and a fried egg for a quick breakfast. This makes a large amount, so you can halve the recipe if you wish. Just use a nine-inch skillet and reduce the bake time by about fifteen minutes.

MAKES ONE 12-INCH ROUND CORN BREAD

¾ cup (1½ sticks) butter, melted, plus more for greasing the skillet
3 cups all-purpose flour, sifted
1½ cups fine-ground cornmeal
3 tablespoons sugar
2 teaspoons baking powder
1½ teaspoons baking soda

2 teaspoons kosher salt
1 cup grated extra-sharp cheddar cheese
1 bunch scallions, green and white parts, thinly sliced
3 large eggs
1½ cups buttermilk
8 ounces sour cream
Steen's Butter (recipe follows), for serving

* Preheat the oven to 325 degrees F. Butter a 12-inch cast-iron skillet and put it in the oven to get hot.

* In a large bowl, whisk together the flour, cornmeal, sugar, baking powder, baking soda, and salt. Mix in the cheddar and scallions. In a medium bowl, whisk together the eggs, buttermilk, sour cream, and melted butter. Add the wet ingredients to the dry ingredients and mix with a rubber spatula until just combined. Do not overmix.

* Pour the batter into the hot skillet and bake until golden brown, about 55 minutes, rotating the pan halfway through baking. Serve hot.

continued

STEEN'S BUTTER

SERVE THIS WITH PRINCESS "HUSH NOW" Hush Puppies (page 39), slathered over corn bread, or on a biscuit sandwich with country ham and a fried egg. It keeps at room temperature for easy spreading for up to one week. Stored covered in the fridge, it keeps indefinitely.

MAKES 2 CUPS

2 cups (4 sticks) unsalted butter, at room temperature

⅔ cup Steen's cane syrup or molasses

* In the bowl of a stand mixer fitted with the whisk attachment, whip the butter until no large lumps remain. Drizzle in the cane syrup and continue to whip until combined.

STEEN'S CANE SYRUP

I . . . took a biscuit off a plate, and punched a hole in it with my finger. Then with a jar of cane syrup, I poured the hole full, waited for it to soak in good, and then poured again. When the biscuit had all the syrup it would take, I . . . went out and sat on the back steps. **–HARRY CREWS**

Steen's cane syrup has been made in southeastern Louisiana for more than 100 years. The caramel color is just a shade lighter than molasses, has no refined sugar, and has a buttered toast flavor. The canes are cooked down in open kettles, and then the juice is concentrated. You can order Steen's online through CajunGrocer.com and Amazon, or substitute molasses, using a little less than what the recipes call for—but if you can, get your hands on some Steen's! It's a versatile pantry ingredient: drizzle it over a warmed split biscuit, granola, oatmeal, or farro breakfast porridge. You can even use it in salad dressings.

SKILLET RAMPS & YUKON GOLD POTATOES
with benton's bacon & toast

As young as eight, I was pulling wild ramps out of the ground. They are found in large patches throughout the Appalachian Mountains and have a garlicky onion flavor. In this recipe, I use Benton's bacon for its extra-smoky flavor, and it goes perfectly with the ramps. Sauté some Yukon Golds in the bacon fat, a touch of butter, poach or fry a couple of eggs, serve 'em over a biscuit or a thick hunk of bread, and you have one good-lookin' country breakfast!

MAKES 4 SERVINGS

1 pound Yukon Gold potatoes

½ pound smoky bacon, such as Benton's, chopped

2 tablespoons unsalted butter

8 ounces wild ramps, cleaned and roots trimmed, or 2 leeks, cleaned thoroughly, pale-green and white parts sliced into half moons

1 tablespoon Texas Pete or Crystal hot sauce

1 tablespoon Worcestershire sauce

4 thick slices rustic bread, or 2 biscuits, cut in half and toasted

4 poached or fried eggs

* Put the potatoes in a large saucepan and fill the pan with enough water to cover. Bring the water to a boil over medium-high heat, and boil the potatoes for 5 to 7 minutes. Drain them and set aside to cool. When the potatoes are cool enough to handle, cut them into bite-size chunks—not too small. Set aside.

* Line a plate with paper towels and set it by the stove. In a large skillet over medium-high heat, sauté the bacon until the fat is rendered and the bacon is crispy. Set it aside to drain on the lined plate. Add the butter to the skillet, swirling it to coat the pan as it melts. Reduce the heat to medium. Add the potatoes and cook until they start to brown, 6 to 7 minutes. Add the ramps and sauté until they're soft, 3 to 4 minutes. Add the bacon back to the skillet along with the hot sauce and Worcestershire. Stir everything until combined.

* To serve, put a slice of bread on each of four plates. Top with one-quarter of the potato-ramp mixture and an egg.

FOR THE BIG POT

BIG LOVE FOR ALL!

WEST COAST–STYLE SHE-CRAB SOUP 147

GO TO CHURCH BRUNSWICK STEW 149

ANY TIME OF YEAR TOMATO SOUP *with biscuit croutons* 150

GRANNY'S GARDEN VEGETABLE SOUP 151

LOADED CHICKEN POTPIE *with biscuit topping* 153

"NOT JUST FOR MONDAY" RED BEANS & RICE 154

SOUTHERN SPAGHETTI SAUCE 155

OUR KITCHEN AT HOME IS SMALL. The kitchen at The Goose is small. Neither kitchen is glamorous and beautifully tiled, ready for the pages of *Bon Appétit* magazine. These kitchens are *small*. They are workhorses, and I make them work. You don't need a pretty kitchen to make amazing food. You don't need the next new gadget or a cute apron. You just need the basics—just like my granny had, and her mother had, and her mother before her. My granny cooked enough food for hundreds, even thousands, of people over the years using an old Hotpoint stove and a Sunbeam hand mixer—not even a KitchenAid stand mixer (although, to be fair, I should point out I really love my KitchenAid).

In my opinion, to be able to entertain, you need just a few quality things:

One very large Dutch oven (bigger than you think)
One stainless steel saucepot for cooking rice
Two large skillets, one cast-iron and one stainless steel
One small nonstick skillet for cooking eggs
One 10-inch chef's knife
One 4-inch paring knife
One good-quality pepper grinder
One microplane zester

A KitchenAid is helpful for baking. Throw in a wooden spoon and a couple of spatulas, and you're good to go. Mostly what matters to me when I entertain is how good the food is and how charismatic the company.

WEST COAST–STYLE SHE-CRAB SOUP

FANCY SHE-CRAB SOUP IS SOMETHING WE always ate with Granddaddy when we went on vacation to North Carolina's Outer Banks and South Carolina's Lowcountry. We were allowed little cups served on doily-lined plates and marveled at its rich, creamy taste. We felt grown up since it had a good amount of sherry stirred in and tiny pink crab roe on top.

In this recipe, I recreate it using the stock left over from making Zevely House Shrimp and Grits (page 91), adding Northwest flair by using flying fish roe. On the West Coast we have Alaskan king and Dungeness crabs instead of the East Coast's blue crabs.

MAKES 6 SERVINGS

½ cup (1 stick) unsalted butter

3 large shallots, diced

½ cup diced celery

½ cup diced sweet onion

½ cup all-purpose flour

½ cup plus 6 tablespoons sherry, divided

4 cups shrimp or crab stock (see page 91)

2 cups whole milk

2 cups heavy cream

Juice from 1 large lemon

2 teaspoons Worcestershire sauce

2 teaspoons Texas Pete or Crystal hot sauce

2 teaspoons kosher salt

½ teaspoon freshly ground black pepper

½ teaspoon Old Bay seasoning

¼ teaspoon smoked paprika

1 bay leaf

1 pound lump crabmeat

6 teaspoons flying fish roe, for garnish

French bread, for serving

* In a large stockpot or Dutch oven over medium heat, melt the butter. Add the shallots, celery, and onion and sauté until the onion is translucent, 5 to 6 minutes. Sprinkle in the flour and stir for 2 to 3 minutes until it is golden brown and smells nutty. Pour in ½ cup of the sherry and the shrimp stock, scraping the bottom of the pan to remove any browned bits. Slowly pour in the milk and cream, reduce the heat to medium low, and simmer until the soup starts to thicken. Stir in the lemon juice, Worcestershire, hot sauce, salt, pepper, Old Bay, paprika, and bay leaf. Taste and adjust the seasoning: depending on how salty your stock was, you might need to add another few teaspoons of salt, as well as hot sauce and Worcestershire. Gently fold in the crabmeat.

* Spoon 1 cup of soup into each of six bowls. Garnish each bowl with 1 teaspoon of roe and 1 tablespoon of sherry. Serve with French bread on the side for dipping.

GO TO CHURCH BRUNSWICK STEW

A FEW BLOCKS FROM GRANNY'S HOUSE, there is a small redbrick church. Every
fall they have a fundraiser and sell vats of Brunswick stew. Overalled men cook
the stew over an open fire in deep black cauldrons, and the women take the tickets,
purchased weeks prior. When Granny died, my father and I found four tickets for
the church's stew in her wallet. We redeemed them and took our Styrofoam cups
of stew to the cemetery, where we toasted Granny and poured a wee bit next to her
marker "just in case."

This is a *thick* stew, especially if you add the pulled pork. If it's too thick for you,
add a few more cups of beef broth at the end of cooking. You can make the whole
recipe at once, roasting the chicken and setting it aside to cool while you start the
stew, but it's easier to cook the chicken separately and have the meat pulled off the
bone and shredded, ready to add after the stew boils. (Or you could cheat and use a
store-bought rotisserie chicken.) One pot of this feeds my family of seven for dinner, with a bit left over for me to have for breakfast.

MAKES 8 SERVINGS

¼ cup extra-virgin
olive oil

2 tablespoons unsalted
butter

1 beef marrowbone

1 pound Yukon Gold
potatoes, diced

1 large sweet
onion, diced

1 cup chopped celery

2 cloves garlic, minced

1 quart (4 cups) beef
stock

1 (28-ounce) can whole
peeled tomatoes
with juice

1 (20-ounce) package
frozen baby lima beans

1 (16-ounce) package
frozen sweet corn

12 to 15 sprigs fresh
thyme, tied with
butcher's twine

1 bay leaf

1 Simple Roast Chicken
(page 57), meat pulled
off the bone and
shredded

2 cups barbecue or
other pulled pork
(optional)

1 cup Central Carolina
Vinegar Sauce
(page 180)

¼ teaspoon cayenne

1 tablespoon kosher salt

1 tablespoon freshly
ground black pepper

French bread,
for serving

* In a large Dutch oven over medium-high
heat, heat the oil and butter. When the butter is
melted and the oil shimmers, sear the marrow-
bone on both sides, then push it to the side of
the pot. Add the potatoes, onion, and celery and
sauté until the onions are translucent, 6 to 7 minutes. Add the garlic and sauté for 1 minute. Add
the beef stock, tomatoes with juice, lima beans,
corn, thyme bundle, and bay leaf. Bring the stew
to a boil, then gently simmer over medium-low
heat. Add the chicken, pork, vinegar sauce, and
cayenne. Cover the pot and simmer the stew,
stirring every 15 minutes, until the potatoes are
soft and the flavors have had time to develop,
65 to 75 minutes. Before serving, remove the
thyme bundle and add the salt and pepper,
seasoning with more to taste. Serve warm with
crusty French bread.

ANY TIME OF YEAR TOMATO SOUP
with biscuit croutons

I GREW UP ON CAMPBELL'S CREAM of tomato soup that my sister and I ate with grilled pimento cheese sandwiches. It was an easy thing for me to heat up for us to eat after school before MJ got home. There's something simple and satisfying about a really good–tasting tomato soup. This one has crunch from the croutons and added tang from the cream cheese. Serve it with grilled "Not Ruth's" Pimento Cheese Spread (page 27) sandwich triangles when your kids come home from school. This soup makes a big batch that you can eat on for a few days, or the recipe can easily be cut in half. I count on two cups per serving as a main course.

MAKES 8 SERVINGS

¼ cup extra-virgin
   olive oil

2 tablespoons unsalted
   butter

2 large sweet onions,
   chopped
   (about 6 cups)

4 carrots, peeled
   and chopped
   (about 2 cups)

6 cloves garlic, smashed

½ ounce torn fresh
   basil leaves (about
   15 leaves)

1 tablespoon kosher salt

2 teaspoons freshly
   ground black pepper

4 (28-ounce) cans whole
   peeled tomatoes
   with juice

4 ounces cream cheese

½ cup half-and-half

Biscuit Croutons (page
   81), for serving

* In large stockpot or Dutch oven over medium-high heat, heat the oil and butter until the butter is melted and the oil shimmers. Add the onions and carrots and sauté until the onions are translucent, about 10 minutes. Add the garlic, basil, salt, and pepper and sauté until the garlic is fragrant but not browned, 3 to 4 minutes. Pour the tomatoes into the pot, then rinse the cans with a bit of water to get all of the tomato juice out and pour into the pot (it ends up equaling about ½ cup). Reduce the heat to medium and simmer until the carrots are soft, about 25 minutes. Add the cream cheese and cook until it's melted, about 10 minutes more.

* Remove the soup from the heat and let it cool for about 20 minutes. Using an immersion blender, puree the soup in the pot or carefully blend the soup in batches in a blender until completely smooth with no chunks remaining. Strain the soup through a sieve using a rubber spatula to push the soup through and back into the pot. Return to the stove over medium-low heat, stir in the half-and-half, and rewarm the soup gently. Taste and adjust the seasoning with additional salt and pepper as needed. Serve with the biscuit croutons on top.

GRANNY'S GARDEN VEGETABLE SOUP

USE WHATEVER GARDEN VEGETABLES ARE FRESH, if you have them, or use high-quality frozen vegetables during the winter. Granny flavored her soup with a beef soup bone but didn't add any meat to the soup (most grocery stores will label bones good for soup as "soup bones"—if you are unsure, ask your butcher). For her it was all about the vegetables. I add fresh okra when it's available. This makes a big batch of soup but it freezes beautifully.

MAKES 8 SERVINGS

¼ cup extra-virgin olive oil

2 tablespoons unsalted butter

1 large beef marrow-bone (soup bone), or 2 to 3 smaller ones

1 pound Yukon Gold potatoes, diced

2 sweet onions, diced

2 cups diced celery

2 quarts (8 cups) beef stock

1 (28-ounce) can diced tomatoes

1 (28-ounce) can whole peeled tomatoes with juice

1 (20-ounce) package frozen baby lima beans

1 (16-ounce) package frozen sweet corn

½ pound fresh okra, sliced into ½-inch rounds (optional)

12 to 15 sprigs fresh thyme tied with butcher's twine

2 bay leaves

3 tablespoons apple cider vinegar

2 tablespoons packed dark brown sugar

4 teaspoons kosher salt

2 teaspoons freshly ground black pepper

French bread, for serving

Texas Pete or Crystal hot sauce, for serving

* In a large Dutch oven over medium-high heat, heat the oil and butter. When the butter is melted and the oil shimmers, sear the beef bone on both sides, then push it to the side of the pot. Add the potatoes, onions, and celery and sauté until the onions are translucent, 6 to 7 minutes. Add the beef stock, tomatoes, lima beans, corn, okra, thyme bundle, and bay leaves. Bring the soup to a boil, then reduce the heat to medium low and gently simmer. Cover the pot three-quarters of the way and simmer the soup for at least 2 hours, but preferably 3 hours, stirring every 30 minutes.

* Add the vinegar, sugar, salt, and pepper and cook for 10 more minutes. Taste for seasoning and adjust with additional salt and pepper. Serve with crusty French bread topped with a dash of hot sauce or vinegar.

LOADED CHICKEN POTPIE
with biscuit topping

THIS IS MY VERSION OF A classic Swanson chicken potpie, which MJ would buy for us as a special treat on the rare evenings we had a babysitter. It's loaded with flavor and vegetables and plenty of savory gravy, all my favorites.

As with the Go to Church Brunswick Stew (page 149), you can make the whole recipe at once, roasting the chicken and cooling it a few hours beforehand, then picking the meat off the bones and making the biscuits while the filling simmers, but sometimes I roast my chicken a day or two ahead of time for convenience. It's also easier to cook the chicken and have the biscuits ready before you make the potpie. The biscuits can be premixed, cut, and kept in the fridge up to one hour before you make the filling.

MAKES 8 SERVINGS

1 cup (2 sticks) unsalted butter

1 pound Yukon Gold potatoes, chopped

1 large sweet onion, chopped

1 leek, cleaned thoroughly, white and pale-green parts sliced into half moons

2½ cups chopped carrots

2 cups chopped celery

1 tablespoon kosher salt

1 teaspoon freshly ground black pepper

1 cup all-purpose flour

1 quart (4 cups) chicken stock

2 chicken bouillon cubes dissolved in 3 cups boiling water

3 tablespoons chopped fresh thyme

1 (16-ounce) bag frozen petite peas

½ cup heavy cream

¼ cup flat-leaf parsley, chopped

1 tablespoon lemon zest

1 Simple Roast Chicken (page 57), meat pulled off the bone and shredded

Unbaked biscuits from ½ recipe Best Buttermilk Biscuits (page 65)

4 tablespoons unsalted butter, melted, for brushing the biscuits

* Preheat the oven to 400 degrees F.

* In a large Dutch oven over medium-high heat, melt the butter. When the butter is melted, add the potatoes, onion, leek, carrots, celery, salt, and pepper and stir to coat the vegetables with the butter. Sauté until the onion is translucent and the vegetables begin to soften, 6 to 7 minutes. Add the flour, stir to coat the vegetables with it, and cook until there is no visible flour, 1 minute. Add the chicken stock, bouillon water, and thyme and stir until the potpie filling starts to thicken, about 5 minutes.

* Turn off the heat and add the peas, cream, parsley, and lemon zest. Stir in the chicken meat and top with the biscuits. Brush the biscuits with the melted butter and bake until they are golden brown and the potpie is bubbling, about 40 to 45 minutes. Cool for 5 minutes before serving.

"NOT JUST FOR MONDAY" RED BEANS & RICE

WHEN WE WERE LITTLE, MJ SERVED us warmed dark-red beans from a can over long-grain white rice. We doused it with ketchup and ate bowlfuls. Nowadays I make it from scratch, though my little ones still eat theirs with ketchup on top. I serve the beans over Coconut Rice (page 139) with extra hot sauce on the side. This dish was originally made in New Orleans on "wash day" Monday. It was something the women could put on the back burner of the stove and let cook for a few hours since it didn't require much attention. Growing up, we had this not just on Mondays but usually Tuesdays as well because there was so much left over. I add the salt toward the end because if you add it early on the beans tend to break apart faster.

MAKES 8 TO 10 SERVINGS

1 pound dried red beans

¼ cup extra-virgin olive oil

1 pound sausage, such as andouille or kielbasa, cut on the bias into 1-inch slices

1 smoked ham hock

2 large sweet onions, chopped

5 ribs celery, chopped

2 large green bell peppers, cored, seeded, and chopped

1 head garlic, peeled and cloves smashed

2 bay leaves

1 tablespoon kosher salt

1½ teaspoons freshly ground black pepper

½ teaspoon cayenne

1½ quarts (6 cups) chicken stock

1 (28-ounce) can diced tomatoes

1 tablespoon white vinegar

Chopped fresh flat-leaf parsley, for garnish

1 bunch scallions, sliced, for garnish

Texas Pete or Crystal hot sauce, for serving

* First, quick-soak the beans. In a large stockpot over high heat, bring 8 cups water to a boil. Add the beans and boil for 1 minute, then cover the pot, take it off the heat, and let it sit for 1 hour. (Alternatively, soak the beans overnight or for at least 8 hours in cold water.) Drain and rinse the beans and set them aside.

* In a large Dutch oven over medium-high heat, heat the oil. When the oil is shimmering, add the sausage and ham hock, browning the meat on both sides. Remove the meat from the pot and set it aside. Add the onions, celery, bell peppers, garlic, bay leaves, salt, pepper, and cayenne and sauté until the onions are translucent, 6 to 7 minutes. Add the beans, chicken stock, tomatoes, and ham hock and bring the mixture to a boil, then reduce the heat to low. Cover the pot halfway and gently simmer the beans until they are soft, about 2 hours. Just before serving, scoop out 3 cups of the beans and puree them in a food processor or blender, or mash with a fork, then stir them back into the pot, along with the sausage and vinegar. Serve over rice sprinkled with parsley and scallions and plenty of hot sauce.

SOUTHERN SPAGHETTI SAUCE

THIS SAUCE CANS BEAUTIFULLY, FREEZES WELL, and makes a great last-minute gift for a new neighbor or friends. Serve it over spaghetti with hunks of French bread and a green salad with Granddaddy's Hard-Boiled Egg Salad Dressing (page 177). As with most pasta sauces, the key is to cook it at a low simmer for three to four hours. It's even better the next day, and cold spaghetti sandwiches (a mound of left-over noodles and sauce served cold between two slices of soft sandwich bread) for breakfast are a favorite in our house.

After dumping the cans of tomatoes into the pot, I always rinse the cans with a bit of water to get all of the juice out, then add this "tomato water" to the pot. It ends up equaling about one cup. I added the butter one day on a whim and love the rich softness it adds to the sauce. You can make a meat version of this sauce by adding in one pound each of browned ground beef and Italian sausage (mild or spicy—I like spicy) during the last hour of cooking. I make this spaghetti once a week in our house; it's a favorite of the kids.

MAKES 2½ QUARTS WITHOUT MEAT OR 3 QUARTS WITH MEAT

¼ cup extra-virgin olive oil

1 large sweet onion, diced

2 large green bell peppers, cored, seeded, and diced

8 ounces button or cremini mushrooms, sliced

6 cloves garlic, smashed

3 teaspoons kosher salt, divided

2 bay leaves

3 tablespoons Italian seasoning

2 teaspoons freshly ground black pepper, divided

1 teaspoon crushed red pepper flakes

¾ cup dry red wine

3 tablespoons sugar

1 (28-ounce) can petite diced tomatoes

1 (28-ounce) can whole peeled tomatoes

1 (28-ounce) can crushed tomatoes

1 (28-ounce) can tomato sauce

1 (6-ounce) can tomato paste

1 ounce whole basil leaves (about 20 leaves), roughly chopped

½ cup (1 stick) unsalted butter

1 pound spaghetti noodles

Freshly grated Parmesan, for garnish

continued

* In a large Dutch oven over medium-high heat, heat the oil. When the oil is shimmering, add the onion and sauté until translucent, 5 to 6 minutes. Add the bell peppers, mushrooms, garlic, and 1 teaspoon of the salt and sauté until the peppers and mushrooms start to soften, 5 to 6 minutes more. Add the bay leaves, Italian seasoning, 1 teaspoon each of the salt and black pepper, and the red pepper flakes and sauté 2 minutes more. Add the wine and sauté until it has evaporated, 2 to 3 minutes. Add the sugar, all the tomatoes plus tomato water, tomato sauce, tomato paste, basil, the remaining 1 teaspoon each salt and pepper, and bring to a boil. Cover the pot halfway and reduce the heat to low. Gently simmer for 3 to 4 hours, stirring every 30 minutes or so. Before serving, add the butter to the sauce and stir to melt it.

* Cook the spaghetti according to the package directions. Serve 1 cup cooked spaghetti with ¾ cup sauce. Top each serving with 3 tablespoons Parmesan.

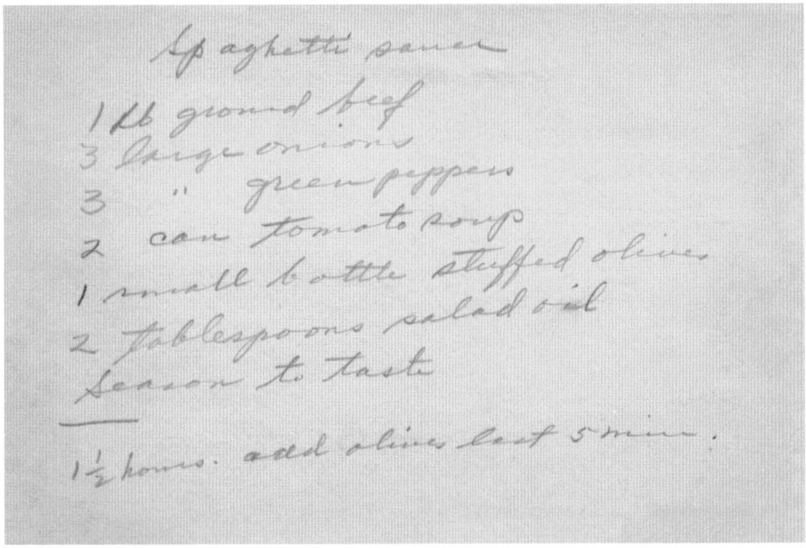

Spaghetti sauce
1 lb ground beef
3 large onions
3 " green peppers
2 can tomato soup
1 small bottle stuffed olives
2 tablespoons salad oil
Season to taste

1½ hours. add olives last 5 min.

ALL ABOUT THE PICKLES

JAR IT UP

GRANNY'S WATERMELON RIND PICKLES 161

BREAD & BUTTER PICKLES *salty & sweet* 162

THE WANDERING GOOSE EXTRA-SPICY DILLS 163

PICKLED RED ONIONS 166

GRANDDADDY'S FAST CUKES IN VIN 166

PICKLED OKRA 167

PICKLED GREEN BEANS 168

CHOWCHOW 169

A CHILD OF THE DEPRESSION living in a small Southern town, Granny canned, pickled, preserved, and "put up" vegetables and fruit all summer long. It didn't matter that she had a cellar full of them already, she kept at it in that steaming-hot kitchen, sterilizing jars and boiling the preserves in a water bath. I can't tell you how many hours I spent standing next to her, sweat rolling down both of our necks, wiping the steaming hot lids and mason jars dry with her soft dish towels as they came out of the water or scrubbing pickling cucumbers or green beans clean before processing. We used the same worn dish towels for years—each year they grew softer and softer.

Nowadays there are many different recipes and ways of making pickles. If I'm making a big batch, I prefer to use the water-bath method (please look up safe canning techniques before starting). But lately it seems I mostly end up making a quick pickle by filling a clean jar with my pickle mixture and then keeping it in the fridge for a week or so. We usually end up eating them before the week is up. Use these recipes as a base for pickling anything and everything! Beets, carrots, radishes, shallots, spring onions, even peaches, grapes and nectarines—they all pickle beautifully and look stunning in a jar on your supper table.

GRANNY'S WATERMELON RIND PICKLES

GRANNY WAS KNOWN FOR THESE PICKLES—sweet and soft and spiced with allspice, ginger, and cloves. She put them up during the summer and gave them as gifts during the holidays. They're great to set out at holiday parties, along with Granny's Crunchy Cheese Straws (page 33) and Spiced Pralines (see page 44). Use a regular watermelon, not a seedless variety, which doesn't have much of a rind to pickle.

This is a two-day process so plan accordingly. Calcium chloride is a firming agent added to replace the lime that was used in the 1950s. It keeps the rind (and other pickled products) crisp.

MAKES 6 PINT JARS

1 very large watermelon (about 20 pounds)

2 tablespoons calcium chloride

5 tablespoons ground ginger

For the pickling syrup:

8 cups sugar

4 cups white vinegar

2½ cups water

½ tablespoon whole allspice berries

½ tablespoon whole cloves

1 cinnamon stick

* Place a bunch of paper towels underneath the watermelon before you begin. This will help to catch all of the juice while you cut it. Using a chef's knife, cut the watermelon in half, then into 1-inch half-moon slices. Cut away the watermelon flesh first, reserving it for eating. Cut the rind into 1½-inch chunks. Using a paring knife, trim the green parts from the white rind and discard.

* In a large plastic container big enough to hold all the rind, mix the calcium chloride with 1 gallon cold water. Add the rinds, cover, and soak overnight in the refrigerator.

* The next day, drain the rinds and rinse them in several changes of cold water. In a large stockpot, whisk the ginger with 1 gallon water and add the rinds. Bring the water to a boil over medium-high heat, then reduce the heat to low and simmer the rinds until you can pierce them with a fork, 50 to 60 minutes.

* While the rinds cook, prepare the pickling syrup. In another large stockpot over medium heat, stir together all the ingredients until the sugar is dissolved. (You can bundle the spices in cheesecloth, or just leave them loose in the syrup.) Keep warm over low heat.

* When the rinds are done simmering, drain them in a colander and add them to the pickling syrup. Turn off the heat and let the pickles sit (not cook) in the hot syrup until the pickles are clear and the syrup is room temperature, about 4 hours. Divide the pickles among six sterilized pint jars and cover with the syrup, leaving ½ inch of headspace. Wipe the rims clean, place the lids on top, and screw on the bands. Process the jars in a water-bath canner according to the manufacturer's instructions.

BREAD & BUTTER PICKLES
salty & sweet

OUR FRONT-OF-HOUSE STAFF ASKS THE KITCHEN for sides of these pickles with their meal. They're great for gifting to friends and family. You can find a crinkle cutter at kitchen supply stores or online; if you don't have one, regular slices are just fine.

MAKES 4 QUART JARS

5 pounds pickling cucumbers, ends trimmed

2 sweet onions, cut in half and then into ¼-inch slices

8 cups cubed ice

½ cup kosher salt

For the pickling liquid:

4 cups apple cider vinegar

3 cups sugar

½ cup cold water

¼ cup yellow mustard seeds

2 tablespoons kosher salt

1 tablespoon freshly ground black pepper

1 tablespoon crushed red pepper flakes

2 teaspoons celery seed

2 teaspoons ground turmeric

* Cut the cucumbers into ¼-inch slices with a crinkle cutter. In a colander with a bowl underneath, toss the cucumbers and onions with the ice and salt, and let them sit in the refrigerator for 6 to 12 hours. This will remove the moisture and make for a crisper pickle. Rinse the cucumbers and onions thoroughly to remove the salt and drain well.

* To prepare the pickling liquid, in large stockpot over high heat, bring all the ingredients to a boil in order to dissolve the sugar and salt. Boil for 2 minutes. Take the pot off the heat and let the liquid cool to room temperature.

* Divide and pack the cucumbers and onions in four glass quart jars, pour the liquid over to cover, lid the jars, and store them in the refrigerator. The pickles will taste best if you let them sit for 1 week before eating. They will keep for up to 1 month.

THE WANDERING GOOSE EXTRA-SPICY DILLS

MY DAD LOVED ANYTHING PICKLED, AND the spicier the better. These are for him. You can use this as a base recipe for pickling all kinds of vegetables, increasing the red pepper flakes for an even spicier brine.

MAKES 4 PINT JARS

2½ pounds whole Kirby
   cucumbers
8 cups cubed ice
½ cup kosher salt

For the pickling liquid:
3 cups apple cider
   vinegar
3 cups water

½ cup kosher salt
½ cup pickling spice
¼ cup sugar
5 cloves garlic, smashed
3 tablespoons dill seed
2 tablespoons crushed
   red pepper flakes
2 tablespoons yellow
   mustard seeds

* In a colander with a bowl underneath, toss the cucumbers with the ice and salt, and let them sit in the refrigerator for 6 to 12 hours. This will remove the moisture and make for a crisper pickle. Rinse the cucumbers thoroughly to remove the salt and drain well.

* To prepare the pickling liquid, in a large stockpot over high heat, combine all the ingredients. Bring the liquid to a boil in order to dissolve the sugar and salt. Boil for 2 minutes. Take the pot off the heat and let the liquid cool to room temperature.

* Divide and pack the cucumbers in four glass pint jars, pour the liquid over to cover, lid the jars, and store them in the refrigerator. The pickles will taste best if you let them sit for 1 week before eating. They will keep for up to 1 month.

PICKLED RED ONIONS

THESE ONIONS ARE QUICK AND EASY to make and look beautiful in a glass quart jar. Serve them on sandwiches, on a platter of smoked salmon, or on top of salads. We serve ours in the Little Gem Salad (page 126).

MAKES 1 QUART JAR

2½ pounds red onions, sliced into ⅛-inch-thick rings

1½ cups cold water

1½ cups champagne vinegar

1½ cups apple cider vinegar

1½ cups sugar

16 sprigs fresh thyme, tied with butcher's twine

3 tablespoons kosher salt

1 tablespoon yellow mustard seeds

1 teaspoon crushed red pepper flakes

* Fill a large bowl with ice water and submerge the onions in it.

* In a large stockpot over high heat, combine the water, vinegars, sugar, thyme bundle, salt, mustard seeds, and red pepper flakes. Bring the liquid to a boil in order to dissolve the sugar and salt. Take the pot off the heat and let the liquid cool to room temperature. Remove and discard the thyme.

* Drain the onions in a colander and put them in a quart jar or a large bowl. Pour the pickling brine over the onions. Cool the pickles in the refrigerator for 12 hours before serving. Lid the jar; they will keep for up to 1 month in the refrigerator.

GRANDDADDY'S FAST CUKES IN VIN

THERE WAS NEVER A TABLE SET at Granddaddy's that did not have these chilled cucumbers floating in cool distilled white vinegar, with ground cracks of black pepper nestled against the pale-green flesh of the cukes, grown by Granddaddy himself. This is an easy and quick pickle to make at the beginning of your supper prep. By the time you're finished cooking, the cukes will have chilled through.

MAKES 1 CUP

1 cucumber

Distilled white vinegar

Freshly ground black pepper

* Peel, halve lengthwise, seed, and slice the cucumber into half moons. Put the slices into a small bowl and pour enough vinegar over them to cover. Season with black pepper to taste (about seven turns of the pepper mill). Refrigerate the cucumbers until well chilled.

PICKLED OKRA

Across the street from Granny and Pop's house lived Valeria. Valeria never married and lived alone. She was a sweet woman and could play the piano like nobody's business. Pop kept her front lawn mowed and fixed little things like a leaking faucet, and in exchange, she let him grow okra in her backyard. When I was a kid, Granny would send me across the street to pick the pods so she could fry them for dinner. These pods were long, green, and tinted red at the tops and bigger than my hand! Granny would dredge them in cornmeal and fry them in a hot cast-iron skillet. She pickled them at the end of the summer with her watermelon rind pickles. Serve them in Bloody Marys or on a po'boy, or just eat them straight from the jar like I do.

MAKES 4 QUART OR 8 PINT JARS

3 pounds fresh
   okra pods

8 cups cubed ice

½ cup kosher salt

For the pickling liquid:

5 cups water

5 cups apple
   cider vinegar

1 head garlic,
   cloves smashed

½ cup kosher salt

½ cup sugar

½ cup pickling spice

2 tablespoons dill seed

2 tablespoons crushed
   red pepper flakes

2 tablespoons yellow
   mustard seeds

* In a colander with a bowl underneath, toss the okra with the ice and salt, and let them sit in the refrigerator for 6 to 12 hours. This will remove the moisture and make for a crisper pickle. Rinse the okra thoroughly to remove the salt and drain well. Cut three slits about ½ inch long into each pod to allow the pickling liquid to penetrate.

* To prepare the pickling liquid, in a large stock-pot over high heat, combine all the ingredients. Bring the liquid to a boil to dissolve the sugar and salt. Boil for 2 minutes. Take the pot off the heat and let the liquid cool to room temperature.

* Divide and pack the okra in four glass quart jars or eight pint jars, pour the liquid over to cover, lid the jars, and store them in the refrigerator. The pickles will taste best if you let them sit for 1 week before eating. They will keep for up to 1 month.

Pop mowing Valeria's grass in his
red Converse, 1970s

PICKLED GREEN BEANS

GREEN BEANS ARE PROLIFIC ALL AROUND the country and easy to pickle. If the beans are extra long I like to can them in a tall one and a half pint jar, if you can find them. Otherwise the standard wide-mouthed pint jars will work just fine. Add one or two whole red chilies for heat and color.

MAKES 8 PINT JARS

3 pounds green beans

8 cups cubed ice

½ cup kosher salt

For the pickling liquid:

5 cups apple
    cider vinegar

5 cups water

1 cup kosher salt

½ cup sugar

½ cup pickling spice

5 cloves garlic, smashed

5 tablespoons dill seed

2 tablespoons crushed
    red pepper flakes

2 tablespoons yellow
    mustard seeds

8 fresh dill sprigs

8 fresh red Thai bird's
    eye chilies

* In a colander with a bowl underneath, toss the green beans with the ice and salt, and let them sit in the refrigerator for 6 to 12 hours. This will remove the moisture and make for a crisper pickle. Rinse the beans thoroughly to remove the salt and drain well.

* To prepare the pickling liquid, in a large stockpot over high heat, combine all the ingredients. Bring the liquid to a boil in order to dissolve the sugar and salt. Boil for 2 minutes. Take the pot off the heat and let the liquid cool to room temperature.

* In a separate large stockpot, bring 2 quarts water to a boil over high heat. Blanch the beans for 2 minutes. Place the beans in an ice-water bath to stop cooking. Drain the beans in a colander and divide and pack them in eight pint jars.

* Place 1 dill sprig and 1 chili in each jar, packing them on the sides. Pour the pickling liquid over to cover, lid the jars, and store them in the refrigerator. The pickles will taste best if you let them sit for 1 week before eating. They will keep for up to 1 month.

CHOWCHOW

I THINK CHOWCHOW IS ONE OF the most underutilized Southern condiments. Growing up, we always had this sweet-and-sour relish as a topping for pinto or red beans. It's basically a way to use up all the extra vegetables from your garden. Some folks call it "end of the season relish." There are most likely more variations of this condiment than any other Southern recipe; in Southern grocery stores, next to the ketchup and mustard, there is an entire row of different varieties of chowchow, a lot of them locally made.

Ours is a chunkier version, more reminiscent of a pickle than a relish. Serve it on "Not Just for Monday" Red Beans and Rice (page 154) or on hot dogs in place of pickle relish. It's also good as a topping for corn bread, black-eyed pea cakes, hamburgers, and collard greens. There's no need to can it, as it keeps in the fridge for one month. You can substitute finely chopped green tomatoes instead of the cabbage if you have some.

MAKES 2 QUART JARS

½ head green cabbage, cored and finely chopped

¼ head cauliflower, cored and finely chopped

½ green bell pepper, cut into ⅛-inch dice

½ red bell pepper, cut into ⅛-inch dice

3 ribs celery, cut into ⅛-inch dice

1 sweet onion, cut into ⅛-inch dice

2 tablespoons kosher salt

For the pickling liquid:

2 cups apple cider vinegar

1 cup cold water

1 cup sugar

1 tablespoon ground turmeric

1 tablespoon yellow mustard seeds

2 teaspoons freshly ground black pepper

½ teaspoon celery seed

½ teaspoon crushed red pepper flakes

* In a large bowl, combine the cabbage, cauliflower, bell peppers, celery, and onion. Toss them with the salt and let them sit in the refrigerator for 1 hour. Rinse and drain the vegetables thoroughly.

* To prepare the pickling liquid, in a large stockpot over high heat, combine all the ingredients. Bring to a boil to dissolve the sugar and salt. Take the pot off the heat and let the liquid cool to room temperature.

* Divide and pack the vegetables among two quart jars. Pour the liquid over to cover, lid the jars, and let them sit in refrigerator for at least 12 hours. The chowchow will keep for up to 1 month.

SAUCES & DRESSINGS

DRESS IT UP

COMEBACK SAUCE 173

SWEET HEAT BBQ SAUCE 176

CREOLE MUSTARD 176

GRANDDADDY'S HARD-BOILED EGG SALAD DRESSING 177

CREAMED BLUE CHEESE DRESSING *for fancy folks* 177

FRENCH RÉMOULADE *for even more fancy folks* 178

HOMEMADE MAYONNAISE 178

ROASTED GARLIC–LEMON VINAIGRETTE 179

CENTRAL CAROLINA VINEGAR SAUCE 180

QUICK & SPICY COCKTAIL SAUCE 180

T HE SAUCES AND DRESSINGS YOU'LL find in this chapter are unique and deserve a place in your fridge. Slathered with Comeback Sauce (page 173), an ordinary burger becomes extraordinary with minimal effort. A dressing is easy and quick to make and tastes better than anything you can buy bottled. Make a double batch of Sweet Heat BBQ Sauce (page 176) and pass out jars for your guests to take home at your next barbecue. These condiments will liven up dishes you're getting bored of or feel like you've hit a rut with.

Southerners have a sauce for everything they eat and many of these are "secret" sauces or dressings. Here you will find nine different sauces, and once you make them, don't be afraid to change them a bit based on your own personal taste. A bit more hot sauce, a touch more lemon juice, or a splash more of vinegar can go a long way.

COMEBACK SAUCE

COMEBACK SAUCE ORIGINATED IN MISSISSIPPI, AND it's called "comeback" because it's so good you'll be coming back for more. You'll find it used as a condiment all over the South. I love my version of it on everything from fried green tomatoes, fried oysters, and burgers to fish and shrimp, steamed or fried. Some folks even use it as a salad dressing. It makes a great sandwich spread and dip for crudités. Make a batch of it and keep it in your fridge for use on anything.

MAKES ALMOST 2 CUPS

1 cup mayonnaise, such as Duke's or Best Foods

½ cup chili sauce, such as Heinz

Juice from 1 large lemon

2 tablespoons canola oil

2 teaspoons Texas Pete or Crystal hot sauce

1 teaspoon Worcestershire sauce

½ teaspoon freshly ground black pepper

¼ teaspoon dry mustard powder

¼ teaspoon onion powder

¼ teaspoon garlic powder

Pinch of kosher salt

* In a blender or food processor, blend all the ingredients until incorporated and smooth. Taste and check for seasoning, adding a bit more salt and hot sauce if desired. Store the sauce in a lidded glass jar in the refrigerator; it will keep for up to 10 days.

Daddy playing basketball in the backyard of our house on Wiley Avenue, Salisbury, North Carolina, 1950s

SWEET HEAT BBQ SAUCE

THIS SAUCE HAS A THICK RICHNESS to it that will have you reaching for it first. It's great as a glaze for fried chicken, roast chicken, collards, shrimp and grits, or just about anything. Double the batch and give half away to your friends.

MAKES ABOUT 4 CUPS

4 cups Texas Pete or Crystal hot sauce

2 cups packed dark brown sugar

1 (12-ounce) bottle amber beer, such as Abita Amber

¼ cup Worcestershire sauce

1 tablespoon dried basil

* In a large pot over medium-high heat, bring the hot sauce up to a slow boil. When it's boiling, whisk in the brown sugar, beer, Worcestershire, and basil and reduce the heat to low. Simmer until the sauce is reduced by one-quarter and is thick and viscous, about 2 hours. Store the cooled sauce in a lidded glass jar in the refrigerator; it will keep indefinitely.

CREOLE MUSTARD

THIS MUSTARD IS POPULAR ALL OVER the South, but in New Orleans, you won't find a pantry without it. Grown in Louisiana, black mustard seeds are spicier and have more tang than the standard yellow European varieties. Creole mustard is great on po'boys, with country ham on a biscuit, or served as a dipping sauce for grilled sausages and smoked pork.

MAKES 3 CUPS

½ cup yellow mustard seeds

½ cup black mustard seeds

2 cups apple cider vinegar

¼ cup sugar

¼ cup creamy Dijon mustard

¼ cup cold water

Kosher salt and freshly ground black pepper

* In a small bowl, soak the mustard seeds in the vinegar overnight. The next day, pulse the mixture in a blender until the seeds are starting to break down a bit. With the blender running, add the sugar in a slow, steady stream. Add the Dijon, water, and salt and pepper to taste, blending until smooth. Store the mustard in a lidded glass jar in the refrigerator; it will keep indefinitely.

GRANDDADDY'S HARD-BOILED EGG SALAD DRESSING

FOR MANY YEARS, THIS WAS THE only salad dressing I knew. Granddaddy made it every single time we ate salad, and MJ and my aunts all made a version of it as well. I never tire of it and company loves it. You can vary it, adding a teaspoon of Creole mustard, chopped fresh garlic instead of granulated, etcetera, but I like it simple. I like smashing the yolks when they are still warm and serving the dressing right after mixing.

MAKES ¾ CUP

3 Perfect Hard-Boiled
Eggs (page 35), halved,
yolks and whites
separated

¼ cup white vinegar

¼ cup extra-virgin
olive oil

2 tablespoons canola oil

½ teaspoon kosher salt

½ teaspoon freshly
ground black pepper

¼ teaspoon granulated
garlic or garlic powder

¼ teaspoon oregano or
Italian seasoning

* In a glass jar with a lid, using a fork, smash the egg yolks, then stir in the vinegar. Add the oils, salt, pepper, garlic, and oregano. Tightly screw the lid on the jar and shake to combine everything. Taste for seasoning and adjust as necessary. Chop the egg whites and use them in your salad. Store the dressing in the lidded glass jar; it will keep for 2 to 3 days in the refrigerator.

CREAMED BLUE CHEESE DRESSING
for fancy folks

THIS DRESSING REMINDS ME (ALMOST) OF a fancy version of buttermilk ranch. It has tartness from the buttermilk and lemon zest and creaminess from the sour cream and mayonnaise. Make this dressing the day before you want to use it—it tastes better after the flavors have time to marry and develop.

MAKES 3 CUPS

1¾ cups sour cream

1 cup buttermilk

½ cup mayonnaise,
such as Duke's or
Best Foods

1 cup blue cheese
crumbles

Zest and juice from
1 large lemon

6 to 8 fresh chives,
chopped

1 teaspoon freshly
ground black
pepper, plus more
for seasoning

½ teaspoon cayenne

Kosher salt

* In a large bowl, whisk the sour cream, buttermilk, and mayonnaise until well incorporated. Whisk in the blue cheese, lemon zest and juice, chives, black pepper, and cayenne. Season to taste with salt and additional black pepper. Store the dressing in a lidded glass jar in the refrigerator; it will keep for up to 10 days.

FRENCH RÉMOULADE
for even more fancy folks

USE THIS ON THE FRIED OYSTER Rich Boys (page 100) and Fried Chicken Po'Boys (page 100), as a side for dipping Aunt Annie's Cornflake Chicken Tenders (page 115), or as a replacement for mayonnaise on a B.L.T.

MAKES 4 CUPS

3½ cups mayonnaise, such as Duke's or Best Foods

1 tablespoon creole or country Dijon mustard

1 tablespoon Texas Pete or Crystal hot sauce

1 medium red onion, finely diced (1 cup)

1 rib celery, finely diced (½ cup)

¼ cup capers, rinsed and chopped

¼ cup chopped fresh flat-leaf parsley

1 scallion, white and green parts, thinly sliced

Kosher salt and freshly ground black pepper

✳ In a large bowl, combine the mayonnaise, mustard, hot sauce, onion, celery, capers, parsley, and scallion. Season to taste with salt and pepper. Store the rémoulade in a lidded glass jar in the refrigerator; it will keep for 2 weeks.

HOMEMADE MAYONNAISE

MAYONNAISE IS SURPRISINGLY EASY TO MAKE, and it tastes better than store bought. (Unless you can get your hands on Duke's, of course.) Add a handful of the Big Herb Blend (page 58) and some chopped fresh garlic for a vegetable aioli dipping sauce.

MAKES 4 CUPS

4 large egg yolks

2 tablespoons cold water

1 tablespoon champagne vinegar

1 tablespoon freshly squeezed lemon juice

1½ teaspoons Dijon mustard

1 teaspoon ground white pepper

3 cups canola oil

✳ In the bowl of a food processor, process the egg yolks, water, vinegar, lemon juice, Dijon, and pepper until smooth. With the motor running, slowly drizzle in the oil through the feed tube until the mixture is emulsified. Store the mayonnaise in a lidded glass jar in the refrigerator; it will keep for 1 week.

ROASTED GARLIC–LEMON VINAIGRETTE

THIS HAS THE PERFECT BALANCE OF garlicky lemony goodness. Use on salads or as a dipping sauce for fried oysters or crudités.

MAKES 2 CUPS

5 cloves garlic, peeled

¾ cup extra-virgin
   olive oil

Zest and juice from
   3 large lemons

1 tablespoon creole or
   Dijon mustard

1 tablespoon honey

Kosher salt

1 cup canola oil

1 tablespoon Big Herb
   Blend (page 58)

Freshly ground
   black pepper

* Preheat the oven to 350 degrees F.

* In a small baking dish or large ramekin, pour the olive oil over the garlic cloves. Roast the garlic in the oven until it's very soft and golden brown, about 35 minutes. Remove the garlic from the oil and set both aside to cool completely.

* When the oil and garlic have cooled, place the garlic in the bowl of a food processor or blender along with the lemon zest and juice, mustard, honey, and a pinch of salt. With the motor running, slowly drizzle the canola oil through the feed tube until the dressing is emulsified, then add the reserved olive oil. Add the herb blend with a few pulses. Season to taste with salt and pepper. Store the dressing in a lidded glass jar in the refrigerator; it will keep for up to 1 week.

KITCHEN TABLE HOT RED "PEPPA SAUCE" PEPPER VINEGAR

On most dining room tables or kitchen counters in the South sits a glass cruet of white vinegar with red chilies inside that folks call "peppa sauce." Used in addition to Texas Pete or Crystal hot sauce, this spicy vinegar adds an acidity that brightens everything from collards to fried foods, and even red beans and rice. You don't need too much, just a few dashes.

To make your own, find a pretty cruet at Goodwill or on eBay. Fill it half way with white vinegar and add 3 to 4 fresh red Tabasco chilies, then top with more vinegar, pushing the chilies down with a chopstick. If you can't find Tabasco chilies, you can substitute Thai bird's eye chilies or any small red spicy chili.

I keep my vinegar on the kitchen counter or dining room table, but you can leave yours in the refrigerator indefinitely. The heat from the chilies will max out after about 6 months, and I just keep topping it off with more vinegar.

CENTRAL CAROLINA VINEGAR SAUCE

THIS VINEGAR SAUCE HAS THE BEST balance of sweet and sour. It's perfect for tossing with your Pulled Pork Butt (page 111) or mixing into Go to Church Brunswick Stew (page 149).

MAKES 1½ CUPS

½ cup apple
   cider vinegar
½ cup apple juice
½ cup ketchup, such
   as Heinz
¼ cup packed dark
   brown sugar

1 teaspoon kosher salt
1 teaspoon freshly
   ground black pepper

* In a small saucepan over low heat, combine all the ingredients. Heat, stirring occasionally, just until the brown sugar is dissolved, about 5 minutes. Taste and check the seasoning, adjusting as necessary. Store the vinegar sauce in a lidded glass jar in the refrigerator; it will keep for up to 2 weeks.

QUICK & SPICY COCKTAIL SAUCE

THIS COCKTAIL SAUCE IS EASY TO make and keeps in the fridge for two weeks. It's great with any fried fish, oysters, and especially shrimp.

MAKES 1 CUP

1 cup ketchup, such
   as Heinz
Juice from 1 large lemon
2 tablespoons horse-
   radish sauce (I prefer
   creamed horseradish)

1 teaspoon Texas Pete
   or Crystal hot sauce
Kosher salt and freshly
   ground black pepper

* In a small bowl, combine the ketchup, lemon juice, horseradish sauce, and hot sauce. Season to taste with salt and pepper. If the sauce is too spicy for your taste, add a touch more ketchup to mellow the flavor. Served chilled. Store the cocktail sauce in a lidded glass jar in the refrigerator; it will keep for up to 2 weeks.

BIG BREAKFAST

NO SERIOUSLY, EAT BREAKFAST

COUNTRY BREAKFAST SAUSAGE *with spice mix* 185

THE WANDERING GOOSE GRANOLA *sour cherries, sesame seeds & steen's cane syrup* 187

SPICY SKILLET POTATOES 188

BLUEBIRD GRAIN FARMS FARRO BREAKFAST PORRIDGE *cinnamon & lemon* 190

BOONVILLE BREAKFAST GRITS 192

BUBBLE & SQUEAK *corned beef brisket with potatoes, onions, poached eggs & spicy bubble sauce* 195

VEGGIE HASH *with poached eggs & red pepper coulis* 197

GRANNY'S PERFECT POACHED EGGS 199

CINNAMON-SUGARED TOAST 199

BREAKFAST TO ME DURING THE workweek usually means I eat at the end of my shift in my car while driving to pick the kids up from school. But on the weekends at home, it's a different story entirely. I almost always make the kids the breakfast of my childhood: bacon and country ham, buttermilk biscuits with strawberry jam, peppery grits, and fried eggs. I remember the feeling I had when I woke up at Granny's with the scent of breakfast permeating my nose. My head would get quiet as I listened to the sounds and smells coming from her kitchen, and I knew that everything would always be okay, no matter what. To change things up a bit, I make breakfast for dinner for my kids once a week. They never know which night I'm serving it, and they all think it's an extra special treat when I do.

COUNTRY BREAKFAST SAUSAGE
with spice mix

THE BREAKFAST SAUSAGE I GREW UP eating at every family get-together was Neese's. A family-owned business in Greensboro, North Carolina, Neese's makes extra-spicy and extra-sage varieties, and The Goose's sausage tastes as close to its extra-spicy as anything. For a big breakfast, serve these with hot biscuits and a platter of scrambled eggs, or serve as a breakfast sandwich on a biscuit topped with a fried egg and extra-sharp cheddar cheese.

MAKES 8 PATTIES

2 pounds ground pork

5 tablespoons Sausage Spice Mix (page 53)

2 tablespoons unsalted butter

* Put the pork in a large bowl and sprinkle the spice mix over it. Using your hands, mix the spices into the meat until no large streaks remain. Still using your hands, portion the sausage into eight equal-sized balls, then use your palm to flatten them into patties. (The patties can be made up to this point and frozen in ziplock freezer bags; thaw them the night before you want to cook them.)

* Line a plate with several layers of paper towels and set it next to the stove. In a large skillet over medium heat, melt the butter. When the butter is foamy, add the sausage patties a few at a time. Cook them until dark brown, 3 to 4 minutes per side. Using a spatula, remove them to the prepared plate to drain. Serve immediately or hold them in a 200-degree-F oven to keep warm while you make the rest.

LIVERMUSH: COUNTRY PÂTÉ

Livermush is a mixture of pig's liver, pig head parts, and cornmeal found almost only in the central part of North Carolina. At Granddaddy's, my cousins and I grew up on Neese's brand livermush, fried in a hot skillet with butter and served on white bread with lots of Duke's mayo and spicy brown mustard. Some folks think German settlers brought it down through the Appalachian Mountains, so it could well be a descendant of Pennsylvania's scrapple. There are festivals held in honor of livermush, so I know I wasn't the only one to grow up with what most folks think of as an oddity. After visiting North Carolina, I always bring some back on the plane.

THE WANDERING GOOSE GRANOLA
sour cherries, sesame seeds & steen's cane syrup

OUR GRANOLA IS ANOTHER OF OUR most requested recipes. While so much commercial granola is overly sweet, ours actually makes you feel healthy as you eat it. We serve it with fresh seasonal fruit, nonfat Greek yogurt, and a hefty drizzle of Muddy Pond sorghum syrup from Tennessee. Make a big batch and gift it in lidded glass jars to your friends and neighbors for a healthy holiday treat.

MAKES 12 CUPS

6 cups old-fashioned oats

2 cups chopped walnuts

1 cup unsweetened coconut flakes

1 cup slivered or sliced almonds

1 cup chopped pecans

½ cup sesame seeds

¾ cup canola oil

½ cup Steen's cane syrup (see page 142) or pure maple syrup

½ cup honey

3 tablespoons packed dark brown sugar

2 teaspoons ground cinnamon

2 teaspoons vanilla extract

2 cups raisins

1 cup dried sour cherries or dried apricots

½ cup currants or dried blueberries

* Preheat the oven to 325 degrees F. Spray a baking sheet with canola cooking spray (or grease it with canola oil) and set it aside.

* In a large bowl, combine the oats, walnuts, coconut, almonds, pecans, and sesame seeds. In a medium saucepan over medium-high heat, combine the oil, cane syrup, honey, brown sugar, cinnamon, and vanilla and cook until the sugar has dissolved and the mixture is starting to simmer, 3 to 4 minutes. Pour the syrup over the dry ingredients and mix with a rubber spatula.

* Spread the granola out on the greased baking sheet and bake until golden brown, 20 to 22 minutes, stirring the mixture three times during baking. Let the granola cool to room temperature, then mix in the raisins, cherries, and currants. Let the granola cool completely before packing it into jars or ziplock bags. Stored in a cool pantry, it will keep for 2 weeks.

SPICY SKILLET POTATOES

MY FRIEND CHRIS REEL (*CHRISREEL*), WHO IS A CHEF, showed me how to make skillet potatoes years ago, and it was then I found out I'd been doing them wrong. He said, "What you want to do is *don't touch them*. Let them form a crust so they lift off the pan by themselves. *Then* stir them." And you know what? He was right—my potatoes have never been better. After the potatoes are cooked, make a well in the middle of the potatoes and fry a few eggs directly in the pan for an easy breakfast. Working in two batches, you can double this to feed a crowd.

MAKES 6 CUPS

2 pounds Yukon Gold potatoes

6 tablespoons extra-virgin olive oil

1 small sweet onion, sliced

¼ cup Texas Pete or Crystal hot sauce

¼ cup Worcestershire sauce

¼ cup (½ stick) unsalted butter, cut into pieces

2 tablespoons Big Herb Blend (page 58)

Kosher salt and freshly ground black pepper

* In a large saucepan over high heat, cover the potatoes with water and bring to a boil. Boil the potatoes for 5 to 7 minutes, then drain them and set aside to cool. When the potatoes are cool enough to handle, cut them into bite-size chunks—not too small.

* In a 12-inch skillet over medium-high heat, heat the oil until it shimmers. Add the potatoes and let them cook for 3 to 4 minutes without stirring. When they start to form a golden-brown crust, you can stir them. Add the onions and cook until the potatoes are golden brown and crunchy all over, 8 to 10 minutes more. Add the hot sauce, Worcestershire, butter, and herb blend and season to taste with salt and pepper. Serve immediately.

BLUEBIRD GRAIN FARMS FARRO BREAKFAST PORRIDGE
cinnamon & lemon

WE MAKE THIS PORRIDGE THE WAY Granny made Cream of Wheat growing up: cooked softly in milk with cinnamon and a touch of lemon. Top it with a drizzle of cream and garnish with fresh fruit and nuts. We use organic whole grain emmer farro from Bluebird Grain Farms, grown in Washington's Methow Valley.

MAKES 3 TO 4 SERVINGS

2 cups whole milk

1 cup emmer farro

2 tablespoons sugar

1 cinnamon stick

1 (2-inch) strip
  lemon peel

Pinch of kosher salt

3 tablespoons heavy
  cream

Fresh fruit and toasted
  pecans, for garnish

* In a small saucepan over medium heat, bring the milk to a gentle simmer. Stir in the farro, sugar, cinnamon stick, lemon peel, and salt. Cover and simmer, stirring often, until the farro is cooked, tender and puffed, 25 to 30 minutes. Serve it drizzled with the cream and garnished with fresh fruit and toasted pecans.

BOONVILLE BREAKFAST GRITS

WE GET OUR GRITS FROM BOONVILLE Flour & Feed Mill, as well as the flour for our biscuits. I love coarse-ground grits, especially the size of the Boonville ones. They use an old stone grind, and the grits are hearty with a toothsome bite. When you make these grits, you need to have a Southerner's mind-set: cook them gentle, patient, and slow.

MAKES 4 SERVINGS

6 cups water

4 teaspoons kosher salt

1 cup stone-ground grits

¼ cup (½ stick) unsalted
   butter, cut into pieces

1 teaspoon freshly
   ground black pepper

* In a large saucepan over high heat, bring the water and salt to a boil. Whisk in the grits, reduce the heat to medium high, and cook for 10 minutes, whisking constantly. Reduce the heat to medium low, add the butter and pepper, and continue to cook for 15 more minutes, whisking every few minutes until the grits are soft and no longer have a crunch to them. Taste for seasoning, adding more salt or pepper if you'd like. Divide the grits between four bowls, or one large bowl for sharing, and serve warm. I like to top mine with an extra pat of butter.

VARIATIONS

SWEET GRITS: Follow the recipe for Boonville Breakfast Grits, reducing the salt to 2 teaspoons, omitting the pepper, and stirring in **2 tablespoons butter** and **4 teaspoons cinnamon sugar** (see Cinnamon-Sugared Toast on page 199) just before serving.

CHEESY GROWN-UP GRITS: Follow the recipe for Boonville Breakfast Grits, stirring in **1 cup grated Gruyère** and **1 cup grated extra-sharp cheddar cheese** just before serving, and garnishing with more grated cheddar and **chopped fresh chives**.

BUBBLE & SQUEAK
corned beef brisket with potatoes, onions,
poached eggs & spicy bubble sauce

THIS DISH ORIGINATED IN ENGLAND AND is found in different versions as a breakfast dish. Usually made with leftover roast from Sunday supper, the meat or sausage makes a squeaking (bubbling), popping sound when cooked in the hot pan, hence the name. (If you've ever cooked a fatty sausage in a hot skillet, you can hear this exact noise.)

Use leftover beef roast or buy a brisket to cook; the bubble sauce is made from blending the liquid that the brisket is cooked in and then reduced to thicken. The sauce is quite spicy, so feel free to use half the can of chipotle peppers instead of the entire thing. Use leftover mashed potatoes if you have them. Since the brisket cooks for six to eight hours, this is a great dish to prep on Saturday night before having friends over for Sunday football. The brisket can also be cooked up to three days before serving.

¼ cup extra-virgin olive oil

1 large sweet onion, chopped

4 carrots, chopped

6 cloves garlic, chopped

2 cups dry red wine, such as cabernet sauvignon

2 quarts (8 cups) chicken stock

1 (28-ounce) can whole peeled tomatoes

1 (7-ounce) can chipotle peppers in adobo sauce

½ ounce fresh thyme tied with butcher's twine or cotton thread

1 bay leaf

5 pounds fresh corned beef brisket, seasoning pack reserved

For the vegetables:

2 pounds Yukon Gold potatoes

1 head green cabbage (2 pounds), outer leaves removed, cored, and cut into 2-inch chunks

½ head purple cabbage (¾ pound), outer leaves removed, cored, and cut into 2-inch chunks

1 sweet onion, sliced

½ cup extra-virgin olive oil

Kosher salt and freshly ground black pepper

4 tablespoons extra-virgin olive oil, divided

2 tablespoons unsalted butter, divided

2 tablespoons Texas Pete or Crystal hot sauce, divided

2 tablespoons Worcestershire sauce, divided

2 tablespoons Big Herb Blend (page 58), divided

Kosher salt and freshly ground black pepper

1 to 2 poached eggs per person, for serving

* Preheat the oven to 250 degrees F.

* In a large Dutch oven over medium-high heat, heat the oil until it shimmers. Add the onion, carrots, and garlic and sauté until the onions are translucent, 3 to 4 minutes. Pour in the wine and cook for 1 to 2 minutes, scraping up any browned bits from the bottom of the pan. Add the stock, tomatoes, peppers, thyme bundle, bay leaf, and reserved seasoning packet. Nestle the brisket in the pot and cover with a lid. Cook in the oven until tender, 6 to 8 hours.

* While the brisket cooks, make the potatoes. In a large saucepan over high heat, cover the potatoes with cold water and bring to a boil. Turn the heat down just a bit and simmer the potatoes until you can pierce them with a fork, about 20 minutes. Drain the potatoes and allow them to cool. When they're cool, cut them into bite-size pieces and set aside.

* When the brisket is done, set it aside to cool and increase the oven temperature to 375 degrees F. Let the brisket cool until you're able to comfortably handle it. Cut against the grain into 1-inch-square pieces and set aside.

* Remove the thyme bundle from the brisket pan. In a food processor or with an immersion blender, puree the cooking liquid and roasted vegetables. Pour the mixture into a medium saucepot and place it over medium heat. Simmer the mixture for 1 hour to reduce and thicken it—this is your "bubble sauce."

* While the sauce simmers, spread the cabbage and onion out on two baking sheets. Drizzle the oil over them and season to taste with salt and pepper. Roast until the cabbage is just beginning to color around the edges, 15 to 20 minutes. Set aside to cool.

* When you are ready to serve, gently warm the sauce in a small saucepan over low heat as needed. Combine the brisket, cabbage, and potatoes into a large mixing bowl.

* In a large sauté pan or Dutch oven over medium-high heat, heat 2 tablespoons of the oil until it shimmers. Add the half of the brisket mixture and sauté everything until hot, 4 to 5 minutes. Stir in 1 tablespoon each of the butter, hot sauce, Worcestershire, and herb blend. Season to taste with salt and pepper. Transfer the mixture to a large bowl. Repeat this process with the remaining ingredients. Mix both batches together and scoop the bubble and squeak into individual cast-iron skillets or onto plates, or pile it onto one large platter. Top with poached eggs and a few tablespoons of the warmed sauce.

VEGGIE HASH
with poached eggs & red pepper coulis

AFTER THE SAWMILL BISCUIT SANDWICH (page 82), our Veggie Hash is the second most popular item on our menu. Full of seasonal veggies, we serve ours in individual cast-iron skillets with poached eggs nestled in the middle and a tangy red pepper coulis on top. Feel free to substitute the veggies depending on the season (pea vines, sweet potatoes, zucchini). If you're missing the meat, you can serve it alongside Country Breakfast Sausage (page 185). Served with Best Buttermilk Biscuits (page 65), this recipe doubles easily to feed a crowd.

MAKES 4 SERVINGS

1 pound Yukon Gold potatoes, cut into ½-inch dice

1 pound turnips, peeled and cut into ½-inch dice

1 pound butternut squash, peeled and cut into ½-inch dice

5 tablespoons extra-virgin olive oil, divided

1 pound red beets, peeled and cut into ½-inch dice

8 ounces button mushrooms, cut into ¼-inch slices

½ yellow onion, cut into thin slices

1 collard green leaf, deveined and thinly sliced (chiffonade) (about 1 cup)

2 tablespoons Worcestershire sauce

1 tablespoon Texas Pete or Crystal hot sauce

1 tablespoon unsalted butter

3 tablespoons Big Herb Blend (page 58)

Kosher salt and freshly ground black pepper

1 to 2 Granny's Perfect Poached Eggs (page 199) per person, for serving

Red Pepper Coulis (recipe follows), for serving

* Preheat the oven to 400 degrees F.

* In a large bowl, toss the potatoes, turnips, and butternut squash together with 2 tablespoons of the oil. Spread the vegetables out in one layer on a baking sheet. On a separate baking sheet, toss the beets in 1 tablespoon of the oil.

* Roast the potatoes, turnips, and squash for 25 minutes, or until you can easily pierce the vegetables with a paring knife, adding the mushrooms after 15 minutes (stir to combine). Roast the beets at the same time but cook them for 40 minutes total. Toss all the vegetables together and set aside.

* In a large cast-iron skillet or sauté pan over medium-high heat, heat the remaining 2 tablespoons oil until shimmering. Add the onion and sauté for 3 minutes, or until translucent and beginning to brown just a bit on the edges. Add the collards and sauté another 3 minutes, or until the collards are wilted. Add in all of the vegetables and sauté until everything is heated through, 3 to 4 minutes. Add the Worcestershire, hot sauce, and butter and stir to combine. Stir in the herb blend, then season to taste with salt and pepper. Serve with poached eggs and red pepper coulis.

continued

RED PEPPER COULIS

MAKES 1½ CUPS

2 (4 ounce) jars pimento
   peppers, drained

2 cloves garlic, peeled

¼ cup red wine vinegar

6 tablespoons canola oil

6 tablespoons extra-
   virgin olive oil

Kosher salt and freshly
   ground black pepper

* Place the peppers, garlic, and vinegar in a blender. With the blender running, slowly drizzle in the oils until emulsified. Season to taste with salt and pepper.

GRANNY'S PERFECT POACHED EGGS

Granny was the one who showed me how to poach an egg. I was watching her bake her usual cake orders, listening to the hum of the dishwasher and the church gospel preaching from Pop's old 1950s radio. I washed out the pot that she had cooked the early morning grits in and filled it with cold water. She instructed me to add a hefty splash of white vinegar and wait for it to come to a simmer. Then she cracked an egg and I watched as it slowly came together, the egg white forming a beautiful soft globe around the yolk. After three minutes she scooped it out with a serrated spoon at just the right moment and set it gently in a small white bowl, saying, with a sweet smile, "There you are, missy!"

MAKES 2 POACHED EGGS

3 tablespoons white
  vinegar
2 large eggs
Kosher salt and freshly
  ground black pepper

* In a medium saucepan over medium-high heat, bring 6 cups water and the vinegar to a slow simmer. Crack the eggs, one at a time, into the pot. Cook for 3 minutes, or until the whites are firm enough for your liking. Season to taste with salt and pepper and serve immediately.

CINNAMON-SUGARED TOAST

My mother, MJ, made this for me, and her mother made it for her when she was a little girl, served with hot tea. I make a large batch of the sugar mixture and keep it in the pantry so the kids can make their own toast.

MAKES 4 SERVINGS

3 tablespoons sugar
4 teaspoons ground
  cinnamon
¼ cup (½ stick) unsalted
  butter, cut into
  tiny squares
4 slices bread

* In a small bowl, mix the sugar and cinnamon. Dot the butter squares all over the bread, sprinkle the cinnamon sugar on top, and toast under a broiler or in a toaster oven until the butter is melted and the cinnamon sugar is bubbling. Serve immediately.

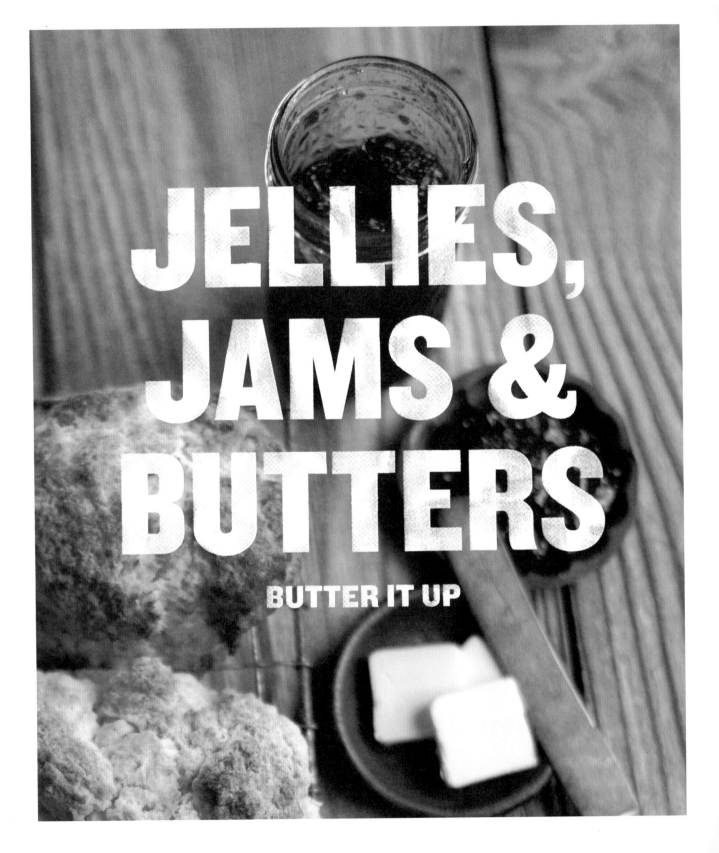

JELLIES, JAMS & BUTTERS

BUTTER IT UP

STRAWBERRY VANILLA PRESERVES 203

GRANNY'S STRAWBERRY FIG PRESERVES 204

PEPPER JELLY 205

TOMATO-APRICOT JAM 208

MATERNAL-SIDE APPLE BUTTER 209

ELLY, JAM, PRESERVES, BUTTERS—all of them have a place in your pantry. Seasons here in the Pacific Northwest tend to be short, so when the berries ripen or the grapes, peaches, and nectarines are ready, I gather my kids and go picking with them. We come home and put up ruby-red strawberry jams, Concord grape pie filling, and smooth apple butter spiced with cinnamon and clove. We have a pantry full of jars ready to hand out to a friend who just stopped by, a new neighbor, or one of the kids' teachers. We use the water-bath method for jellies and jams, and have a pressure canner for canning fresh tuna, spaghetti sauces, chili, and stews. It's something fun to do with your kids, and it's nice to be able to grab a jar of preserves for a quick snack on a split biscuit or toast.

From early on, Southern families depended on home preservation for survival. In the rural South, families had gardens and could be self-sufficient if need be. Preserving was a way to protect food from spoiling but also to preserve its fresh taste, texture, and nutritional value. Granny canned anything and everything, letting not a thing go to waste. Nowadays, preserving has shifted from something you had to do to something you want to do. Food is celebrated in the South and gifting food, such as a jam or jelly you made yourself, is always welcomed with big smiles and a jar of something for you in return. When Granny passed she had a pantry full of not only her own preserves but those gifted to her as well.

STRAWBERRY VANILLA PRESERVES

MY HUSBAND AND I PICKED STRAWBERRIES from a local organic farm two years ago and made this jam. We made so much of it, we still have some in the pantry. It's delicious spread on toast with thick cream cheese or between a biscuit with a hefty chunk of melted butter.

If you want to use vanilla sugar instead of regular sugar, for every cup of sugar, mix in the scraped seeds from two vanilla beans, along with the pods. Allow the pods to infuse the sugar for as long as you can. I have vanilla sugar that's been infusing for five years!

Note: Before you make the jam, use Pomona's calcium powder to make the calcium water called for in the recipe. In a small bowl or jar with a lid, combine one-half teaspoon calcium powder and one-half cup water. This makes enough calcium water for several batches of jam. Store it in the fridge and shake well before using. It will last for several months. Pomona's Universal Pectin is available at natural food stores and online.

MAKES 16 HALF-PINT JARS

8 to 9 pints strawberries

Juice from 2 large lemons

2 tablespoons Pomona's
  calcium water

4 vanilla beans,
  cut lengthwise

4 cups sugar or
  vanilla sugar

4 teaspoons Pomona's
  Universal Pectin
  powder

* Sterilize your jars, prepare your bands and lids, and have all your canning tools ready.

* Hull the strawberries and cut the largest berries in half. Leave the smaller ones whole if you like a chunky texture, or halve them too. You want about 16 cups berries.

* In a large stockpot, combine the berries, lemon juice, and calcium water. Scrape out the vanilla seeds with a sharp paring knife and add them to the pot, along with the pods.

* In a medium bowl, stir together the sugar and pectin powder.

* Over medium-high heat, bring the fruit mixture to a boil, stirring frequently to prevent scorching, then add the pectin mixture. Reduce the heat to low and simmer for 20 to 25 minutes.

* Ladle the jam into sterilized jars, leaving ¼ inch of headspace. Wipe the rims clean, place the lids on top, and screw on the bands. Process the jars in a water-bath canner according to the manufacturer's instructions. Store in the refrigerator or pantry for up to 1 year.

GRANNY'S STRAWBERRY FIG PRESERVES

GRANNY ALWAYS HAD THIS JAM IN her fridge, made with figs from the huge Celeste tree in her backyard. She had more of this jam than anything else in her cellar, so I always got to take a jar home. She made regular strawberry jam as well, but I think she made this more because the figs were free and the Jell-O was cheap. One spoonful and I'm back in her kitchen, at her round table with the green linoleum floor. This is her original recipe, the only directions and measurements she wrote down. I like to store the jam in little half-pint quilted jelly jars. This recipe can easily be doubled or tripled.

MAKES 4 HALF-PINT JELLY JARS

3 cups fresh figs, mashed
3 cups sugar

1 (3-ounce) package
strawberry Jell-O

* Sterilize your jars, prepare your bands and lids, and have all your canning tools ready.

* In a saucepot over medium-high heat, stir the figs, sugar, and Jell-O packet together. Bring the mixture to hard boil and cook for 3 to 5 minutes.

* Skim off any foam. Ladle the jam into sterilized jars, leaving ¼ inch of headspace. Wipe the rims clean, place the lids on top, and screw on the bands. Process the jars in a water-bath canner according to the manufacturer's instructions. Store in the refrigerator or pantry for up to 1 year.

Granny and my sister, Chelsea, in Granny's backyard, Salisbury, North Carolina, 1976

PEPPER JELLY

ONCE YOU TRY IT, YOU WILL use this pepper jelly for so many things! It's beautiful given as gifts around the holidays in quilted crystal jelly jars. It's perfect dolloped on fried oysters and adds tang to a fried chicken sandwich. Make a batch, give out half for gifts, and keep the rest for yourself.

MAKES 6 HALF-PINT JARS

1 yellow bell pepper, seeded and cut into ⅛-inch dice (trimmings, seeds, and core reserved)

1 red bell pepper, seeded and cut into ⅛-inch dice (trimmings reserved)

1 orange bell pepper, seeded and cut into ⅛-inch dice (trimmings reserved)

½ cup white vinegar

½ cup apple cider vinegar

2 quarts (8 cups) water

6 cups sugar

1 teaspoon freshly ground black pepper

1 teaspoon crushed red pepper flakes

1 bay leaf

3 gelatin packets, such as Knorr

* Sterilize your jars, prepare your bands and lids, and have all your canning tools ready.

* In a small saucepan over high heat, combine the reserved pepper trimmings and the vinegars and bring to a boil. Turn off the heat and let the trimmings steep for 30 minutes.

* In a food processor, puree the vinegar mixture and strain it into a medium saucepot. Discard the trimmings. Add the water, sugar, black pepper, red pepper flakes, and bay leaf, and cook over medium heat until the mixture is reduced by a third, 25 to 30 minutes.

* Meanwhile, in a large skillet over medium heat, lightly sauté the peppers for 2 to 3 minutes, making sure not to brown them.

* Remove the bay leaf from the saucepot and add the sautéed peppers. Let the mixture cool just a bit, about 10 minutes, then sprinkle the gelatin evenly over the top and stir to combine.

* Cool the jelly in the refrigerator for 3 to 4 hours, stirring it periodically to suspend the peppers evenly. Ladle the jelly into sterilized jars, leaving ¼ inch of headspace. Wipe the rims clean, place the lids on top, and screw on the bands. Process the jars in a water-bath canner according to the manufacturer's instructions. Store in the refrigerator or pantry for up to 1 year.

My daddy, John Thomas Earnhardt, 1952

TOMATO-APRICOT JAM

At the end of summer, I had a pile of apricots that were on their way out and too many Sungold tomatoes lying around. I couldn't bear to waste them, so I came up with this jam. I love it served with a cheese plate at parties or on country ham biscuits or Bacon, Cheddar, and Scallion Biscuits (page 72).

Note: Before you make the jam, use Pomona's calcium powder to make the calcium water called for in the recipe. In a small bowl or jar with a lid, combine one-half teaspoon calcium powder and one-half cup water. This makes enough calcium water for several batches of jam. Store it in the fridge and shake well before using. It will last for several months. Pomona's Universal Pectin is available at natural food stores and online.

MAKES 6 HALF-PINT JARS

3 tablespoons extra-virgin olive oil

¼ cup diced shallot

2 pints mixed cherry tomatoes, preferably from the farmers' market, hulled

1 pound apricots, halved and pitted

2 cups sugar

1 tablespoon calcium water

1 tablespoon Pomona's Universal Pectin powder

* Sterilize your jars, prepare your bands and lids, and have all your canning tools ready.

* In a large sauté pan or Dutch oven over medium heat, heat the olive oil. Add the shallots and sauté them until they are somewhat translucent but not brown, 3 to 4 minutes. Add the cherry tomatoes and sauté until they start to break down, about 6 minutes. Add the apricots and simmer over medium heat until the tomatoes and apricots start to incorporate. Add the sugar, calcium water, and pectin and continue simmering until the jam registers 220 degrees F on a candy thermometer, 25 to 35 minutes. Strain the jam through a fine-mesh strainer, pushing down with a spatula to get rid of seeds.

* Ladle the jam into sterilized jars, leaving ¼ inch of headspace. Wipe the rims clean, place the lids on top, and screw on the bands. Process the jars in a water-bath canner according to the manufacturer's instructions. Store in the refrigerator or pantry for up to 1 year.

MATERNAL-SIDE APPLE BUTTER

I *LOVE* APPLE BUTTER. TO ME, nothing says easy, quick, after-school snack like toast or a biscuit smeared thick with apple butter. It cooks for a long time, so make your time worth the effort and plan on giving some away. This recipe is from my Aunt Susie, and she's made this for as long as I can remember. This butter is super good served on a charcuterie plate, spread onto a grilled cheese and bacon sandwich, layered between stacks of pancakes, or simply smeared on toast.

MAKES 9 HALF-PINT JARS

6 pounds tart apples, such as Granny Smith

5 cups sugar

5 cups apple cider or apple juice

1 tablespoon freshly squeezed lemon juice

1 tablespoon ground cinnamon

1½ teaspoons ground allspice

1½ teaspoons ground cloves

1 teaspoon kosher salt

* Sterilize your jars, prepare your bands and lids, and have all your canning tools ready.

* Peel and core the apples, then cut them into 1-inch chunks.

* In a large Dutch oven over high heat, combine all of the ingredients. Bring the mixture to a boil, then reduce the heat to low. Cover the pot halfway with the lid, allowing the steam to escape and the liquid to reduce. Simmer for 5 hours, stirring every 30 minutes. Taste for seasoning, adding a touch more cinnamon as needed. Cool the mixture to room temperature.

* In a food processor, puree the apple butter until smooth.

* Ladle the butter into sterilized jars, leaving ¼ inch of headspace. Wipe the rims clean, place the lids on top, and screw on the bands. Process the jars in a water-bath canner according to the manufacturer's instructions. Store in the refrigerator or pantry for up to 1 year.

My maternal grandmother, Eleanore Bonner Corbett, 1940s

BIG CAKES & BUNDTS

BIGGER IS BETTER

"BOB'S LAST MEAL" CHOCOLATE CAKE 213

HAPPY BIRTHDAY CAKE 214

BROWNED BUTTER BANANA BUNDT CAKE 216

HUCKLEBERRY CARDAMOM BUNDT CAKE 217

BROWNSTONE FRONT CAKE 219

GRANNY'S KITCHEN TABLE CAKE
with bittersweet chocolate frosting 222

LUSTY LEMON LAYER CAKE
with lemon cream cheese frosting 225

SOUTHERN COCONUT CAKE
with coconut cream cheese frosting 227

UNCLE RAY'S FRESH APPLE CAKE
with buttermilk soda frosting 229

SHORTCAKES *strawberries with elderflower syrup* 230

7UP BUNDT CAKE 232

A compromise is the art of dividing a cake in such a way that everyone believes he has the biggest piece.

THE SIMPLICITY OF A BUNDT CAKE or the impressive quality of a big layer cake are two things I never tire of. I like to be able to hold a piece of a thick, chunky Bundt in my hand, adorned with nothing more than a quick sifting of confectioners' sugar. (It's easy to nibble on while driving between soccer practices and games.) And nothing else quite makes for a grand entrance like a three-layered frosted cake. When the cake comes out after supper, so do the ooohs and ahhhs.

Make sure your layers have cooled completely before you frost the cake. Also, trim away any domed top with a long serrated knife so that your layers stack evenly and don't slide. For the frosting, make sure to not put too much in the middle layers—you'll need enough for the sides and the top. (Although sometimes I like to frost the layers thick in the middle and top and leave the sides unadorned—sans any frosting.) For garnishing, I use sprinkles, sanding sugar, or edible flowers from my garden.

For buttering a cake pan, I do what Granny always did: butter the pan with room-temperature butter, line it with a circle of parchment paper, then coat it again with more butter.

For chocolate cakes, use the same technique but dust the pan with cocoa powder at the end. The cocoa powder makes chocolate cakes come out with ease.

"BOB'S LAST MEAL" CHOCOLATE CAKE

MY FRIEND BOB WAS IN HIS late eighties when I brought him a slice of this cake. His watery eyes lit up after the first bite, and he said, "Well now, *that* is a good cake." The next day over dinner I asked him what he would want to eat for his last meal. He became quiet for a moment, his eyes looking toward the ceiling squinting with thought. He then fixed his eyes on mine and said, "That cake you fed me yesterday. *That's* what I would want." I promptly named this cake after him. These cake layers are especially delicate so be careful when you flip them out of the cake pans.

MAKES ONE 3-LAYER, 9-INCH FROSTED CAKE

1½ cups (3 sticks) unsalted butter, at room temperature, plus more for greasing

3½ cups all-purpose flour

4 teaspoons ground cinnamon

2 teaspoons kosher salt

2 teaspoons baking soda

2 teaspoons cayenne

2 teaspoons ground cardamom

1½ teaspoons ancho chili powder

12 ounces bittersweet chocolate

1½ cups Dutch-process cocoa powder

1 tablespoon instant espresso powder

1½ cups boiling water

2 cups sour cream, at room temperature

2 tablespoons vanilla extract

4 cups packed dark brown sugar

10 large eggs, at room temperature

1 recipe Bittersweet Chocolate Frosting (page 222)

* Thoroughly butter three 9-inch cake pans, making sure to coat the sides, and line the bottoms with parchment paper. Butter the parchment and set the pans aside. Line three baking sheets with parchment paper and set them aside. Preheat the oven to 350 degrees F.

* In a large bowl, sift the flour, cinnamon, salt, baking soda, cayenne, cardamom, and chili powder together. In a medium bowl, combine the chocolate, cocoa, espresso powder, and boiling water, stirring until smooth. Stir in the sour cream and vanilla.

* In the bowl of a stand mixer fitted with the paddle attachment, cream the butter and brown sugar on medium-high speed until light and fluffy. Add the eggs one at a time, scraping down the bowl after every two eggs. Reduce the speed to low. Add the flour mixture and the chocolate mixture in three alternating batches, beginning and ending with the flour. Scrape down the sides of the bowl again and pour the batter evenly into the prepared pans.

* Bake until the cake springs back when you touch the center with your finger, and it is pulling away from the sides of the pan just a bit (the cake will have small cracks forming along the outermost edges), about 45 minutes, rotating the pans front to back and top to bottom halfway through baking. Let the cakes cool in the pans until you can touch the pans comfortably, about 15 minutes, then flip the cakes out onto the lined baking sheets to cool completely before frosting.

* Frost between the layers, around the sides, and on top of the cake with the chocolate frosting.

HAPPY BIRTHDAY CAKE

I ALWAYS GOT SPRINKLES ON MY vanilla-chocolate swirl from the Mister Softee trucks when I was little, and wanted a cake and frosting that reminded me of the vanilla ice cream with rainbow sprinkles smashed into it. This is a cake that you should have enough of to serve a slice for breakfast. At our house we always have a store-bought cupcake in the morning for the kids' birthdays (mostly to remind them of how much better their real birthday cake will be later after supper) and one slice of leftover birthday cake for breakfast the day *after* their birthday as a sweet reminder.

MAKES ONE 3-LAYER, 9-INCH FROSTED CAKE

2¼ cups (4½ sticks) butter, at room temperature, plus more for greasing

5 cups all-purpose flour

1½ teaspoons kosher salt

1½ teaspoons baking powder

1 teaspoon baking soda

1½ cups buttermilk

2 tablespoons vanilla extract

3 cups sugar

7 large eggs, at room temperature

1 cup rainbow sprinkles

For the frosting:

2½ cups (5 sticks) unsalted butter, at room temperature

2 pounds confectioners' sugar, sifted

1 tablespoon vanilla extract

1 tablespoon heavy cream

Rainbow sprinkles, for decorating

* Thoroughly butter three 9-inch cake pans, making sure to coat the sides, and line the bottoms with parchment paper. Butter the parchment and set the pans aside. Line three baking sheets with parchment paper and set them aside. Preheat the oven to 325 degrees F.

* In a large bowl, sift the flour, salt, baking powder, and baking soda together. In a small bowl, combine the buttermilk and vanilla.

* In the bowl of a stand mixer fitted with the paddle attachment, cream the butter and sugar on medium-high speed until light and fluffy. Add the eggs one at a time, scraping down the bowl after every two eggs. Reduce the speed to low. Add the flour mixture and the buttermilk mixture in three alternating batches, beginning and ending with the flour. Mix in the sprinkles. Scrape down the sides of the bowl again and pour the batter evenly into the prepared pans.

* Bake until the cake springs back when you touch the center with your finger, and it is pulling away from the sides of the pan just a bit, 30 to 40 minutes, rotating the pans front to back and top to bottom halfway through baking. Let the cakes cool in the pans until you can touch the pans comfortably, about 15 minutes, then flip the cakes out onto the lined baking sheets to cool completely before frosting.

* While the cakes cool, make the frosting. In the clean bowl of the stand mixer, mix the butter and sugar until no clumps remain. Add the vanilla and cream and blend until smooth. Frost between the layers, around the sides, and on top of the cake with the frosting. Garnish the top of the cake with the sprinkles. Sometimes I even add them to the sides as well for an extra-special presentation.

BROWNED BUTTER BANANA BUNDT CAKE

THIS IS MY DAUGHTER'S FAVORITE PASTRY from The Goose. The addition of browned butter gives this cake a richness unlike any other banana bread you've had. Use the blackest bananas you can; they are what provides the intense banana flavor. Don't bother with yellow or green ones. I like this sliced when it's steaming hot, smeared with butter or Steen's Butter (page 142).

MAKES 1 BUNDT CAKE

1 cup (2 sticks) unsalted
  butter, plus more
  for greasing
2¾ cups all-purpose
  flour
2 cups sugar
2 teaspoons baking soda
2 teaspoons kosher salt

2 cups (about 5 large)
  very ripe (preferably
  black) smashed
  bananas
12 ounces sour cream
4 large eggs
1 tablespoon vanilla
  extract

* Preheat the oven to 325 degrees F. Thoroughly butter a Bundt pan and set it aside.

* In a small saucepan over medium-high heat, melt the butter. Bring it to a boil and continue to cook, whisking constantly. Keep your eye on it; it will start to foam. You want to watch for the browned bits that will begin to form on the bottom. If you can't see the bottom of the pan, take the butter off the heat for a second and take a look. Keep cooking until there are dark-brown—but not burned—bits on the bottom of the pan. The butter will smell nutty. Pour it into a metal bowl to cool.

* In a large bowl, sift the flour, sugar, baking soda, and salt. In another large bowl, whisk the bananas, sour cream, eggs, and vanilla. Whisk the browned butter into the wet ingredients, then whisk the wet ingredients into the dry, mixing until no visible clumps of flour remain.

* Pour the batter into the prepared pan and bake until the cake is dark brown on top and springs back when you push on it with your finger, 65 to 70 minutes. Let it cool in the pan for 20 minutes (or until you can comfortably hold it), then flip it out onto a serving plate. Serve warm, or cool completely and wrap in plastic wrap. The Bundt will keep for 3 to 4 days well wrapped. Reheat cold slices in a 300-degree-F oven for 6 minutes.

HUCKLEBERRY CARDAMOM BUNDT CAKE

I RARELY ENJOY WHOLE WHEAT FLOUR in baked goods, but using a small portion of it works perfectly in this recipe, lending this cake a heartiness without making it overly dense. I love it warm with a thick smearing of butter. If you can't find huckleberries, use fresh or frozen blueberries, or even sour cherries.

MAKES 1 BUNDT CAKE

1½ cups (3 sticks) unsalted butter, at room temperature, plus more for greasing

2½ cups all-purpose flour

¾ cup whole wheat pastry flour

2 teaspoons ground cardamom

2 teaspoons kosher salt

1 teaspoon baking powder

1 teaspoon baking soda

¾ cup sour cream

¾ cup buttermilk

1 tablespoon vanilla extract

1½ cups packed dark brown sugar

3 large eggs, at room temperature

1½ cups fresh or frozen huckleberries or blueberries

Confectioners' sugar, for dusting

* Thoroughly butter a Bundt pan and line a baking sheet with parchment paper. Set them aside. Preheat the oven to 350 degrees F.

* In a large bowl, sift the flours, cardamom, salt, baking powder, and baking soda together. In a small bowl, combine the sour cream, buttermilk, and vanilla.

* In the bowl of a stand mixer fitted with the paddle attachment, cream the butter and sugar on medium-high speed until light and fluffy. Add the eggs one at a time, scraping down the bowl after each addition. Reduce the speed to low. Add the flour mixture and the sour cream mixture in three alternating batches, beginning and ending with the flour. Fold in the huckleberries. Scrape down the sides of the bowl again and pour the batter into the prepared pan.

* Bake until the cake springs back when you push on it with your finger and a skewer inserted comes out clean, 45 to 55 minutes. Let it cool in the pan for 20 minutes (or until you can comfortably hold it), then flip it out onto the lined baking sheet to cool completely. Once the Bundt is completely cool, dust it with sifted confectioners' sugar.

BROWNSTONE FRONT CAKE

I LEARNED THIS CAKE FROM THE grandmother I never knew, by way of my aunts' hands and touch. They learned to make it from their mother, my grandmother Ellie, who passed away when I was two. She was only fifty, still beautiful and full of life and laughter. Granddaddy never remarried after she died, so I knew she was something else. My aunts served this cake at every single Thanksgiving and Christmas at Granddaddy's and at most family gatherings. This cake is by far our most popular at The Goose.

MAKES ONE 3-LAYER, 9-INCH FROSTED CAKE

1½ cups (3 sticks) unsalted butter, at room temperature, plus more for greasing

4½ cups all-purpose flour

1½ teaspoons kosher salt

2 ounces unsweetened chocolate, chopped into small pieces

¾ cup boiling water

1½ teaspoons baking soda

3 cups sugar

5 large eggs, at room temperature

1 tablespoon vanilla extract

1½ cups buttermilk, at room temperature

For the frosting:

2 cups (4 sticks) unsalted butter

4 cups packed dark brown sugar (about 28 ounces)

1 (12-ounce) can evaporated milk

8 cups sifted confectioners' sugar (about 2 pounds)

* Thoroughly butter three 9-inch cake pans, making sure to coat the sides, and line the bottoms with parchment paper. Butter the parchment and set the pans aside. Line three baking sheets with parchment paper and set them aside. Preheat the oven to 325 degrees F.

* In a medium bowl, sift the flour and salt together. In a small bowl, pour the boiling water over the chopped chocolate and whisk until the chocolate is melted. Add the baking soda (the chocolate mixture will puff up) and whisk until combined.

* In the bowl of a stand mixer fitted with the paddle attachment, cream the butter and sugar on medium-high speed until light and fluffy. Add the eggs one at a time, beating well after each addition, then add the vanilla. Scrape down the sides of the bowl. Add the flour mixture and the buttermilk in three alternating batches, beginning and ending with the flour. Scrape down the bowl well. Add the melted chocolate and mix until just combined. Be sure to scrape down the bottom of the bowl to incorporate all of the chocolate. Pour the batter evenly into the prepared pans.

* Bake until the cake springs back when you touch the center with your finger, and it is pulling away from the sides of the pan just a bit, 30 to 40 minutes, rotating the pans front to back and top to bottom halfway through baking. Let the cakes cool in the pans until you can touch the pans comfortably, about 15 minutes, then flip the cakes out onto the lined baking sheets to cool completely before frosting.

continued

* After the cakes are cool, make the frosting. In a large saucepan over medium-high heat, melt the butter. When it is completely melted, whisk in the brown sugar. Cook, whisking constantly, until the sugar is completely incorporated with the butter. Whisk in the evaporated milk. Continue whisking until the mixture comes to a boil, then continue to boil until the temperature registers 185 to 190 degrees F on a candy thermometer, 5 to 7 minutes.

* Put the confectioners' sugar in the bowl of a stand mixer fitted with the whisk attachment. With the mixer running, pour the butter mixture into the bowl in a steady stream. Mix on low until the confectioners' sugar is combined and no lumps remain, scraping the bowl down once. The frosting will have the consistency of honey and should still be very hot.

* With an offset spatula, frost the cooled cake layers. The frosting will ooze from the middle layers at first, but as you get to the final layer and the sides, it will start to set. Frost the sides last. You want to work very quickly while the frosting is hot because once it cools off, it becomes too stiff to work with. If this happens, you can add 1 to 2 tablespoons of boiling water to the frosting to bring it back, but that will only buy you a few extra minutes, so work quickly! Once you frost the top and sides, try to avoid going back over the frosting. It quickly forms a coating as it cools, and if you fuss, it can become a bit messy. But no worries because the cake will still taste just as good!

ON FROSTING THE BROWNSTONE

This cake took me many frosting attempts before I felt I understood it. Boiled sugar frostings aren't made much nowadays and I had no real directions to work from, just some scribbled notes I could barely read. Respect the difficulty but don't give in to the fear of making it, because it is by far one of the most unique-tasting cakes you'll ever have. I served it to a best friend on her birthday, cracked open on top from mistakenly frosting it while the layers were still warm. Years later she still talks about that cake saying it's the best birthday cake she ever had. This cake comes from Valdese, North Carolina, the town Granddaddy lived in—just a few miles from where I was born in Hickory. We think a version of this cake came over with the Italian Waldensians that settled in Valdese in the late 1800s.

Pour two to three big scoopfuls of the warm frosting over the layers.

Spread the frosting quickly.

Add the final layer, top or bottom side up, whichever is smoother.

Pour a bit more frosting on the top than you did on the middle layers.

Let the frosting pour over the sides.

Using an offset spatula, go over the frosting just once or twice to achieve a smooth result.

GRANNY'S KITCHEN TABLE CAKE
with bittersweet chocolate frosting

GRANNY KEPT A 1950s ALUMINUM-COVERED CAKE pan with a black Bakelite knob on her kitchen table. When my sister and I would visit her, there was always this three-layer yellow cake with chocolate fudge frosting underneath it. She usually already had many orders for her birthday cakes or wedding cakes or pound cakes, but she almost always found the time to make this cake for us.

As a restaurant owner who sees how hard it is to balance my time when we get cake orders in on top of everything else we have to bake and prep, I truly appreciate what it must have taken for her to make our visit to her house even more memorable. This cake is moist with extra eggs that give it a rich yellow color. Our frosting uses Callebaut bittersweet chocolate, so it packs the perfect punch of chocolate flavor. In honor of Granny, from whom I learned how to be kind, caring, and giving to strangers and relatives alike, I made my version of this memory called Granny's Kitchen Table Cake. I hope she would be proud.

MAKES ONE 3-LAYER, 9-INCH FROSTED CAKE

2¼ cups (4½ sticks) butter, at room temperature, plus more for greasing

5 cups all-purpose flour

1½ teaspoons kosher salt

1½ teaspoons baking powder

1 teaspoon baking soda

1½ cups buttermilk

2 tablespoons vanilla extract

3 cups sugar

7 large eggs, at room temperature

For the frosting:

2 cups bittersweet chocolate chips, such as Callebaut

½ cup (1 stick) unsalted butter

1 cup sour cream

1 tablespoon vanilla extract

2 teaspoons kosher salt

28 ounces confectioners' sugar, sifted

1 to 2 tablespoons light or dark corn syrup

Sprinkles, for decorating (optional)

* Thoroughly butter three 9-inch cake pans, making sure to coat the sides, and line the bottoms with parchment paper. Butter the parchment and set the pans aside. Line three baking sheets with parchment paper and set them aside. Preheat the oven to 325 degrees F.

* In a large bowl, sift the flour, salt, baking powder, and baking soda together. In a small bowl, combine the buttermilk and vanilla.

* In the bowl of a stand mixer fitted with the paddle attachment, cream the butter and sugar on medium-high speed until light and fluffy. Add the eggs one at a time, scraping down the bowl after every two eggs. Reduce the speed to low. Add the flour mixture and the buttermilk mixture in three alternating batches, beginning and ending with the flour. Scrape down the sides of the bowl again and pour the batter evenly into the prepared pans.

* Bake until the cake springs back when you touch the center with your finger, and it is pulling away from the sides of the pan just a bit, 30 to 40 minutes, rotating the pans front to back and top to bottom halfway through baking. Let the cakes cool in the pans until you can touch the pans comfortably, about 15 minutes, then flip the cakes out onto the lined baking sheets to cool completely before frosting.

* While the cakes cool, make the frosting. Over a saucepan of simmering water, stack a metal or glass bowl, making sure it fits snugly and the water doesn't touch the bottom. Put the chocolate and butter in the bowl and stir until fully melted and smooth. Transfer the chocolate mixture to the bowl of a stand mixer fitted with the paddle attachment, and mix in the sour cream, vanilla, and salt on medium speed. Add the confectioners' sugar and enough corn syrup to make the frosting smooth. Frost between the layers, around the sides, and on top of the cake with the frosting. Decorate with the sprinkles.

Granny and Pop a year before they were married, May 1937

THE SWEET REMAINS

Granny died in February 1994, less than two weeks shy of her seventy-eighth birthday. No one expected it. Not that anyone is ever ready, but we all were thinking it was Pop who would go first, as he was in the VA hospital slowly having his last breath taken out of him by colon cancer. Granny was still baking for customers between trips to see Pop every day. I was there often during this time and would follow her around, helping when I could.

The last weekend I spent with her we hugged hard, her soft white curls brushing my cheek, the fresh scent of her Dove soap enveloping me. She handed me a bag full of frozen garden vegetables, as she hadn't been cooking all that much with Pop in the hospital and it's what she had on hand. She never let me leave without food of some kind or another.

Granny, now the sweet remains of my memory that I can still touch and feel and smell and hear her voice like it was a day ago. Granny, who stands by my side even now: I carry her with me, the sweet remains.

LUSTY LEMON LAYER CAKE
with lemon cream cheese frosting

WITH PILES OF ZEST, THIS CAKE packs a clear punch of lemon flavor without relying on extract. The egg whites make it soft and fluffy, and the buttermilk makes it tender. It's perfect for a baby shower or wedding rehearsal dinner. Garnish it with edible flowers; bachelor's buttons are super cute on top.

MAKES ONE 3-LAYER, 9-INCH FROSTED CAKE

1½ cups (3 sticks) unsalted butter, at room temperature, plus more for greasing

5½ cups all-purpose flour

1½ tablespoons baking powder

1 tablespoon kosher salt

3 cups buttermilk, at room temperature

2 tablespoons vanilla extract

4 cups sugar

Zest from 7 large lemons

7 large egg whites

For the frosting:

20 ounces cream cheese, at room temperature

1 cup (2 sticks) unsalted butter, at room temperature

Zest from 3 large lemons

7 cups confectioners' sugar, sifted

1 tablespoon vanilla extract

* Thoroughly butter three 9-inch cake pans, making sure to coat the sides, and line the bottoms with parchment paper. Butter the parchment and set the pans aside. Line three baking sheets with parchment paper and set them aside. Preheat the oven to 325 degrees F.

* In a large bowl, sift the flour, baking powder, and salt together. In a small bowl, combine the buttermilk and vanilla.

* In the bowl of a stand mixer fitted with the paddle attachment, cream the butter, sugar, and lemon zest on medium-high speed until light and fluffy. Add the egg whites one at a time, scraping down the bowl after each addition. Reduce the speed to low. Add the flour mixture and the buttermilk mixture in three alternating batches, beginning and ending with the flour. Scrape down the sides of the bowl again and pour the batter into the prepared pans.

* Bake until the cake springs back when you touch the center with your finger, and it is pulling away from the sides of the pan just a bit, 30 to 40 minutes, rotating the pans front to back and top to bottom halfway through baking. The cakes will be puffed and golden brown on top. Let the cakes cool in the pans until you can touch the pans comfortably, about 15 minutes, then flip the cakes out onto the lined baking sheets to cool completely before frosting.

* While the cakes cool, make the frosting. In the clean bowl of a stand mixer, mix the cream cheese, butter, and lemon zest until no lumps remain. Add the confectioners' sugar and vanilla and mix until smooth. Frost between the layers, around the sides, and on top of the cake with the frosting.

SOUTHERN COCONUT CAKE
with coconut cream cheese frosting

LIKE MOST SOUTHERN BAKERS, GRANNY MADE a coconut cake. The *Salisbury Post* wrote about it after she died: "Oh goodness, her coconut cake! It teased you with its taste and demanded a second piece to make sure it really was as good as you thought it was. And of course it never was. It was always better." There was no recipe when she passed, so I created one from memory. It's as close as I can get to hers and it's darn good.

MAKES ONE 3-LAYER, 9-INCH FROSTED CAKE

2¼ cups (4½ sticks) unsalted butter, at room temperature, plus more for greasing

5 cups all-purpose flour

1½ tablespoons baking powder

2 teaspoons kosher salt

1 teaspoon baking soda

1½ cups canned coconut cream or coconut milk from 1 (19-ounce) can, such as Mae Ploy

1 tablespoon vanilla extract

1 tablespoon almond extract

1 tablespoon coconut extract

3 cups sugar

7 large eggs, at room temperature

2¼ cups (7 ounces) sweetened coconut flakes

For the frosting:

20 ounces cream cheese, at room temperature

1 cup (2 sticks) unsalted butter, at room temperature

7 cups confectioners' sugar

1 tablespoon vanilla extract

1 tablespoon coconut extract

1½ teaspoons almond extract

2¼ cups (7 ounces) sweetened coconut flakes, toasted, for decorating (see note)

* Thoroughly butter three 9-inch cake pans, making sure to coat the sides, and line the bottoms with parchment paper. Butter the parchment and set the pans aside. Line three baking sheets with parchment paper and set them aside. Preheat the oven to 325 degrees F.

* In a large bowl, sift the flour, baking powder, salt, and baking soda together. In a small bowl, combine the coconut cream and extracts.

* In the bowl of a stand mixer fitted with the paddle attachment, cream the butter and sugar on medium-high speed until light and fluffy. Add the eggs one at a time, scraping down the bowl after every two eggs. Reduce the speed to low. Add the flour mixture and the coconut cream mixture in alternating batches, beginning and ending with the flour. Mix in the coconut flakes. Scrape down the sides of the bowl again and pour the batter evenly into the prepared pans.

continued

* Bake until the cake springs back when you touch the center with your finger, and it is pulling away from the sides of the pan just a bit, 30 to 40 minutes, rotating the pans front to back and top to bottom halfway through baking. Let the cakes cool in the pans until you can touch the pans comfortably, about 15 minutes, then flip the cakes out onto the lined baking sheets to cool completely before frosting.

* While the cakes cool, make the frosting. In the clean bowl of the stand mixer, mix the cream cheese and butter until no lumps remain. Add the confectioners' sugar and extracts and blend until smooth. Frost between the layers, around the sides, and on top of the cake with the frosting. Decorate the top and sides of the cake with the toasted coconut.

Note: Toast the coconut flakes on a baking sheet at 300 degrees F until golden brown, about 10 minutes, stirring every 3 to 4 minutes. Be sure the coconut is completely cool before decorating the cake.

Uncle Ray on his first birthday with Aunt Becky, 1946

UNCLE RAY'S FRESH APPLE CAKE
with buttermilk soda frosting

GRANNY MADE THIS APPLE CAKE HUNDREDS of times over the years, and like so many others, it was a cake she could conjure up on a whim. Fresh apple cake is a Southern specialty; super-dense and moist, it's unlike any regular Bundt cake you've ever had. The baking-soda frosting is quite unique, and I've never seen it anywhere else. Uncle Ray tested and tried a bunch of recipes to recreate hers, and this one is pretty close.

MAKES 1 BUNDT CAKE

Softened butter,
    for greasing
3 cups all-purpose flour
1 tablespoon ground
    cinnamon
1 teaspoon baking soda
1 teaspoon kosher salt
½ teaspoon freshly
    grated nutmeg
¼ teaspoon ground
    cloves
2 large or 3 small tart
    apples, peeled, cored,
    and diced (3 cups)
1 cup toasted pecan
    pieces

1 cup sweetened
    coconut flakes
3 large eggs
2 cups sugar
1¼ cups canola or
    vegetable oil

For the frosting:
1 cup sugar
½ cup (1 stick) unsalted
    butter
½ cup buttermilk
½ teaspoon baking soda

* Thoroughly butter a Bundt pan and line a baking sheet with parchment paper. Set them aside. Preheat the oven to 325 degrees F.

* In a large bowl, sift the flour, cinnamon, baking soda, salt, nutmeg, and cloves. Add the apples, pecans, and coconut.

* In the bowl of a stand mixer fitted with the paddle attachment, beat the eggs and sugar on medium-high speed until light and fluffy, 3 to 4 minutes. With the mixer running, add the oil in a steady stream. Pour the egg mixture into the flour mixture and stir until combined. Pour the batter into the prepared pan and bake until a skewer inserted comes out clean, 55 to 65 minutes.

* After removing the cake from the oven, make the frosting. In a large saucepan over high heat, bring the sugar, butter, buttermilk, and baking soda to a boil for 1 minute. Pour the frosting over the hot cake and let it sit for 1 hour before flipping the cake out of the pan onto the lined baking sheet.

SHORTCAKES
strawberries with elderflower syrup

IN THE LATE 1970s MY SISTER and I stayed with my daddy in Lewisburg, West Virginia, one summer in an old barn with no running water and an honest-to-goodness outhouse out back. On a visit, Granny promptly made strawberry shortcake using teeny wild strawberries that my sister and I harvested from the hillside. I never forgot the taste of those little berries and how different it was from the ones I was used to. The elderflower syrup is a nod to how the countryside smelled and felt during that summer when I was six.

MAKES NINE 2½- TO 3-INCH SHORTCAKES

4 pints fresh strawberries, hulled and halved

½ cup sugar, divided

3 tablespoons elderflower syrup (found at Ikea or in specialty stores)

4 cups all-purpose flour

2 tablespoons baking powder

2 teaspoons kosher salt

1½ cups (3 sticks) unsalted butter, chilled and cut into ½-inch dice

4 large eggs

1 cup heavy cream

1 tablespoon vanilla extract

1 recipe Egg Wash (page 31)

Turbinado sugar, for sprinkling

Whipped Cream (recipe follows), for serving

Fresh mint leaves, for garnish

* In a large bowl, toss the strawberries gently with ¼ cup of the sugar and the elderflower syrup. Set aside to macerate while you make the shortcakes and cream.

* Preheat the oven to 400 degrees F. Line a baking sheet with parchment paper.

* In the bowl of a stand mixer fitted with the paddle attachment, mix the flour, remaining ¼ cup sugar, baking powder, and salt on low speed. Add the butter and mix until it resembles small peas. In a medium bowl, whisk together the eggs, cream, and vanilla. With the mixer running, add the egg mixture, mixing only until just blended.

* Turn the dough out onto a lightly floured surface and form it into a disk 1½ to 2 inches thick. Use a biscuit cutter to cut out nine 2½- to 3-inch rounds. Place them on the lined baking sheet. Brush the tops with the egg wash and sprinkle with turbinado sugar. Bake until puffed and golden brown on top, 20 to 25 minutes.

* To assemble the dessert, cut each shortcake in half. Place the bottom half in a serving bowl. Add a large dollop of whipped cream, then a large scoop of strawberries, followed by another large dollop of whipped cream. Place the shortcake top back on and serve. Garnish with fresh mint.

WHIPPED CREAM

MAKE 4 CUPS

2 cups heavy cream
3 tablespoons sugar
2 teaspoons vanilla
  extract

* In the bowl of a stand mixer fitted with the whisk attachment, beat the cream and sugar on medium-high speed until soft peaks begin to form, 3 to 4 minutes. Add the vanilla and continue whisking until firm peaks form, about 2 minutes. Do not overbeat or the cream will turn to butter.

7UP BUNDT CAKE

At Granny and Pop's house, as kids we were allowed soda, but only when there was a family get-together. Granny bought glass bottles of 7Up, Coke, and Cheerwine. I loved the tiny emerald-green glass bottle of 7Up pulled from an ice-filled cooler that would numb my skinny sun-browned arm. I drank the bottle straight without stopping once to tilt my head back upright. Drinking it this way made my eyes tear up, but I didn't care; it was summertime at Granny's. Pop grilled barbecue chicken, and the older cousins played basketball, while the adults took nips of vodka from paper cups. This cake reminds me of those hot, sticky summers spent in Granny and Pop's backyard.

MAKES 1 BUNDT CAKE

1 cup (2 sticks) unsalted butter, at room temperature

3 cups all-purpose flour

1 teaspoon kosher salt

½ teaspoon baking powder

½ teaspoon baking soda

¾ cup 7Up

¼ cup buttermilk

1 tablespoon vanilla extract

3 cups sugar, divided

3 tablespoons zest plus ¼ cup juice from 3 to 4 large limes

1 tablespoon zest plus ¼ cup juice from 2 large lemons

4 large eggs

For the frosting:

2 cups sifted confectioners' sugar

⅓ cup 7Up

* Thoroughly butter a Bundt pan and line a baking sheet with parchment paper. Set them aside. Preheat the oven to 325 degrees F.

* In a medium bowl, sift the flour, salt, baking powder, and baking soda. In a small bowl, mix the 7up, buttermilk, and vanilla.

* In the bowl of a stand mixer fitted with the paddle attachment, cream the butter, 2 cups of the sugar, and the citrus zests on medium-high speed until light and fluffy. Add the eggs one at a time, scraping down the bowl after each addition. Reduce the speed to low. Add the flour mixture and 7Up mixture in three alternating batches, beginning and ending with the flour. Pour the batter into the prepared pan and bake for 50 minutes, or until a skewer inserted comes out clean.

* In a small saucepan over medium heat, warm the remaining 1 cup sugar with the citrus juices, stirring occasionally, until the glaze is clear and the sugar is dissolved, 3 to 4 minutes.

* While the cake is still in the pan, use a skewer to poke holes all over the top. Pour the glaze slowly over the cake while it's still warm, allowing the syrup to soak into the holes. Set the cake aside to cool for 20 minutes before flipping it out onto a serving plate.

* To make the frosting, in a medium bowl, whisk the confectioners' sugar and 7Up until smooth. Add 2 to 3 tablespoons more 7Up if you need to thin out the frosting; you want it smooth enough to drizzle on top. Drizzle the frosting over the cooled cake.

PIES & TARTS

IT'S JUS' PIE

CONCORD GRAPE TART 237

SOUR CHERRY HAND PIES 238

APPLE ROSEMARY GALETTE 241

RHUBARB GALETTE *with orange blossom water* 242

SWEET TEA CHESS PIE 243

LEMON BUTTERMILK CHESS PIE 244

CHOCOLATE CHILI CHESS PIE 247

KEY LIME PIE *with saltine cracker crust* 248

TARTE Á LA BOUILLIE 249

IES, TARTS, GALETTES—WHICHEVER ONE YOU pick, as long as you have a good dough to fall back on, any of these fillings are sure to please. Pies shouldn't look perfect. Your crimp should be a bit off all the way around, your lattice uneven, and your filling spilling out over the sides of your pie. Have fun with it: of all the pies and tarts I've ever eaten in my life, the messy ones were by far the best.

Many of these ingredients are made using pantry staples—eggs, sugar, cornmeal, flour, and buttermilk—and make it easy for you to throw a pie together at the last minute. Buttermilk adds a tangy richness to fillings, and fruit fillings can be changed depending on the seasons. Kids love rolling out pie dough and can become expert crimpers in no time flat!

CONCORD GRAPE TART

As kids we ate muscadine grapes off Granddaddy's vines, and nothing other than the Concord has as much of a magical, floral taste. Concord grapes arrive in the Pacific Northwest in early September, and are only around for a few weeks. They have a short shelf life once picked, and I order as many flats of them as I can. Everyone in the kitchen pitches in to squeeze the skins off of these slip-skin grapes. Concords are highly regarded by pie folks: their short season and the difficulty of separating each skin from the grape makes them taste all that much better. Buy as many as you can and keep this filling stored in jars, or make as many tarts as you can during September. I use a French tart pan here, but you can use a regular pie tin and it works just as well.

MAKES ONE 11-INCH TART

1 recipe Liquored Pie
 Dough (page 105)
2 pounds Concord
 grapes, peeled
 (skins reserved)
1 cup sugar
3 tablespoons instant
 tapioca

1 recipe Egg Wash
 (page 31)
Turbinado sugar,
 for sprinkling
Vanilla bean ice cream,
 for serving

* Shape the dough into two disks. Wrap each in plastic wrap and refrigerate for 1 hour.

* In a small saucepot over medium-high heat, cook the grapes for 5 minutes. Add the sugar and tapioca, and cook, stirring frequently to prevent scorching, until the grapes are starting to look a bit opaque, about 10 minutes. Reduce the heat and simmer the mixture until the grapes break down a bit, 6 to 7 more minutes. Using a spatula, push the mixture through a fine-mesh strainer into a large bowl to get all the seeds out. Discard the seeds. Stir the reserved grape skins into the bowl with the pulp. Set it aside to cool.

* Preheat the oven to 400 degrees F.

* Remove one of the dough disks from the refrigerator and, on a lightly floured surface, roll it out into a 12-inch circle ¼ inch thick. Fit it into the bottom of an 11-inch fluted tart pan with a removable bottom. Let the extra dough hang over the sides; you will trim it later. Put the pan in the freezer and chill until the dough is firm, 15 to 20 minutes.

* Pour the cooled filling into the chilled crust. Remove the other disk of dough from the refrigerator and roll it out to into a 11-inch circle ¼ inch thick. Using a ½-inch pastry cutter, cut out five to six small circles to vent the pie as it cooks. Position the top crust over the filling and trim the edges of both the top and bottom dough flush with the pan. You can use a rolling pin and go over the sides of the pan to cut off the extra dough. Brush the tart with egg wash and sprinkle the top with turbinado sugar. Bake until golden brown, 30 to 40 minutes, reducing the oven temperature to 375 degrees F after 20 minutes. Serve warm with vanilla bean ice cream.

SOUR CHERRY HAND PIES

WE BAKE OFF EXACTLY EIGHT OF these each day, and often customers are upset if they arrive in the afternoon and there isn't one left. Some customers have taken to calling in the morning and having us reserve one for them in the afternoon. We prep them in big batches and freeze.

Note: When making these, you might have a little bit of dough left over. I like to make mini galettes, or stuff the hand pies with a bit of savory filling such as Loaded Chicken Potpie (page 153) filling or even the Brunswick stew (see page 149).

MAKES 8 LARGE HAND PIES

1 pound frozen pitted
    sour cherries
¾ cup sugar
3 tablespoons instant
    tapioca
2 teaspoons almond
    extract

1 recipe Liquored Pie
    Dough (page 105)
1 recipe Egg Wash
    (page 31)
Turbinado sugar,
    for sprinkling

* In a small saucepot over medium-high heat, cook the cherries, sugar, tapioca, and almond extract until the cherries are bubbling. Continue cooking for about 20 minutes, or until the syrup is thick and bubbly. Remove the filling from the stove and chill it in the refrigerator until you're ready to make the pies, about 2 hours.

* Refrigerate the dough for 1 hour. Portion the chilled dough into 8 equal disks (about 3 ounces each). On a lightly floured surface, roll them out into 6-inch circles ¼ inch thick. Scoop a few tablespoons of chilled filling into each circle, leaving a 1-inch border. Brush the border with egg wash, fold the dough over to make a half-moon shape, and crimp the sides. Freeze the pies until firm, 30 to 40 minutes. At this point, the pies can be wrapped and kept in the freezer for up to 6 months so you can bake them off as desired.

* When you're ready to bake the pies, preheat the oven to 425 degrees F. Brush the tops of the pies with egg wash and sprinkle them with turbinado sugar. Arrange them on a baking sheet and bake until they are dark golden brown, 22 to 25 minutes, rotating the sheet halfway through baking (don't worry if some of the filling bubbles out—this is okay).

APPLE ROSEMARY GALETTE

I'VE MADE THIS GALETTE FOR MORE than ten years now and I never get tired of it. So many of my baked goods have savory components, and this is another one of them. Feel free to change up the rosemary with another herb or leave it out if you wish. This galette is perfect with vanilla ice cream and Salty Whiskey Caramel Sauce (page 269).

MAKES ONE 12-INCH GALETTE

1 recipe Liquored Pie
    Dough (page 105)
6 tablespoons unsalted
    butter
4 to 5 tart apples,
    peeled, cored, and cut
    into ¾-inch slices
Pinch of kosher salt
¼ cup packed dark
    brown sugar

½ teaspoon ground
    cinnamon
Leaves from 3 sprigs
    fresh rosemary,
    chopped
1 recipe Egg Wash
    (page 31)
Turbinado sugar,
    for sprinkling

* Refrigerate the dough for 1 hour. On a lightly floured surface, roll the chilled dough out into a 16-inch circle ¼ inch thick. Place it on a parchment paper–lined baking sheet and chill it in the refrigerator while you make the filling.

* In a large skillet over medium-high heat, melt the butter. Add the apples and salt. Increase the heat to high and sauté the apples until they start to brown, 5 to 6 minutes. Add the brown sugar, cinnamon, and rosemary, and sauté for another 2 to 3 minutes. Spread the filling out on a baking sheet to cool.

* Preheat the oven to 425 degrees F.

* After the filling has cooled, remove the dough from the refrigerator. Spread the filling evenly over the round, leaving a 2-inch border around the edge. Starting at one side, fold the 2-inch border of dough over the filling all the way around, leaving a gap in the middle where the filling shows. Brush the dough with egg wash and sprinkle it with turbinado sugar. Bake until the crust is dark golden brown, 35 to 45 minutes.

RHUBARB GALETTE
with orange blossom water

I GROW RHUBARB IN MY GARDEN at home, and the two huge bushes I have produce so much during the spring that I'm constantly filling bags of it to bring to The Goose. I love its tart, sour flavor and especially love it combined with orange blossom water. If you like a sweeter dessert, add a half cup more sugar.

MAKES ONE 12-INCH GALETTE

1 recipe Liquored Pie
    Dough (page 105)
5 cups rhubarb cut into
    ½-inch slices (about
    1¼ pounds)
1 cup sugar
Juice from 1 navel
    orange
1½ teaspoons orange
    blossom water

Pinch of kosher salt
1 recipe Egg Wash
    (page 31)
Turbinado sugar,
    for sprinkling
Whipped Cream
    (page 231), or vanilla
    bean ice cream,
    for serving

* Refrigerate the dough for 1 hour. On a lightly floured surface, roll the chilled dough out into a 16-inch circle ¼ inch thick. Place it on a parchment paper–lined baking sheet and chill it in the refrigerator while you make the filling.

* In a large bowl, toss the rhubarb with the sugar, orange juice, orange blossom water, and salt. Let the filling macerate for 30 minutes.

* After 30 minutes, preheat the oven to 400 degrees F and remove the chilled dough from the refrigerator.

* Using a slotted spoon, transfer the filling to the center of the dough, leaving any liquid in the bowl. Spread the filling evenly over the round, leaving a 2-inch border around the edge. Starting at one side, fold the 2-inch border of dough over the filling all the way around, leaving a gap in the middle where the filling shows. Brush the dough with egg wash and sprinkle it with turbinado sugar. Bake the galette until the crust is golden brown and the filling is bubbling, 40 to 45 minutes. Serve with whipped cream or vanilla bean ice cream.

SWEET TEA CHESS PIE

I LOVE THIS PIE AND THE hint of black tea flavor it gives. It's perfect for an afternoon snack and interesting enough to bring to a potluck.

MAKES ONE 9-INCH PIE

½ recipe Liquored Pie Dough (page 105)

4 large eggs

1½ cups sugar

½ cup powdered iced tea mix, such as Lipton

½ cup buttermilk

2 tablespoons all-purpose flour

1 tablespoon yellow cornmeal

1 teaspoon zest plus 1 tablespoon juice from 1 large lemon

2 teaspoons vanilla extract

Pinch of kosher salt

½ cup (1 stick) unsalted butter, melted

* Refrigerate the dough for 1 hour. On a lightly floured surface, roll the chilled dough out into an 11-inch circle ¼ inch thick. Fit it into a 9-inch pie plate. Crimp the edges and chill in the freezer while you make the filling.

* In a large bowl, whisk the eggs, sugar, iced tea mix, buttermilk, flour, cornmeal, lemon zest and juice, vanilla, and salt. Whisk in the melted butter until well blended. Set aside while you parbake the shell.

* Preheat the oven to 375 degrees F.

* Cut a circle of parchment paper to fit over the crust and place it on top. Add dried beans or pie weights on top of the parchment. Bake for 12 minutes, then remove the beans and parchment, and bake the crust for another 3 minutes. The crust should be lightly golden brown on the edges and a pale tan on the bottom.

* Reduce the oven temperature to 350 degrees F.

* Pour the filling into the parbaked crust and bake until it's set and no longer jiggly in the middle, 35 to 45 minutes.

LEMON BUTTERMILK CHESS PIE

CHESS PIE MOST LIKELY ORIGINATED FROM England, and there are recipes for it appearing as far back as the 1700s. Some folks think the name comes from the pie chest the warm pies were placed in to cool. Others think at one time a Southern cook was asked what kind of pie she was serving, to which she replied, "It's jus' pie." If you're familiar with Southern accents, "jus'" could have easily morphed into "chess" over the years. I love this version with blueberries or huckleberries.

MAKES ONE 9-INCH PIE

½ recipe Liquored Pie Dough (page 105)

4 large eggs

1½ cups sugar

½ cup buttermilk

¼ cup juice plus 1 tablespoon zest from 2 medium lemons

2 tablespoons all-purpose flour

1 tablespoon cornmeal

2 teaspoons vanilla extract

Hefty pinch of kosher salt

½ cup (1 stick) butter, melted

1 cup fresh blueberries or huckleberries (optional)

* Refrigerate the dough for 1 hour. On a lightly floured surface, roll the chilled dough out into an 11-inch circle ¼ inch thick. Fit it into a 9-inch pie plate. Crimp the edges and chill in the freezer while you make the filling.

* In a large bowl, whisk the eggs, sugar, buttermilk, lemon juice and zest, flour, cornmeal, vanilla, and salt. Whisk in the melted butter until well blended. Set aside while you parbake the shell.

* Preheat the oven to 375 degrees F.

* Cut a circle of parchment paper to fit over the crust and place it on top. Add dried beans or pie weights on top of the parchment. Bake for 12 minutes, then remove the beans and parchment, and bake the crust for 3 minutes more. The crust should be lightly golden brown on the edges and a pale tan on the bottom.

* Reduce the oven temperature to 350 degrees F.

* Pour the filling into the parbaked crust. Add the blueberries and bake until it's set and no longer jiggly in the middle, 35 to 45 minutes.

VARIATION

LEMON SAFFRON BUTTERMILK CHESS PIE: Try this variation if you want to add a savory component to this recipe. Simply omit the blueberries and add **1 teaspoon saffron** to the filling. I love the minerality it brings to the pie, and the color is out of this world. Lightly bruise the saffron between your fingers before adding it to the filling.

CHOCOLATE CHILI CHESS PIE

CHOCOLATE PECAN PIE IS ONE OF my favorites, but I wanted a spicy version without nuts. I love the balance of sweet and spicy heat. After your first bite, the chili spice lingers a few moments but is not too overpowering, and the hint of cinnamon adds a nice warmth. Serve this with a big dollop of Whipped Cream (page 231).

MAKES ONE 9-INCH PIE

½ recipe Liquored Pie
   Dough (page 105)
⅔ cup bittersweet
   chocolate chips
½ cup (1 stick) unsalted
   butter
2 tablespoons unsweet-
   ened cocoa powder
½ teaspoon crushed red
   pepper flakes
3 large eggs

1 cup sugar
¾ cup evaporated milk
2 tablespoons all-
   purpose flour
1 tablespoon vanilla
   extract
¼ teaspoon ground
   cinnamon
Hefty pinch of
   kosher salt

* Refrigerate the dough for 1 hour. On a lightly floured surface, roll the chilled dough out into an 11-inch circle ¼ inch thick. Fit it into a 9-inch pie plate. Crimp the edges and chill in the freezer while you melt the chocolate.

* Over a saucepan of simmering water, stack a metal or glass bowl, making sure it fits snugly but the water doesn't touch the bottom. Put the chocolate, butter, cocoa, and red pepper flakes in the bowl and stir until fully melted and smooth. Keep warm over low heat while you parbake the shell.

* Preheat the oven to 375 degrees F.

* To parbake the shell, cut a circle of parchment paper to fit over the crust and place it on top. Add dried beans or pie weights on top of the parchment. Bake for 12 minutes, then remove the beans and parchment, and bake the crust for another 3 minutes. The crust should be lightly golden brown on the edges and a pale tan on the bottom.

* Reduce the oven temperature to 350 degrees F.

* In a large bowl, whisk the eggs, sugar, milk, flour, vanilla, cinnamon, and salt. Add the chocolate mixture to the filling and mix until well blended. Pour the filling into the parbaked crust and bake until it's set and no longer jiggly in the middle, about 40 minutes. The crust will be a bit puffed and starting to crack.

KEY LIME PIE
with saltine cracker crust

TRIPS TO THE OUTER BANKS OF North Carolina as a child were always magical—tidelands, sand dunes, and the wide-open Atlantic. We stayed in Duck, just north of Kill Devil Hills where the Wright brothers completed the first flight. All day long my sister, cousins, and I collected shells and swam almost endlessly in the warm ocean. For supper we had cups of she-crab soup, platters of fried seafood, and *always* key lime pie for dessert. I wanted a savory component for the crust, so I made a saltine cracker crust since saltines were a staple in my house growing up. (You can use saltines or Ritz crackers interchangeably.) Garnished with freshly whipped cream and buttered saltine cracker crumbs, this pie is one of my favorites.

MAKES ONE 9-INCH PIE

2¾ cups saltine crackers (about 1½ sleeves)

3 tablespoons sugar

½ cup (1 stick) butter, melted

2 ounces cream cheese, at room temperature

1 (14-ounce) can sweetened condensed milk

2 large egg yolks

1 tablespoon zest plus ½ cup juice from 4 to 5 limes

½ teaspoon orange blossom water

½ recipe Whipped Cream (page 231)

* In the bowl of a food processor, crush the saltines. Leave some larger pieces; you don't want the crackers to turn to dust. Pulse in the sugar and then the melted butter. Transfer the crumb mixture to a 9-inch pie tin, reserving ¼ cup. Wash the food processor bowl to use for the filling.

* Using your hands, press the crumb mixture into the pie tin, pressing up to form the sides. The crust will still seem a bit loose. Place the crust in freezer for 10 minutes while you make the filling.

* In the bowl of the food processor, pulse the cream cheese, condensed milk, egg yolks, and lime zest until smooth. Add the lime juice and orange blossom water and pulse until combined.

* Preheat the oven to 325 degrees F.

* On a baking sheet, spread the reserved cracker crumbs and toast until golden brown, about 10 minutes. Meanwhile, bake the pie crust until golden brown, 20 minutes. Set both aside to cool.

* Pour the filling into the cooled crust and bake for 15 to 20 minutes, or until the filling is set and no longer jiggly in the middle.

* Cool the pie at room temperature. Once cooled, add the whipped cream to the top of the pie, allowing the crust edges to show. Smooth over the whipped cream with an offset or rubber spatula, then sprinkle the reserved cracker crumbs over the top. Serve immediately or store in the refrigerator for up to 3 days. The crust might soften a bit but the pie will be just as delicious.

TARTE Á LA BOUILLIE

TARTE Á LA BOUILLIE (PRONOUNCED "BOO-YEE") is a boiled custard pie that originated in southern Louisiana. It's a classic Cajun dessert most known by the older generation; I like to think of it as a New Orleans version of chess pie. Lots of folks make them around the holidays, but any time of the year is good for me. This pie is one of the most unique tasting pies I've ever eaten. I like to serve mine with big slices of brûléed bananas on the side. You can make some fancy leaf decorations out of the top dough or cover in a simple lattice.

For brûléeing the bananas, cut two bananas into thirds and then halve each piece and place on a baking sheet. Sprinkle with sugar and, using a blowtorch (or the broiler in your oven), broil until the bananas are bubbling and caramelized, three to four minutes.

MAKES ONE 9-INCH PIE

For the crust:

1 cup sugar

6 tablespoons unsalted butter, at room temperature

2 cups all-purpose flour

1 teaspoon baking powder

¼ cup whole milk

1 teaspoon vanilla extract

2 cups whole milk

3 large egg yolks

1 cup sugar

1 (12-ounce) can evaporated milk

1 tablespoon vanilla extract

1 whole vanilla bean

½ teaspoon kosher salt

¼ teaspoon freshly grated nutmeg

¾ cup all-purpose flour

¼ cup (½ stick) unsalted butter, at room temperature

1 recipe Egg Wash (page 31)

* To make the crust, in the bowl of a stand mixer fitted with the paddle attachment, blend the sugar and butter on medium-high speed until light and fluffy, 3 to 4 minutes. Reduce the speed to low and add the flour and baking powder until combined. The mixture should resemble coarse meal. With the mixer on low, add the milk and vanilla and mix until combined. Turn the dough onto a lightly floured surface and knead five to six times until smooth. Form the dough into a 1-inch-thick disk and wrap it in plastic wrap. Chill it in the refrigerator while you make the custard.

* In a large saucepan over medium heat, scald the milk by bringing it almost to a boil, then reduce the heat to low and keep the milk warm.

* In the bowl of a stand mixer fitted with the whisk attachment, beat the egg yolks on medium-high speed until thick, 3 to 4 minutes. With the mixer running, add the sugar and mix until light

continued

and fluffy, 3 to 4 minutes, then mix in the evaporated milk, vanilla extract, vanilla bean, salt, and nutmeg until combined. Reduce the speed to low and mix in the flour. Whisking constantly, gradually add ¼ cup of the hot milk at a time to the egg mixture, until the milk is all incorporated. Whisk the egg mixture into the saucepan over low heat, stirring constantly with a rubber spatula until thick and smooth, 10 to 12 minutes. Take the pan off the heat and stir in the butter until it's melted and incorporated. Set the custard aside to cool completely, pressing plastic wrap on the surface so the custard doesn't form a skin.

* When the custard is cool and the dough is chilled, preheat the oven to 350 degrees F.

* Remove the dough from the refrigerator, divide it into two portions (with one portion being just a tad bit bigger than the other). Shape the portions into disks, and on a lightly floured surface, roll the larger disk out into a 10-inch circle ¼ inch thick. Fit it into the bottom of a 9-inch pie tin and chill in the refrigerator until firm, about 20 minutes.

* Remove the chilled shell from the refrigerator and pour the custard into it. Roll out the second dough disk into a 10-inch circle ¼ inch thick and cut it into ¾-inch strips. Arrange the top crust pieces in a lattice and seal and crimp the sides. Brush the top with the egg wash and bake until lightly brown, 35 to 45 minutes. Let the pie cool to room temperature before slicing. I like to eat mine with a big slice of brûléed banana on the side.

COOKIES, BARS & BREAD PUDDING

BIG TREATS

BEST CHOCOLATE CHIP COOKIE IN SEATTLE 255

SMOKED CHOCOLATE CHIP COOKIES *bacon & ruffles* 256

CHOCOLATE CHERRY OAT COOKIES *with toffee bits* 258

CHOCOLATE CHIP WALNUT TOFFEE COOKIES 259

CRACKLIN' COOKIES *chicken skin & toffee bits* 261

CHARLIE BROWN COOKIES *peanut butter & chocolate at its best* 263

AUNT CHUBBY BARS *peanut butter & jelly* 264

GOOEY BUTTER CAKE BARS 266

BITTERSWEET CHOCOLATE BREAD PUDDING
with salty whiskey caramel sauce 267

EVERY COOKIE HAS ITS OWN distinct personality, formed at the hands of its baker. I personally like my cookies big and a bit flatter (but not too thin) and crunchy on the outside but soft on the inside. To me, a cookie should have craggy tops and a caramel-y, buttery smell and taste. I like my cookies not too sweet and often with a savory component added.

The bars are a fun change from cookies and easy to make to take to a potluck. The bread pudding is something easy to make for a sit-down dinner party. Plated with a pile of whipped cream and hefty drizzles of Salty Whiskey Caramel Sauce (page 269), you'll be making the recipe (and variations of it) over and over again.

ON BAKING COOKIES

Every oven is different, so keep an eye on your cookies religiously during the last three minutes of baking. Just as they start to turn golden brown around the edges and are forming a tiny bit of crackle on top, pull them out. At The Goose, we bake multiple trays at a time, but when I cook at home, I never have luck baking on multiple racks and I have to bake them in batches, using two baking sheets each time. Learn the personality of your oven, and your cookies will come out perfect every time. If you do happen to overbake them, don't throw them out! Break them into crumbles and serve them over vanilla ice cream.

These cookies all use a three-ounce scoop, making large four- to five-inch cookies. I usually space mine on the baking sheets evenly apart with six cookies per baking sheet. If you prefer a smaller cookie, use a smaller scoop, but remember to cut your baking time down as they will cook a lot faster. You can also make the dough, scoop it into balls, and then freeze the cookie balls in ziplock bags. No need to thaw them out before baking, just add one to two minutes onto your bake time. Frozen, unbaked cookies will keep for three months in the freezer.

BEST CHOCOLATE CHIP COOKIE IN SEATTLE

I'VE MADE THOUSANDS OF COOKIES OVER the years, and these chocolate chip ones are my favorite. One year, they even beat out every other bakery in town for Seattle's best. Topped with *fleur de sel*, they have the perfect balance of salty and sweet. These cookies are easy to overbake, so remember: they cook a lot more on the baking sheet once you pull them out of the oven.

MAKES 2 DOZEN 4-INCH COOKIES

4½ cups all-purpose flour

2 teaspoons kosher salt

1 teaspoon baking soda

1½ cups (3 sticks) unsalted butter, at room temperature

2 cups packed dark brown sugar

1 cup granulated sugar

2 large eggs, at room temperature

1 large egg white, at room temperature

1 tablespoon vanilla extract

1 (20-ounce) bag bitter-sweet chocolate chips (see note)

* Preheat the oven to 350 degrees F and line two baking sheets with parchment paper.

* In a large bowl, sift the flour, salt, and baking soda together and set it aside.

* In the bowl of a stand mixer fitted with the paddle attachment, cream the butter and sugars together on medium-high speed until light and fluffy. Add the eggs and egg white one at a time, scraping down the bowl after each addition. Add the vanilla. Reduce the speed to low and gradually add the flour mixture. Do not overmix. Fold in the chocolate chips.

* Working in batches (you'll have to complete this process twice), use a 3-ounce scoop to scoop the dough and drop them on the lined baking sheets, gently pressing down the cookies to flatten them a bit. The cookies will spread when baking, so evenly space six cookies per baking sheet. Bake until the cookies are golden brown around the edges, 14 to 16 minutes, rotating the sheets halfway through baking. Using a spatula, transfer the cookies to a wire rack to cool.

> **Note:** Look for the Ghirardelli 20-ounce bags of bittersweet chocolate chips. If you can't find them, subsitute a 16-ounce bag.

SMOKED CHOCOLATE CHIP COOKIES
bacon & ruffles

QUITE REGULARLY THERE ARE TIMES WE are simultaneously baking off trays of bacon in the oven and mixing a batch of cookie dough in the mixer. I'm not ashamed to admit that more often than not I eat a stack of bacon with cookie dough smeared on top for breakfast. I could make a little appetizer platter out of mounded cookie dough with crunchy bacon sprinkled on top and Ruffles on the side for dipping. Nothing better for that salty-sweet fix! You can use regular bittersweet chips that aren't smoked in this recipe, and it's just as good.

MAKES 2 DOZEN 4-INCH COOKIES

4½ cups all-purpose flour

2 teaspoons kosher salt

1 teaspoon baking soda

1½ cups (3 sticks) unsalted butter, at room temperature

2 cups packed dark brown sugar

1 cup granulated sugar

2 large eggs, at room temperature

1 large egg white, at room temperature

1 tablespoon vanilla extract

1 (20-ounce) bag bittersweet chocolate chips, cold smoked (see note)

8 ounces bacon, cooked crispy, drained, and chopped

1 (8-ounce) bag original Ruffles potato chips

* Preheat the oven to 350 degrees F and line two baking sheets with parchment paper.

* In a large bowl, sift the flour, salt, and baking soda together and set it aside.

* In the bowl of a stand mixer fitted with the paddle attachment, cream the butter and sugars together on medium-high speed until light and fluffy. Add the eggs and egg white one at a time, scraping down the bowl after each addition. Add the vanilla. Reduce the speed to low and gradually add the flour mixture. Do not overmix. Add the chocolate chips and bacon and mix for three or four turns. Add the Ruffles, letting the mixer turn just once or twice.

* Working in batches (you'll have to complete this process twice), use a 3-ounce scoop to scoop the dough and drop them on the lined baking sheets, gently pressing down the cookies to flatten them a bit. The cookies will spread when baking, so evenly space six cookies per baking sheet. Bake until the cookies are golden brown around the edges, 14 to 16 minutes, rotating the sheets halfway through baking. Using a spatula, transfer the cookies to a wire rack to cool.

COLD SMOKING

Cold smoke adds a gentle, lingering smoke taste to sweet and savory foods (and drinks) where you least expect it. I cold smoke chocolate, peanut butter, sugars, salts, butter, oats, and all kinds of things that I then incorporate into my baked goods. Handheld versions are available online and at any kitchen supply store, and they are relatively inexpensive and easy to use. Or better yet, make your own. Once you start cold smoking, it's hard to stop.

CHOCOLATE CHERRY OAT COOKIES
with toffee bits

I WANTED A COOKIE THAT WAS similar to an oatmeal cookie but had other components: sour and sweet and chocolaty. These are amazing on their own, or made into an ice cream sandwich. Or overcook them by a few minutes and crumble them over a bowl of ice cream.

MAKES 3 DOZEN 4-INCH COOKIES

3½ cups all-purpose flour

2 teaspoons kosher salt

2 teaspoons baking soda

1¾ cups (3½ sticks) unsalted butter, at room temperature

1¾ cups packed dark brown sugar

1½ cups granulated sugar

2 large eggs, at room temperature

2 teaspoons vanilla extract

4 cups old-fashioned oats

2 cups dried sour cherries

2 cups bittersweet chocolate chips

1 (10-ounce) bag Skor toffee bits, or 1 (8-ounce) bag Heath Bits

* Preheat the oven to 350 degrees F and line two baking sheets with parchment paper.

* In a large bowl, sift the flour, salt, and baking soda together and set it aside.

* In the bowl of a stand mixer fitted with the paddle attachment, cream the butter and sugars together on medium-high speed until light and fluffy. Add the eggs one at a time, scraping down the bowl after each addition. Add the vanilla. Reduce the speed to low and gradually add the flour mixture. Do not overmix.

* Transfer the mixture to a large bowl and, using your hands, mix in the oats, cherries, chocolate chips, and toffee bits until well incorporated. (Some stand mixer bowls aren't big enough to accommodate the extra ingredients here.)

* Working in batches (you'll have to complete this process three times), use a 3-ounce scoop to scoop the dough and drop them on the lined baking sheets, gently pressing down the cookies to flatten them a bit. The cookies will spread when baking, so evenly space six cookies per baking sheet. Bake until the cookies are golden brown around the edges, 14 to 16 minutes, rotating the sheets halfway through baking. Using a spatula, transfer the cookies to a wire rack to cool.

CHOCOLATE CHIP WALNUT TOFFEE COOKIES

I DON'T USUALLY LIKE NUTS IN baked goods unless it's a pecan pie or pecan bars; to me, the nut flavor overpowers the other ingredients. But these cookies, which Mama MJ loves, have the perfect balance of meaty walnuts and sweet toffee bits. Feel free to substitute pecans or another favorite nut.

MAKES 3 DOZEN 4-INCH COOKIES

4 cups all-purpose flour

2 teaspoons kosher salt

1 teaspoon baking soda

1½ cups (3 sticks) unsalted butter, at room temperature

2 cups packed dark brown sugar

1 cup granulated sugar

2 large eggs, at room temperature

1 large egg white, at room temperature

1 tablespoon vanilla extract

1 (20-ounce) bag bittersweet chocolate chips

1 (10-ounce) bag Skor toffee bits, or 1 (8-ounce) bag Heath Bits

12 ounces chopped walnuts

* Preheat the oven to 350 degrees F and line two baking sheets with parchment paper.

* In a large bowl, sift the flour, salt, and baking soda together and set it aside.

* In the bowl of a stand mixer fitted with the paddle attachment, cream the butter and sugars together on medium-high speed until light and fluffy. Add the eggs and egg white one at a time, scraping down the bowl after each addition. Add the vanilla. Reduce the speed to low and gradually add the flour mixture. Do not overmix.

* Transfer the mixture to a large bowl and, using your hands, mix in the chocolate, toffee bits, and walnuts until well incorporated. (Some stand mixer bowls aren't big enough to accommodate the extra ingredients here.)

* Working in batches (you'll have to complete this process three times), use a 3-ounce scoop to scoop the dough and drop them on the lined baking sheets, gently pressing down the cookies to flatten them a bit. The cookies will spread when baking, so evenly space six cookies per baking sheet. Bake until the cookies are golden brown around the edges, 14 to 16 minutes, rotating the sheets halfway through baking. Using a spatula, transfer the cookies to a wire rack to cool.

Every week, when my boys were little, we would bake for our garbage man, Adolpho. It was our ritual, and we would tie the pastries onto the garbage can if we weren't home to hand-deliver them. We did this for 5 years until we moved. At our new house, I introduced us to our new garbage man, Jeff. We ended up baking for Jeff for over 6 years. When my son Oscar was 3, I asked him who he wanted to invite to his birthday party, and Jeff was at the top of the list!

CRACKLIN' COOKIES
chicken skin & toffee bits

ONE MORNING AT THE GOOSE, I'd made a batch of cookie dough and was scooping it into rounds to bake while I watched my prep cook trim the fat and skin from the chicken thighs he was deboning, then throw them in the compost. It was so much waste, I couldn't bear it, so I saved the scraps of skin, rendered them in the oven, and added them to the cookie dough. Delicious! You can render your own skins or make it easier and buy a bag of pork rinds—a.k.a. *chicharrónes*—to add the savory crunch. Either way, they provide unexpected salty-but-sweet crunchy goodness.

MAKES 2 DOZEN 4-INCH COOKIES

4½ cups all-purpose
   flour

2 teaspoons kosher salt

1 teaspoon baking soda

1½ cups (3 sticks)
   unsalted butter, at
   room temperature

2 cups packed dark
   brown sugar

1 cup granulated sugar

2 large eggs, at room
   temperature

1 large egg white, at
   room temperature

1 tablespoon vanilla
   extract

1 (20-ounce) bag bitter-
   sweet chocolate chips

1 (10-ounce) bag Skor
   toffee bits, or
   1 (8-ounce) bag
   Heath Bits

7 ounces Chicken
   Cracklin's (recipe
   follows), or 1 (7-ounce)
   bag pork rinds, such as
   Guerrero *Chicharrón
   de Cerdo*

* Preheat the oven to 350 degrees F and line two baking sheets with parchment paper.

* In a large bowl, sift the flour, salt, and baking soda together and set it aside.

* In the bowl of a stand mixer fitted with the paddle attachment, cream the butter and sugars together on medium-high speed until light and fluffy. Add the eggs and egg white one at a time, scraping down the bowl after each addition. Add the vanilla. Reduce the speed to low and gradually add the flour mixture. Do not overmix. Fold in the chocolate chips, toffee bits, and cracklin's.

* Working in batches (you'll have to complete this process twice), use a 3-ounce scoop to scoop the dough and drop them on the lined baking sheets, gently pressing down the cookies to flatten them a bit. The cookies will spread when baking, so evenly space six cookies per baking sheet. Bake until the cookies are golden brown around the edges, 14 to 16 minutes, rotating the sheets halfway through baking. Using a spatula, transfer the cookies to a wire rack to cool.

continued

CHICKEN CRACKLIN'S

CRACKLIN'S ARE SKIN (USUALLY CHICKEN OR PORK) rendered of its fat and fried or roasted until nothing is left but the crunchy skin. Plates of them sat on stovetops when I was growing up, a quick bite to eat as you were running outside to play. Most often rendered in large cast-iron cauldrons outside, I've created an easier version you can make in your oven at home. Serve these in bowls at parties, with Comeback Sauce (page 173) on the side. Save up chicken skins over time (store in the freezer) as you trim your birds, or ask your butcher, who will sometimes give you a bag of skins for free or at a low cost.

MAKES 7 OUNCES

2 pounds chicken skins

* Preheat the oven to 300 degrees F and line two baking sheets with parchment paper.

* Put the skins in one layer on a baking sheet (you can crowd them as they will shrink considerably). Cover with another sheet of parchment paper then weigh down the skins with another baking sheet on top. Repeat this with all the chicken skin, and keep layering until you have three or four pans stacked on top of each other. Roast the skins, pouring off any fat that has accumulated, for 45 minutes.

* Unstack the baking sheets, remove the parchment paper, and roast the skins on the separated sheets until they're crispy, about 10 more minutes. Drain on a paper towel–lined plate.

CHARLIE BROWN COOKIES
peanut butter & chocolate at its best

CUSTOMERS ALWAYS ASK HOW THESE COOKIES got their name. When we lived in Richmond, my dad would take my sister and me for ice cream. We always went to the same store, and I always got the same flavor: Charlie Brown, which was dark chocolate with thick swirls of salty peanut butter. I tried and tried to order another flavor, perusing the glass cold case, envious of my little sister who ordered the bubble gum flavor. But alas, the Charlie Brown always made it into my hand.

Note: This dough is a bit loose after mixing. Place the cookie dough bowl in the fridge for thirty minutes until the dough is a bit firmer and easier to scoop.

MAKES 2 DOZEN 4-INCH COOKIES

1 pound bittersweet chocolate chips

1½ cups (3 sticks) unsalted butter, at room temperature

3 cups all-purpose flour

1½ cups Dutch-process cocoa powder

2 teaspoons kosher salt

1½ teaspoons baking soda

6 large eggs

4 cups sugar

1½ tablespoons vanilla extract

3 (10-ounce) bags peanut butter chips

* Preheat the oven to 350 degrees F and line two baking sheets with parchment paper.

* Over a saucepan of simmering water, stack a metal or glass bowl, making sure it fits snugly and the water doesn't touch the bottom. Put the chocolate and butter in the bowl and stir until fully melted and smooth. Set the mixture aside.

* In a medium bowl, whisk together the flour, cocoa, salt, and baking soda and set aside.

* In the bowl of a stand mixer fitted with the paddle attachment, cream the eggs and sugar on medium-high speed until light and fluffy. Add the vanilla and the melted chocolate. Reduce the speed to low and gradually add the flour mixture. Fold in the peanut butter chips. Place the bowl in the refrigerator for 30 minutes.

* Working in batches (you'll have to complete this process twice), use a 2-ounce scoop to scoop the dough and drop them on the lined baking sheets, gently pressing down the cookies to flatten them a bit. The cookies will spread when baking, so evenly space six cookies per baking sheet. Bake until the cookies are starting to crack and lose their shiny appearance, 14 to 16 minutes, rotating the sheets halfway through baking. Using a spatula, transfer the cookies to a wire rack to cool.

AUNT CHUBBY BARS
peanut butter & jelly

AUNT CHUBBY, GRANNY'S OLDEST SISTER—A.K.A. EVA MAE—wasn't chubby, at least when I knew her. But she was a chubby baby and didn't grow out of it until she was twelve or thirteen; by then the nickname had been around for so long it stuck. Aunt Chubby was actually a teeny tiny, dainty Southern lady who would laugh easily and crack jokes with us. These bars are thick and chubby with peanut butter and jelly, and named for her.

MAKES 16 BARS

3 cups all-purpose flour

1½ teaspoons kosher salt

1 teaspoon baking soda

1 cup (2 sticks) unsalted butter, at room temperature, plus more for greasing

1½ cups sugar

2 large eggs, at room temperature

1 (16.3-ounce jar) extra-crunchy peanut butter, such as Skippy (see note)

1 tablespoon vanilla extract

2 cups raspberry freezer jam or jarred raspberry preserves

* Preheat the oven to 350 degrees F and butter a 10-inch square pan.

* In a large bowl, sift the flour, salt, and baking soda together and set aside.

* In the bowl of a stand mixer fitted with the paddle attachment (or mix by hand in a bowl), cream the butter and sugar on medium-high speed. Add the eggs one at a time, scraping down the bowl after each addition. Add the peanut butter and vanilla and mix until combined. Reduce the speed to low and gradually add the flour mixture. Do not overmix.

* Using a small offset spatula or your fingers (I use my fingers), spread a little bit more than half of the batter into the bottom of the pan, pressing with your fingers to form a bottom crust, about 1 inch up the sides. Spread the jam over the crust. Top with the remaining batter, tearing off individual pieces about 2 inches square and flattening them, then piecing them together like a puzzle. (It is not necessary for the entire top to be covered completely.) Bake until golden brown, 35 to 40 minutes. Cool completely before cutting into sixteen bars, otherwise the cake doesn't have time to set up and the jam will ooze out everywhere.

Note: Try to avoid natural peanut butters if you can. You need the added sugar in the commodity brands for this recipe.

GOOEY BUTTER CAKE BARS

MY DEAR FRIEND TRACY (WHO IS also from North Carolina and now lives in Seattle) loves, loves, *loves* these bars—the recipe is from her grandmother "Gemma" Myra, of Madison, North Carolina. She talked about them for a few years after we first met before I ever tried them. To be honest, I wasn't sure about them at first when she told me the recipe called for a box of cake mix. But don't knock it until you try it, folks, because these things are good!

Southern cooks see no problem with breaking the rules, such as using a prepackaged food as an ingredient (for example, see Prince's Southern Iced Tea on page 273). Keep in mind though that it must be an *ingredient*, not the dish itself. I love the shiny, crunchy top crust that forms as you bake these bars.

MAKES 16 BARS

1 box yellow butter cake mix, such as Betty Crocker

½ cup (1 stick) unsalted butter, at room temperature, plus more for greasing

3 large eggs, divided

1 pound confectioners' sugar

1 (8-ounce) package cream cheese, at room temperature

2 teaspoons vanilla extract

* Preheat the oven to 350 degrees F. Butter a 9-by-13-inch pan.

* In the bowl of a stand mixer fitted with the paddle attachment (or mix by hand in a bowl), combine the cake mix, butter, and 1 of the eggs and mix on medium speed until the batter has the consistency of cookie dough. Using your fingers, press the dough into the pan.

* In the clean bowl of a stand mixer fitted with the paddle attachment, thoroughly beat together the remaining 2 eggs on medium-high speed. Reduce the speed to low and mix in the confectioners' sugar, cream cheese, and vanilla until combined, then beat well for about 1 minute more. Pour the batter over the dough in the pan, spreading it evenly with a spatula.

* Bake until the cake is golden, a little crusty on top, and jiggles only a bit, 30 to 35 minutes. Cool completely and cut into sixteen bars.

BITTERSWEET CHOCOLATE BREAD PUDDING
with salty whiskey caramel sauce

THIS IS AN EASY DESSERT TO make and one your company will love. We make it every week for Fried Chicken Friday. You can add butterscotch, toffee, or peanut butter chips; sautéed apple slices; or almost anything you want to this versatile bread pudding. I often vary what's inside, but it almost always has bittersweet chocolate. We cut large rectangles and serve them with whipped cream.

   Tip: This recipe uses ten egg yolks. Save the egg whites to make Lusty Lemon Layer Cake (page 225). You can also make this the day before and rewarm in a 300-degree-F oven just before serving.

MAKES 8 TO 10 SERVINGS

2 baguettes, cut into
   1-inch pieces (about
   16 cups), or 7 *banh
   mi* buns
5 cups half-and-half
1 cup heavy cream
1½ cups sugar
10 large egg yolks
3 large eggs
2 tablespoons vanilla
   extract

2 cups bittersweet
   chocolate chips
1 recipe Whipped
   Cream (page 231),
   for serving
1 recipe Salty Whiskey
   Caramel Sauce (recipe
   follows), for serving
Fleur de sel, for garnish

* Preheat the oven to 325 degrees F.

* Put the bread pieces on a baking sheet and toast until the bread is dry and no longer soft, about 5 minutes. Set them aside and leave the oven on.

* In a large mixing bowl, whisk the half-and-half, heavy cream, sugar, egg yolks, eggs, and vanilla until thoroughly combined. Add the bread to the bowl and toss to coat the pieces completely. Spread half of the bread pieces in the bottom of a 9-by-13-inch pan. Sprinkle the chocolate chips over the top in an even layer. Finish with the remaining bread pieces and pour any remaining egg mixture on top.

* Cover the pan with aluminum foil and bake for 45 minutes. Remove the foil, rotate the pan 180 degrees, and bake until the pudding is golden brown and puffed on top, 45 to 50 minutes more. Remove from the oven and serve warm with whipped cream and caramel sauce. Garnish with a sprinkling of *fleur de sel*.

continued

SALTY WHISKEY CARAMEL SAUCE

BE EXTRA CAREFUL WHEN YOU MAKE this recipe, as the sugar gets superhot and can burn you. Use pot holders and stand back from the saucepot.

MAKES 5 CUPS

4 cups sugar

2 cups water

2 cups heavy cream

1 cup (2 sticks) unsalted
  butter, each stick cut
  into 4 pieces

¼ cup whiskey

1 tablespoon vanilla
  extract

1 tablespoon *fleur de sel*

* In a large saucepot over medium-high heat, bring the sugar and water to a boil—*do not stir*. Once the sugar water comes to a boil, start brushing down the sides of the pan with a clean pastry brush dipped in water; this will help prevent the sugar from crystallizing. Continue to boil, brushing down the sides of the pot every 5 minutes or so but not touching the sugar. Once the caramel starts to darken, watch it closely: you want a nice deep-amber color, but you don't want it to get too dark and burn.

* Once it's a dark amber, after about 30 minutes, take the pot off the heat and immediately but *slowly* pour in your cream, using a whisk to stir. Be careful! The sugar will bubble and steam. Once the cream is added, immediately whisk in the butter, whiskey, vanilla, and *fleur de sel*. Keep whisking until the butter has melted and is completely incorporated. If you have trouble melting the butter completely, you can place the pot over low heat and whisk until incorporated.

* Take the pot off the heat and let the sauce cool to room temperature. Store it in a lidded glass jar. I keep mine in the refrigerator indefinitely, but it usually doesn't last too long, either at the restaurant or my house. Warm before serving by placing the jar of sauce in a saucepot of hot water for a few minutes.

FOR
SIPPIN'
YOU COULD USE A DRINK

PRINCE'S SOUTHERN ICED TEA *not too sweet* 273

OLD DOMINICAN HANGOVER HELPER 275

CARROT-APPLE-BEET-GINGER SQUEEZE 275

THE WANDERING GOOSE EASY MICHELADA MIX 276

ECAUSE IT'S SO HOT DOWN THERE, Southerners drink a lot of everything: sweet tea, lemonade, Coke, Mello Yello, 7Up, Cheerwine, whiskey, whiskey with soda, whiskey with lemonade, and whiskey with iced tea. Basically anything they drink, they add whiskey to. And anything they drink has to have a lot of ice.

When company comes over, invited or uninvited, you always, *always* offer them a drink right away. Granny made a pitcher of iced tea every morning first thing, and it sat on her counter all day, ready to be poured into a glass full of ice and offered to company. In their younger years, Granny and Pop and their extended family and friends drank vodka with 7Up. I remember them holding paper cups of clear liquid, me asking what was inside, and them laughing and saying, "Why, that's jus' 7Up!"

PRINCE'S SOUTHERN ICED TEA
not too sweet

THE SOUTH'S MOST UBIQUITOUS DRINK (other than whiskey) is sweet tea, which is black tea steeped long and strong, so it's able to hold up to the copious amounts of sugar added. I like my tea not too sweet and came up with this recipe after eating at Prince's restaurant in Myrtle Beach, South Carolina. Prince was an older African American man, tall and charming, and he ran a restaurant out of his house. I asked him once how he made his tea and he hinted that he added a bit of "something secret," but he never would tell me. I maddeningly tested all kinds of ways of making iced tea, then stumbled upon adding *powdered iced tea mix* to replace part of the sugar. Perfect! For a fancy presentation, garnish the glasses with a sugar-coated rim and fresh mint.

MAKES 3 QUARTS

8 small or 4 large bags black tea, such as Lipton's or Luizanne

½ cup Lipton iced tea mix

⅓ cup sugar

Pinch of baking soda

4 cups cold water

4 cups ice

* In a saucepot bring 4 cups of water to a boil. Add the tea bags and turn off the heat. Let the tea steep for 8 minutes. Remove the tea bags and pour the tea into a large pitcher. Add the Lipton tea mix and sugar, stirring until they are dissolved. Stir in the baking soda. Add the cold water and ice. Store in the refrigerator for 2 to 3 days.

OLD DOMINICAN HANGOVER HELPER

PEOPLE IN THE RESTAURANT BUSINESS TEND to drink a lot, much more than most folks. Which means they also tend to be hungover a lot, much more than most folks. Mike Law, our first chef when we opened The Goose, is both a Southerner and a restaurant guy. He loves whiskey, as do most Southerners. So we needed a drink for those mornings when Mike had had too much whiskey, but still had to work the busy line (which was often). He came up with this drink (he's half Dominican, hence the name), and I tweaked it a bit to get it to where it is now. It's good, whether you're hungover or not.

MAKES 8 CUPS

6 cups good-quality orange juice

1 fresh pineapple, peeled, cored, and cut into 2-inch chucks

2 cups fresh or frozen blueberries

1 jarred pickled jalapeño

* Combine all the ingredients in a blender and blend until smooth. Serve immediately or store in the refrigerator for up to 2 days.

CARROT-APPLE-BEET-GINGER SQUEEZE

THE COOKS MAKE HUGE CONTAINERS OF this juice, and every time, they give me a little glass to taste. To me, it's the perfect balance of earthy vegetable flavor with a bit of sweetness from the apples and spiciness from the fresh ginger. At The Goose, we use the Breville 850-watt juicer—nothing too fancy or expensive, but it does the job.

MAKES 4 CUPS

3 tart apples, such as Granny Smith

4 large carrots

1 large red beet

1 (1-inch) piece ginger

Pinch of kosher salt

* In a juicer, process the apples, carrots, beet, and ginger according to the manufacturer's instructions. Stir in the salt. Serve immediately or store in the refrigerator for up to 2 days.

THE WANDERING GOOSE EASY MICHELADA MIX

A *MICHELADA* IS A POPULAR MEXICAN beverage of beer mixed with lime and tomato or Clamato juice. We serve a lot of them at breakfast and brunch and during our Fried Chicken Friday dinners. To make our version, dampen the rim of a pint glass with a cut lime, then roll the glass in kosher salt and pepper (you could also use La Valentina chili and lime powder), fill it three-quarters full with Dixie Lager beer, and top it with this mix. Garnish with a lime wedge.

You can also drink the mix as is, with no beer, or add vodka and some Pickled Okra (page 167) and Pickled Green Beans (page 168) for a fabulous version of a Bloody Mary. I love the extra lime juice our version has.

MAKES 6 CUPS

1 (46-ounce) bottle original V-8 juice

¼ cup Texas Pete or Crystal hot sauce

¼ cup Worcestershire sauce

¾ cup juice from about 5 limes

Kosher salt and freshly ground black pepper

* In a pitcher that holds at least 2 quarts, stir together the V-8 juice, hot sauce, Worcestershire, and lime juice. Season with salt and pepper to taste.

MINI COCA-COLAS WITH SALTY PEANUTS

I've heard stories of Southern farmers as early as the 1930s grabbing a bottle of Coke and dumping peanuts in it for a snack as they rode their tractors around the fields. Try it: take a few sips from a supercold 6-ounce bottle of Coke to allow room for the peanuts. Add a handful of boiled or salted peanuts. By the time you get to the bottom of the bottle, the peanuts are softer and ready to eat. It's a quick, salty-sweet fix.

(Top): Me, 1970s; (Bottom): At the James River with my cousins Holly
and Marjie and my sister, Chelsea, Richmond, Virginia, 1970s

A BIG LOVE THANK-YOU

I learned a lot from writing this book.

I learned that memories fade as you get older, and they are different for all of us. What I can see, smell, and hear so clearly—almost touch—my aunts, uncles, and cousins remember nothing about. A memory that is very distinct to me will be recalled completely differently by my sister, who stood right next to me at the time, or a cousin who was in the same room. I wish I had written down so much more than I did. I also realize that I learned from more family members than I'd thought.

From Aunt Susie, who made cooking look like an effortless dance, I learned how to stay calm and collected in the kitchen. From Aunt Dee-Dee, I learned how to be excited about *the whole process* of cooking. She could cook something she had served us kids a hundred times and turn around from the bubbling pot and say, "Aren't you so excited? *Boy*, it sure is going to be *good*! I can't wait! Can you?" She could have served us North Carolina red-dirt pies, and, with her enthusiasm, they would have been the most savory, scrumptious pies ever. To this day, Aunt Dee-Dee's passion for food has not dwindled one iota.

From my mama, MJ, I learned the basics. MJ was a single mom working full-time, but she still took the time to show me what she did know and gave me building blocks to grow from. Without her, I wouldn't have many of my recipes today.

From my many cousins, aunts and uncles, great-aunts and great-uncles, Mee-Maws and Dee-Das, Big Mamas and Little Mamas, I learned that when someone cooks you something, you should go out of your way to not only thank them, but also convince them it's by God the best thing you have ever eaten in your life! Yes, the compliments should abound.

From all of them gathered together, I learned to love bustling surroundings. It's to no one's surprise that I replaced my childhood extended family with my present-day restaurant family. Like slipping into Virginia's wide James River, I eased into the chaos of a restaurant's buzz and hum, noise and laughter, humor and heat, and the messy, dirty craziness of it all.

When I was little at Granddaddy's house, I would step out back on his redbrick pathway—the periwinkle tickling my ankles, lightning bugs flying in languid, delicate swirls near my outstretched hand, bullfrogs croaking in the deep. I would turn and look back at the house, with life inside its every lit-up window, shouts and laughter coming from different rooms, the soft clink of the dishwasher running, a door being slammed, the garage door trembling closed, and the summer-night breeze pushing my thick blond hair to the left side of my mosquito-bitten temple.

All of this, *all* of it, is one big messy life full of memories and feelings, scents and sounds. This was the shift in my childhood, standing on Granddaddy's brick pathway, where I started to remember things for the rest of my life; it was at this point when the magnolia scent married into my skin and never left. Much of our memories are insignificant, mediocre little spots and blurbs that at the time you would have never thought would be a memory for you. Pay attention to it all.

Stop to hear the wind move the leaves on the trees; be a good person; do something for someone else not just once in awhile but every day and don't ever expect anything back from that. Simply give it *all you have*, y'all. Your blood, your bones, your guts, your grit. It is by far the most beautiful thing to share with our children. Our friends. Our family. Give it all you've got, y'all.

ACKNOWLEDGMENTS

Without these folks it simply would not have been possible to write this cookbook. (No joke, y'all.)

Thank you to my immediate family, comprised of Maxwell, Oscar, Josie June, Zac, Coen, and Livi (and puppy, Augustus "Gus," and rabbit, Biscuit). Thank you for giving up our dining room table for over a year so I could write this thing. I'm back now and can start feeding y'all proper at the table again.

To my dear best friends, Tracy and Jon Haaland, who have never missed a single birthday party I ever threw for my kids, and who, when I said I needed help testing recipes, both dropped what they were busy doing (making stunning handmade leather bags—Chemical Wedding Bags) and jumped right in, taking detailed notes and going back over and over a recipe until we had it right. These recipes wouldn't work without their skills. And thanks to Tracy again for reminding me that the South and what we were brought up in is all a messy and crazy patchwork nut job that makes you laugh until you snort and is (almost) pee-your-pants funny.

To my best girlfriends, Auntie Maureen, Auntie Jasmine, Auntie Cheryl, Auntie Tracy, and Auntie Annie (who are called "Aunties" by my children), just because y'all are beautiful and magnificent, and my kids and I are stronger because of you.

To Josephine, for being the most beautiful seventy-nine-year-old I ever did see and for taking care of Olive and loving her like she isn't a dog (which she isn't).

To all my current staff and all of the previous staff that have always made my job that much easier, y'all *rock*.

To my editor, Susan Roxborough, who took on this project and told me I wasn't alone and let me have a bit of a freak-out without blinking an eye when I thought I wouldn't be able to make my word count, and then didn't blink her other eye when I was way over my word count. To Sarah Hanson, for believing in me and what I do, and to all of the staff at Sasquatch Books, especially Anna Goldstein and Em Gale, y'all should be so proud of yourselves and the job you are doing.

To Bob Prince, Dani Cone, and Mike and Liz McConnell, this restaurant wouldn't exist without your guidance, support, and belief in me from day one.

To Jim Henkens, for your photographer's eye and finding beauty in the every day.

To Mama MJ, for raising me to be a strong and compassionate woman, and for taking the time to pass on what you learned from your mama. I know now what it must have taken for you to raise two daughters as a single mom, and you know what? You did all right, Mama, if I do say so myself.

To my sister, Chelsea, for sharing all of that big, wonderful world of a childhood we had together. Wow.

To Uncle Ray, always the first in the family to answer my email questions, your stories and storytelling are world-class! Your humor, laughter, and love, especially after Daddy died, mean the world to me; I can't even express how much. Thank you, *thank you*, Uncle Ray.

To Aunt Becky, for sending the recipes you had and for being a rock to your family. You're stronger than most.

To Aunt Kay, for sending me recipes, writing stories (you remembered so much!), and giving me so much to work with. This book could not have been done without you and your beautiful memories of Granny.

To Richard and Jon, Mikelaw, Chrisreel, and Matttice, you boys are my Southern brothers through and true.

To Sallie, Terri, and Tom Davis, for eating my food for all those years. I love you all.

To Carly, Tiffany, and Rachelle (and all the other bakers I've had side-by-side with me), for baking like champs.

To Jesse and Keri, for gently and never on purpose reminding me what my life would be like without kids. I'm sometimes envious.

To Zac, my true blue, for pushing me when I needed it, and for letting me be the first to shove a biscuit into your mouth. (And no, I'm not the reason you gained thirty pounds after we met, sorry!)

To all of our customers, who continue to come back day after day. The Wandering Goose wouldn't be a restaurant without all of you.

And finally, to my daddy, John Thomas Earnhardt, the best daddy a little girl could want for. Thank you for showing me the way and repeating all of the stories over and over again. I so wish you were here to hold my hand and laugh. I miss you, Daddy.

INDEX

Note: Photographs are indicated by *italics*.

A

Angel Biscuits, 79–80
apples
    Apple Rosemary Galette, *240*, 241
    Carrot-Apple-Beet-Ginger Squeeze,
    274, 275
    Maternal-Side Apple Butter, 209
    Uncle Ray's Fresh Apple Cake, 229
Apricot-Tomato Jam, 208
author's personal story, 1–20

B

bacon
    Bacon, Cheddar, and Scallion
    Biscuits, 72
    B.O.L.T. (Bacon, Fried Oysters,
    Lettuce, and Tomato), 102, *103*
    Angels on Horseback, 42–43
    Maple, Bacon, and Date Biscuits, *66*, 67
    Smoked Chocolate Chip Cookies,
    256–257, *257*
Banana Bundt Cake, Browned Butter, 216
Bars, Aunt Chubby, 264, *265*
Bars, Gooey Butter Cake, 266
BBQ Sauce, Sweet Heat, 176
Beans and Rice, "Not Just for Monday"
    Red, 154

beef
    Bubble and Squeak, *194*, 195–196
    MJ's Chipped Beef on Toast, 50
Birthday Cake, Happy, 214, *215*
biscuits, 60–87
biscuits, day-old, uses for, 70
Biscuit Sandwich Suggestions, Big,
    82, *83–87*
Blue Cheese Dressing, Creamed, 177
Bread and Butter Pickles, 162
Bread Pudding, Bittersweet Chocolate,
    267–269, *268*
breakfast, 182–199
Brownstone Front Cake, *218*, 219–220, *221*
Brunswick Stew, Go to Church, *148*, 149
Bubble and Squeak, *194*, 195–196
Buttermilk Biscuits, Best, *64*, 65
butters
    Maternal-Side Apple Butter, 209
    Steen's Butter, 142
    Whipped Honey Butter, 116, *116*

C

Caffe Vita, 56
Cake Bars, Gooey Butter, 266
cakes and Bundts, 210–233
cane syrup, Steen's, 142
Caramel Sauce, Salty Whiskey, 269
Carrot-Apple-Beet-Ginger Squeeze,
    274, 275
Charlie Brown Cookies, 263

Cheese Spread, "Not Ruth's" Pimento, *26*, 27
Cheese Straws, Granny's Crunchy, *32*, 33
Cherry Hand Pies, Sour, 238, *239*
chess pies. *See* pies and tarts
chicken
 Aunt Annie's Cornflake Chicken Tenders, 115–116
 Big Love Buttermilk Fried Chicken, 95–96, *97*
 Chicken Cracklin's, 262
 "Fried Chicken Friday" dinners, 96
 Fried Chicken Po' Boys, 100
 Go to Church Brunswick Stew, *148*, 149
 Loaded Chicken Potpie, *152*, 153
 Simple Roast Chicken and Pan Gravy, 57–58, *59*
Chipped Beef on Toast, MJ's, 50
chocolate
 Best Chocolate Chip Cookie in Seattle, 255
 Bittersweet Chocolate Bread Pudding, 267–269, *268*
 "Bob's Last Meal" Chocolate Cake, 213
 Charlie Brown Cookies, 263
 Chocolate Cherry Oat Cookies, 258
 Chocolate Chili Chess Pie, *246*, 247
 Chocolate Chip Walnut Toffee Cookies, 259
 Cracklin' Cookies, *260*, 261–262
 Granny's Kitchen Table Cake, 222–223
 Smoked Chocolate Chip Cookies, 256–257, *257*
Chowchow, 169
Cinnamon Rolls, Biscuit, *76*, 77–78, *78*
Cinnamon-Sugared Toast, 199
Coca-Colas with salty peanuts, mini, 276
Cocktail Sauce, Quick and Spicy, 180
Coconut Cake, Southern, *226*, 227–228
Coconut Rice, 139
cold smoking, 257

coleslaw
 Granny's Salisbury Red Slaw, *136*, 137
 Wandering Goose White Slaw, The, 139
Collards, Smoky Meat, 130–131, *131*
Comeback Sauce, 173
Angels on Horseback, 42–43
cookies, bars, and bread pudding, 252–269
cookies, tips for baking, 254
cooking, considerations for, 21
Corn Bread, Hot Skillet, 141–142
Cornmeal Dredge, 98
Crab Soup, West Coast–Style She-, 147
Croutons, Biscuit, 81

D
Dills, The Wandering Goose Extra-Spicy, 163
drinks, 270–276

E
eggs
 Country Caviar, 34–35, *35*
 Egg Wash, 31
 Granddaddy's Hard-Boiled Egg Salad Dressing, 177
 Granny's Perfect Poached Eggs, 199
 Perfect Fried Eggs, 55
 Perfect Hard-Boiled Eggs, 35

F
Farro and Collard Green Salad, Bluebird Grain Farms, 128, *129*
Farro Breakfast Porridge, Bluebird Grain Farms, 190, *191*
Fig Preserves, Granny's Strawberry, 204
Fish Fry, Friday Night, *112*, 113–114
flour, types of, 65

food, beginning and ending with, 117
French Rémoulade, 178

G

Galette, Apple Rosemary, *240*, 241
Galette, Rhubarb, 242
Garlic–Lemon Vinaigrette, Roasted, 179
Granola, The Wandering Goose, *186*, 187
Grape Tart, Concord, 237
gravy, 46–59
Green Beans, Pickled, 168
Greens, Granny's Mess of Soft, 127
grits
    Basic Grits, 92
    Boonville Breakfast Grits, 192, *193*
    Cheesy Grown-Up Grits, 192
    Grits and Grillades, 94
    Sweet Grits, 192
    Zevely House Shrimp and Grits,
        91–92, *93*

H

ham
    Angel Biscuits, 79–80
    Country Ham with Redeye Gravy, *54*, 55
Hangover Helper, Old Dominican, 275
Hash, Veggie, 197–198, *198*
Herb Blend, Big, 58, *58*
Huckleberry Cardamom Bundt Cake, 217
Hush Puppies, Princess "Hush Now,"
    39–41, *40*

I

Iced Tea, Prince's Southern, 273

J

jellies, jams, and butters, 200–209, *206–207*

K

Key Lime Pie, 248
Kitchen Table Cake, Granny's, 222–223

L

Lemon Buttermilk Chess Pie, 244, *245*
Lemon Layer Cake, Lusty, *224*, 225
Lemon Saffron Buttermilk Chess Pie, 244
Lemon Vinaigrette, Roasted Garlic–, 179
livermush, 185

M

Mac and Cheese, Pimento "Not Your
    Mama's," 134, *135*
Maple, Bacon, and Date Biscuits, *66*, 67
Mayonnaise, Homemade, 178
Michelada Mix, The Wandering Goose
    Easy, 276
Mushroom Gravy, 49
Mustard, Creole, 176

O

Okra, Double-Order Fried, 122, *123*
Okra, Pickled, 167
Onion Dip, Walla Walla Sweet, 28–29, *29*
Onions, Pickled Red, 166
onions, sweet, 125
outdoor cooking, 114
oysters
    B.O.L.T. (Bacon, Fried Oysters,
        Lettuce, and Tomato), 102, *103*
    Angels on Horseback, 42–43
    Crunchy Cornmeal-Fried Oysters, 98, *99*
    Fried Oyster Rich Boys, 100, *101*

P

parties, cooking for, 41
Peas, Lowcountry Sea Island Red, *124*, 125
peppers
    Mama Lil's Peppers and Tillamook Cheddar Biscuits, 74, *75*
    "peppa sauce" pepper vinegar, 179
    Pepper Jelly, 205
    Red Pepper Coulis, 198
pickles, 158–169, *164–165*
Pie Dough, Liquored, 105
pies and tarts, 234–251
pork
    Grits and Grillades, 94
    Pulled Pork Butt, *110*, 111
Porridge, Bluebird Grain Farms Farro Breakfast, 190, *191*
potatoes
    Granddaddy's Fancy New Potatoes, 140
    MJ's Potato Salad, 121
    Skillet Ramps and Yukon Gold Potatoes, 143
    Spicy Skillet Potatoes, 188, *189*
pot liquor, 131
Potpie, Loaded Chicken, *152*, 153
Pralines, Spiced, 44, *45*

R

Ramps and Yukon Gold Potatoes, Skillet, 143
Rémoulade, French, 178
Rhubarb Galette, 242
Rice, Coconut, 139
Rice and Red Beans, "Not Just for Monday," 154

S

salad dressings
    Creamed Blue Cheese Dressing, 177
    Granddaddy's Hard-Boiled Egg Salad Dressing, 177
salads
    Biscuit Croutons, 81
    Bluebird Grain Farms Farro and Collard Green Salad, 128, *129*
    Granny's Salisbury Red Slaw, *136*, 137
    Little Gem Salad, 126
    Tomato and Cucumber Salad, 138
    Wandering Goose White Slaw, The, 139
    Watermelon Salad, 140
Salmon Pie, Smoked, 104–105
sandwiches
    Big Biscuit Sandwich Suggestions, 82, *83–87*
    B.O.L.T. (Bacon, Fried Oysters, Lettuce, and Tomato), 102, *103*
    Fried Chicken Po' Boys, 100
    Fried Oyster Rich Boys, 100, *101*
sauces and dressings, 170–180, *174–175*
sausage
    Country Breakfast Sausage, 185
    Sausage and Sage Biscuits, 73
    Sausage Spice Mix, 53
    Sawmill Gravy, 52–53
Sawmill Gravy, 52–53
Sea Island Red Peas, Lowcountry, *124*, 125
7Up Bundt Cake, 232, *233*
Shortcakes, 230–231, *231*
Shrimp, "Granddaddy's Coming to Visit" Peel and Eat, 108, *109*
Shrimp and Grits, Zevely House, 91–92, *93*
side dishes, 118–143
Sigala brothers, 53
Sleeping Dogs, Home-Wrecker, 30–31, *31*

snacks and starters, 22–45
sorghum syrup, 138
soups and stews, 144–157
Southern names, 6
Spaghetti Sauce, Southern, 155–157, *156*
Spice Mix, Sausage, 53
Squid, Pickle, and Lemon Plate,
  Fried, 37–38
Steen's Butter, 142
Steen's cane syrup, 142
strawberries
  Granny's Strawberry Fig Preserves, 204
  Shortcakes, 230–231, *231*
  Strawberry Vanilla Preserves, 203
supper, 88–116
Sweet Potato Biscuits, 71

tomatoes
  Any Time of Year Tomato Soup, 150
  Broiled Garden Tomatoes, *132*, 133
  Cornmeal Fried Green Tomatoes, 25
  Little Gem Salad, 126
  Red Tomato Cheddar Pie, 106, *107*
  Southern Spaghetti Sauce, 155–157, *156*
  Tomato and Cucumber Salad, 138
  Tomato-Apricot Jam, 208

V

Vegetable Soup, Granny's Garden, 151
Veggie Hash, 197–198, *198*
Vinaigrette, Roasted Garlic–Lemon, 179
vinegar, "peppa sauce" pepper, 179
Vinegar Sauce, Central Carolina, 180

T

Tart, Concord Grape, 237
Tarte á la Bouillie, 249–250, *251*
Taylor Shellfish, 102
Tea, Prince's Southern Iced, 273
Texas Pete hot sauce, 43
Toast, Cinnamon-Sugared, 199

W

Wandering Goose, The, about, 17–20
Watermelon Rind Pickles, Granny's, 161
Watermelon Salad, 140
Whipped Cream, 231
Whiskey Caramel Sauce, Salty, 269

Granny and my daddy, 1950

CONVERSIONS

VOLUME			LENGTH		WEIGHT	
UNITED STATES	METRIC	IMPERIAL	UNITED STATES	METRIC	AVOIRDUPOIS	METRIC
¼ tsp.	1.25 ml		⅛ in.	3 mm	¼ oz.	7 g
½ tsp.	2.5 ml		¼ in.	6 mm	½ oz.	15 g
1 tsp.	5 ml		½ in.	1.25 cm	1 oz.	30 g
½ Tbsp.	7.5 ml		1 in.	2.5 cm	2 oz.	60 g
1 Tbsp.	15 ml		1 ft.	30 cm	3 oz.	90 g
⅛ c.	30 ml	1 fl. oz.			4 oz.	115 g
¼ c.	60 ml	2 fl. oz.			5 oz.	150 g
⅓ c.	80 ml	2.5 fl. oz.			6 oz.	175 g
½ c.	125 ml	4 fl. oz.			7 oz.	200 g
1 c.	250 ml	8 fl. oz.			8 oz. (½ lb.)	225 g
2 c. (1 pt.)	500 ml	16 fl. oz.			9 oz.	250 g
1 qt.	1 l	32 fl. oz.			10 oz.	300 g

TEMPERATURE				WEIGHT (cont.)	
OVEN MARK	FAHRENHEIT	CELSIUS	GAS	11 oz.	325 g
Very cool	250–275	130–140	½–1	13 oz.	375 g
Cool	300	150	2	14 oz.	400 g
Warm	325	165	3	15 oz.	425 g
Moderate	350	175	4	16 oz. (1 lb.)	450 g
Moderately hot	375	190	5	1½ lb.	750 g
	400	200	6	2 lb.	900 g
Hot	425	220	7	2¼ lb.	1 kg
	450	230	8	3 lb.	1.4 kg
Very Hot	475	245	9	4 lb.	1.8 kg

MAMA GOOSE

HEATHER EARNHARDT grew up in the Piedmont of North Carolina, the Lowcountry of South Carolina, the foothills of the Appalachian Mountains, and on the bayou of New Orleans. Her heroes are chef Edna Lewis and the character Augustus McCrae, and she thinks that everything about morals, values, empathy, and courage can be learned from the Lonesome Dove series. She loves the voice of novelist Shelby Foote along with the other voices of Southern men and women who have the gift of good storytelling.

She made her way to Seattle in 1997, when the Speakeasy Café was where she wrote email and the Comet Tavern and Ernie Steele's were where she drank beer. She feels just as at home by the ocean as she does in the mountains and thinks no smell is better than that of a warm tomato plant vine. She has never owned a microwave and prefers mindful (some might say "mindless") tasks like peeling a case of apples or zesting forty-five lemons. Her cooking style is founded on the memories and stories of her Southern childhood where the acts of generosity and love learned from her extended family run deep in her veins.

Heather is the owner of The Wandering Goose in Seattle where her Southern-belle roots shine through in her baking and cooking style, which is big, loud, full of flavor, and rambunctious—yet refined underneath. She lives in the city's Columbia City neighborhood with her husband where she tries to teach the art of good manners to their five children. They keep chickens, bees, a dog named Gus, a rabbit named Biscuit, and a big wild garden. She has been known to exist purely on raw cookie dough and good Southern literature—and she's just fine with that.